Georges Bernanos' Debt to Thérèse of Lisieux

Mary Frances Catherine Dorschell

Mellen University Press
Lewiston/Queenston/Lampeter

Library of Congress Cataloging-in-Publication Data

Dorschell, Mary Frances Catherine
    Georges Bernanos' debt to Thérèse of Lisieux / Mary Frances Catherine Dorschell.
        p.   cm.
    Includes bibliographical references and index.
    ISBN 0-7734-2266-8 (hardcover)
    1. Bernanos, Georges, 1888-1948--Criticism and interpretation.
2. Thérèse, de Lisieux, Saint, 1873-1897--In literature.
3. Thérèse, de Lisieux, Saint, 1873-1897--Influence.
4. Spirituality in literature.   I. Title.
PQ2603.E5875Z677   1996
843'.912--dc20   95-47721
                                                                                CIP

A CIP catalog record for this book is available from the British Library.

Copyright © 1996 Mary Frances Catherine Dorschell

All rights reserved. For information contact

  The Edwin Mellen Press   The Edwin Mellen Press
        Box 450   Box 67
  Lewiston, New York   Queenston, Ontario
  USA 14092-0450   CANADA L0S 1L0

The Edwin Mellen Press, Ltd.
Lampeter, Dyfed, Wales
UNITED KINGDOM SA48 7DY

Printed in the United States of America

DEDICATION

To the memory of my parents

TABLE OF CONTENTS

ABBREVIATIONS i
ACKNOWLEDGEMENT v
FOREWORD, GUY GAUCHER vii
FOREWORD, WILLIAM BUSH xi
AUTHOR'S PREFACE xvii
INTRODUCTION - THÉRÈSE, BERNANOS, AND THE CRITICS . . . 3

PART ONE
EXPLICIT EVIDENCE OF THÉRÈSE OF LISIEUX' PRESENCE IN BERNANOS' WORK

CHAPTER 1 - FIRST EXPLICIT EVIDENCE (1905-1930) 17
    Explicit Evidence prior to *L'Imposture* (1927) 17
    L'Imposture and *La Joie* (1926-1929) 23
    "Jeanne, relapse et sainte" (1929) 30

CHAPTER 2 - EXPLICIT EVIDENCE IN THE SECOND PERIOD
    (1931-1938) 33
    The Crucible of Suffering 34
    "Tout est grâce" (1934-1936) 40
    Les Grands Cimetières sous la lune (1937-1938) 46
    Preface for *Louis le Cardonnel, pèlerin de l'invisible* (1938) 52

CHAPTER 3 - EXPLICIT EVIDENCE IN THE LAST DECADE
    (1939-1948) 57
    The Brazilian "Exile" (July, 1938-June, 1945) 58
        i)   Heroic Childhood 59
        ii) *Lettre aux Anglais* (1940-1942) 62

iii) "Discours pour le baptême de l'avion brésilien 'Jeanne d'Arc'" (1943) 65
"The Final Years" (June, 1945-July, 1948) 65
   i)   "Nos amis les saints" and "Derniers appels" (1947) . . 67
   ii) Dialogues des Carmélites (1947-1948) 68

PART TWO
IMPLICIT EVIDENCE OF THÉRÈSE OF LISIEUX' PRESENCE IN BERNANOS' WORK

CHAPTER 4 - A NATURAL AFFINITY: EARLY WRITING AND SHORT STORIES (1905-1930) 75
Early Correspondence (1905-1926) 76
"Ecrits de jeunesse": premiers essais romanesques (1907-1914) . . 83
"La Malibran" (1913) 84
"Madame Dargent" and "Dialogue d'ombres" (1922-1928) 88

CHAPTER 5 - PARALLEL AND REVERSE IMAGES OF THÉRÈSE IN SOUS LE SOLEIL DE SATAN (1919-1926) 93

CHAPTER 6 - TOWARDS AN INCARNATION OF THÉRÈSE (1926-1930) 107
"Saint Dominique"(1926) 107
"Jeanne, relapse et sainte" (1929) 109
La Grande peur des bien pensants (1931) 111
L'Imposture and La Joie (1926-1929) 112

CHAPTER 7 - REVERSE IMAGES OF THÉRÈSE IN UN MAUVAIS RÊVE, UN CRIME (1931-1935), AND MONSIEUR OUINE (1931-1940) 131

    Un mauvais rêve and *Un crime* 132
    Monsieur Ouine 141

CHAPTER 8 - THERESIAN SPIRITUALITY ON THE SUPERNATURAL LEVEL IN JOURNAL D'UN CURÉ DE CAMPAGNE (1934-1936) 163

CHAPTER 9 - THERESIAN SPIRITUALITY ON THE NATURAL LEVEL IN NOUVELLE HISTOIRE DE MOUCHETTE (1936-1937) 185

CHAPTER 10 - REFORMERS AND SAINTS: "FRÈRE MARTIN" (1943) AND "NOS AMIS LES SAINTS" (1947) 203
    "Frère Martin" 204
    "Nos amis les saints" 208

CHAPTER 11 - BERNANOS' SPIRITUAL TESTAMENT: DIALOGUES DES CARMÉLITES (1947-1948) 215

CONCLUSION - "DANS LA DOUCE PITIÉ DE DIEU" 239
BIBLIOGRAPHY 245
INDEX 263

ABBREVIATIONS

Ang   Bernanos, Georges. Lettre aux Anglais. Paris: Gallimard, 1946.

"BT"   Gaucher, Guy, o.c.d. "Bernanos et Sainte Thérèse de l'Enfant-Jésus." La Revue des Lettres Modernes 56-57 (1960) "Etudes bernanosiennes" 1: 228-268.

Che   Bernanos, Georges. Le Chemin de la Croix-des-âmes. Nouvelle édition, complétée, corrigée et annotée par Brigitte et Jean-Loup Bernanos d'après les manuscrits. Augmentée de tous les articles et messages écrits au Brésil. Monaco: Editions du Rocher, 1987.

---. Correspondance inédite, recueillie par Albert Béguin, choisie et présentée par Jean Murray, o.p. Paris: Plon, 1971.
Corr.I   Tome I. 1904-1934 Combat pour la vérité.
Corr.II   Tome II. 1934-1948 Combat pour la liberté.

Corr.III   ---. Correspondance inédite, recueillie, choisie, annotée et présentée par Jean-Loup Bernanos. Paris: Plon, 1983. Tome III. 1904-1948 Lettres retrouvées.

Cré   ---. Le crépuscule des vieux. Paris: Gallimard, 1956.

CSG   Thérèse de l'Enfant-Jésus et de la Sainte-Face. Conseils et souvenirs. Recueillis par Soeur Geneviève de la Sainte Face, soeur et novice de sainte Thérèse de l'Enfant-Jésus. Paris: Editions du Cerf, 1988.

DE   ---. J'entre dans la vie: derniers entretiens. Paris: Editions du Cerf, 1973.

EE   Bridel, Yves. L'esprit d'enfance dans l'oeuvre romanesque de Georges Bernanos. Paris: Minard Lettres Modernes, 1966. "Thèmes et Mythes No 10."

Fra   Bernanos, Georges. Français, si vous saviez 1945-1948. Paris: Gallimard, 1961.

"FM"   "Frère Martin." Présenté par Albert Béguin. Esprit 183 (octobre 1951): 433-445.

HA   Thérèse de l'Enfant-Jésus et de la Sainte-Face. Histoire d'une âme: manuscrits autobiographiques. Paris: Editions du Cerf et Desclée de Brouwer, 1972.

IE   Gaucher, Guy, o.c.d. Georges Bernanos ou l'invincible espérance. Paris: Plon, 1962.

Len   Bernanos, Georges. Le lendemain, c'est vous!. Paris: Plon, 1969.

Lib   ---. La liberté pour quoi faire?. Paris: Gallimard, 1953.

LT   Thérèse de l'Enfant-Jésus et de la Sainte-Face. Une course de géant: lettres. Edition intégrale. Paris: Editions du Cerf et Desclée de Brouwer, 1977.

OE,I   Bernanos, Georges. Oeuvres romanesques, suivies de Dialogues des Carmélites. Préface par Gaëtan Picon. Texte et variantes établis par Albert Béguin. Notes par Michel Estève. Paris: Gallimard. "Bibliothèque de la Pléiade," 1984.

OE,II   ---. Essais et écrits de combat. Tome I. Textes présentés et annotés par Yves Bridel, Jacques Chabot et Joseph Jurt sous la direction de Michel Estève. Paris: Gallimard, "Bibliothèque de la Pléiade," 1971.

"R-M"   Raymond-Marie, Soeur, s.s.a. "Bernanos et l'esprit d'enfance." Carmel 4 (1959): 292-317.

RP   Thérèse de l'Enfant-Jésus et de la Sainte-Face. Théâtre au Carmel: "récréations pieuses." Paris: Editions du Cerf et Desclée de Brouwer, 1985.

S*   Bernanos, Georges. Sous le soleil de Satan. Première édition conforme au manuscrit original. Texte établi et annoté par William Bush. Paris:

Plon, 1982.

SE — Bush, William. <u>Souffrance et expiation dans la pensée de Bernanos</u>. Paris: Minard Lettres Modernes, 1962. "Thèmes et Mythes No 8."

Sp — Speaight, Robert. <u>Georges Bernanos: A Study of the Man and the Writer</u>. London: Collins and Harvill Press, 1973.

"T" — Tobin, Michael Robinson. "Thérèse de Lisieux and Bernanos' First Novel." <u>French Forum</u> 10.1 (1985): 84-96.

von B — Balthasar, Hans Urs von. <u>Le chrétien Bernanos</u>. Trad. Maurice de Gandillac. Paris: Editions du Seuil, 1956.

VS — Bernanos, Georges. <u>La vocation spirituelle de la France</u>. Inédits rassemblés et présentés par Jean-Loup Bernanos. Paris: Plon, 1975.

ACKNOWLEDGEMENT

*It is with sincere gratitude that I would like to thank
Mgr Guy Gaucher and Professor William Bush
for their guidance and encouragement in my research
and for their generosity in writing the forewords for
<u>Georges Bernanos' Debt to Thérèse of Lisieux</u>.*

AVANT-PROPOS

Guy Gaucher

Evêque Auxiliaire de Bayeux et Lisieux

Lisieux, France

La thèse de Soeur Mary Frances Dorschell sur la dette de Bernanos envers Thérèse de Lisieux est pour moi beaucoup plus qu'un travail littéraire. Lorsque j'étais jeune étudiant en lettres à la Sorbonne, je découvris avec émerveillement tout ce que devait ce très grand écrivain, ce très puissant chrétien à la "petite" Sainte de Lisieux. J'ai eu bien du mal à croire - mais les textes étaient là - que cet homme si libre avait pu se mettre à l'école de cette jeune fille.

J'avais alors tenté une étude sur l'influence de la spiritualité thérésienne dans le roman La Joie. Il est vrai que Chantal de Clergerie était bien la soeur d'âme de la carmélite normande. J'espérais alors continuer ce travail pour toutes les oeuvres bernanosiennes. Mais les événements de la vie ne m'ont pas permis de mener à bien cette entreprise.

C'est pourquoi le remarquable travail d'analyse de Soeur Dorschell a été une joie pour moi. Quelqu'un, au-delà de l'océan, avait mené l'enquête d'une manière exhaustive, depuis les premiers écrits bernanosiens - dès 1913 - jusqu'à son chef d'oeuvre, Dialogues des Carmélites de 1947-48.

L'auteur n'a négligé aucun texte, a réalisé une étude d'une grande précision qui aboutit à une démonstration que l'on ne peut contester et qui vérifie au-delà de toute espérance la phrase de Urs von Balthasar qui ouvre son livre: "Sainte Thérèse est partout présente dans l'oeuvre de Bernanos." J'imagine que ce grand théologien, à la culture encyclopédique, aurait lu avec joie une telle étude si documentée.

Pour ma part, elle m'a amplement confirmé dans mes intuitions de jeunesse. Je disais que ce travail n'est pas seulement un précieux apport à la littérature. Il apporte une vision de l'homme, de notre civilisation, de notre monde qui ouvre sur de très vastes horizons.

La hantise de Georges Bernanos fut la vérité et la liberté de l'homme. Ses romans et ses oeuvres de combat rejoignent l'actualité la plus essentielle concernant le destin de l'humanité. Qu'un homme d'une telle qualité humaine et spirituelle, d'un tel regard libre sur le monde ait pu trouver un remède au désespoir dans les écrits et les paroles d'une petite carmélite obscure, morte de tuberculose à vingt-quatre ans, apporte une lumière dans nos nuits. Quand on les traverse, "on rencontre une autre aurore," disait-il.

Il faut remercier Soeur Mary Frances Dorschell de nous livrer ces trésors qui nous renvoient à la lecture des oeuvres de celui derrière lequel elle s'efface. Mais elle a été comme une sourcière qui fait jaillir la Source. Je souhaite que beaucoup s'y abreuvent.

Translation of the above:

The thesis of Sister Mary Frances Dorschell on Bernanos' debt to Thérèse of Lisieux is much more than a literary exercise for me. While studying literature in my student days at the Sorbonne, I discovered, to my amazement, all that that very great and powerful Christian writer owed to the "little" saint of Lisieux. Though it was difficult for me to believe that a man as independent as Bernanos could actually have been a disciple of that very young woman, the texts were there.

I therefore attempted a study of the influence of Theresian spirituality on Bernanos' novel, La Joie, since its heroine, Chantal de Clergerie, is indeed a soul-sister of the young Norman Carmelite. I hoped even at the time to continue my study to include the whole of Bernanos' work. Circumstances, however, did not allow this.

That is why this remarkable study by Sister Dorschell has been a great joy for me. On the other side of the Atlantic someone else has carried out this study in a truly exhaustive way, beginning with the first Bernanosian writings - in 1913, even - and going all the way through to his masterpiece, Dialogues des Carmélites.

Not a single text has been neglected in this very thorough study. The results are an incontestable demonstration justifying, beyond anything anyone could have hoped for, Urs von Balthasar's statement: "Saint Thérèse is present throughout the work of Bernanos." I can only imagine the joy with which that great theologian, given his encyclopedic culture, would have read this well-documented work.

As for myself, my own youthful intuitions on the subject have now been amply confirmed by this study. I would further say that it is not only a precious contribution to literary studies, but also contributes to our vision of man, of our civilization and of our world, opening out on such vast horizons.

Ideas on truth and on man's freedom haunted Georges Bernanos. His novels and non-fictional writings are thus still relevant to the most essential contemporary questions concerning the destiny of mankind today. That a man of such human and spiritual qualities, and of such independence in looking at the world, could seek in the words of an obscure little Carmelite nun, dying of tuberculosis at twenty-four years of age, an answer to his despair, therefore causes our own nights to be less dark. And, as he himself said, it is after coming through those nights that "we find another dawn."

We are very grateful to Sister Mary Frances Dorschell for having given us these precious discoveries which send us back to the works of him before whom she is always so self-effacing. Like a diviner she has caused a new spring to flow. I hope that many will drink of it.

                    Trans. William Bush
                            Professor of French Literature
                            The University of Western Ontario
                            London, Canada

FOREWORD

William Bush
Professor of French Literature
The University of Western Ontario
London, Canada

In *Georges Bernanos' Debt to Thérèse of Lisieux* Dr. Mary Frances Dorschell has done far more than merely trace an "influence" since Georges Bernanos' ties with St. Thérèse of Lisieux defy the limits of what one generally terms, "influence." These extraordinary ties extend not only across Bernanos' entire work but, as Professor Dorschell suggests with reasonable justification, may actually go back as far as 1913. Whatever it may be with their beginnings, these ties are, as is demonstrated, profoundly rooted in the spiritual and psychological depths of Bernanos' own inner life from which emerged that author's powerful and inimitable imaginary world.

The most startling aspects of this work are the numerous proofs Dr. Dorschell offers us of how the exact opposite of Theresian spirituality consistently served as a model for Bernanos' great sinners, whether Simone Alfieri or Monsieur Ouine, in both of whom the author sought, allegorically, to present the sin of the modern world. Having found in Thérèse of Lisieux what he esteemed to be an authentic model of the Christian life - which for Bernanos was nothing less than "*theosis*," that is man's actual participation in the divine life - the author took as it were the other side of the coin to show the corresponding vice. The spirit of childhood is answered by the spirit of old age; youth's risk of "all or nothing," by the prudence and indecisive compromise of maturity.

Yet Dr. Dorschell has avoided, as did Bernanos himself, simplistic, summary contrasts. For in Bernanos' imaginary world, as in life itself, the two sides are never really separable, but interconnected within each personality by countless networks of associations. Astounding reactions can be mysteriously triggered, suddenly metamorphosing virtue into vice, or vice into virtue. Yet, even then, Dr. Dorschell shows us, the Theresian ideal ever remained Bernanos' touchstone and surest measure.

It may be useful to recall that Dr. Dorschell is, of course, dealing with a writer of great standing. Quite paradoxically she is also dealing with what is, on the one hand, a commonplace in Christian history while, on the other hand, something rare indeed in literature, particularly modern literature.

Historically, whether in the Greek or the Latin Church, the Christian faithful have always considered themselves part of a vast, extended family stretching back to the beginnings of Christianity. Given Christianity's insistence that death has been conquered, its adherents have ever regarded its holy ones as eternally present in God and therefore living, dynamic presences who touch the lives of those who, with fear of God, with faith and love, draw near them to seek their help. From the earliest Christian history the power of the holy dead, especially those martyred for the faith, has been recognized and their blessing and protection invoked. That Bernanos would have been "influenced" by a saint who both died and was canonized in his own lifetime is therefore a commonplace.

What is not a commonplace is that this great creative genius, whom André Malraux called "*the greatest novelist of his time*," displayed such singularity in his whole-hearted interior devotion to this one, particular saint. Thérèse of Lisieux indeed eclipsed all other Christian saints in his life. In her he discovered, both for himself and for his powerful interior world, a place of sure repose.

This fusion of two souls through their mutual love of identical aspects of man's life in God is therefore far more than one of "influences." Rather must it be understood as the deepest sort of psychic communion whereby a neophyte soul finds a true guide in a more experienced soul of similar temper.

For the Christian, of course, Jesus Christ Himself is always the only final and true guide. Yet both the Latin and Greek Churches have always insisted on the importance of the spiritualized humanity of those who are His, beginning with the Holy Virgin and coming down through the saints who, in the course of Christian history, have forsaken all to follow Him. Moreover, within those thousands upon thousands of saints, as in any extended family, there will always be, for each member, certain ones to whom one's own heart is more drawn than to others.

For the heart plays a large role in this affair. Bernanos' Christian heart vibrated to Thérèse of Lisieux's spiritual orientation, so firmly fixed on the double foundation of Johannine and Pauline teaching. In that orientation to God, as understood by the young Carmelite, nought is sought, cherished, nor allowed to prevail that is not Love itself. Such an orientation, a perfect answer to the seemingly innate spiritual longing of both Bernanos and the little Carmelite, seems to have caused Bernanos' soul to respond from its very depths, and in a completely unique way, to the young saint's great sister soul, movingly present in all her writings.

That Bernanos attempted to allow for other saints, and in a quite major way, is evident in his first novel, <u>Sous le soleil de Satan</u>. He had obviously aimed there to give a superior role to that male saint canonized in the same month of April, 1925, in which the little Thérèse was raised to the altars: Jean-Marie Vianney, the curé of Ars. He actually calls Donissan, the hero of <u>Sous le soleil de Satan</u>, a "new curé of Ars" and attempts to fathom the mystery behind that famous wonder-worker's physical struggles with the devil, behind his frightening self-flagellations, as well as his deep sense of being a total failure as a priest.

This attempt on Bernanos' part failed, however. In the midst of the composition of his first novel his preoccupation with "the little Thérèse" began to impose itself, even if <u>Sous le soleil de Satan</u> were not supposed to be dedicated to her at all, but rather to her male counterpart, canonized the same month as she.[1] Nor does Bernanos' treatment of St. Dominic, or even of Joan of Arc, in any way measure up to the intimate, interior and on-going communion he always enjoyed with Thérèse of Lisieux. After the success of <u>Sous le soleil de Satan</u> in 1926, she would be enthroned at the centre of the author's creative imagination as a sort of measure by which all was thenceforth to be evaluated, be it good or evil, vice or virtue.

In 1960, in the first issue of the *Revue des Lettres Modernes'* "*études bernanosiennes*" series, Monseigneur Guy Gaucher launched the idea of "*an exhaustive work*" on Bernanos and the young Carmelite. It is an honour, thirty-four years later, to be associated with a work so perfectly and explicitly answering those hopes articulated in 1960. As Monseigneur Gaucher so rightly anticipated at that time, such a study "*would give astonishing results.*" It will be the reader's privilege to discover these "*astonishing results*" in this well-written and very useful volume by Dr. Dorschell.

NOTES

FOREWORD

[1] See Michael R. Tobin, "Thérèse of Lisieux and Bernanos' First Novel," *French Forum*, vol. 10, no. 1, Jan 1986, pp. 84-96.

AUTHOR'S PREFACE

At the time of the death of Thérèse of Lisieux from tuberculosis on September 30, 1897 at the age of twenty-four in the Carmel of Lisieux Georges Bernanos was nine years old. A year later, the first edition of the <u>Histoire d'une âme</u> was printed, and in less than ten years, the Carmelites of Lisieux were already preparing Thérèse's cause for beatification. By June of 1914, Pius X had declared privately to a missionary bishop that Thérèse was the greatest saint of modern times[1] and her cause for beatification had been formally introduced in Rome. During World War I, Thérèse was called the "darling" of the French troops in the trenches and her beatification in April, 1923, quickly followed by her canonization in May, 1925, was exceptional! Two years after canonization, Thérèse was declared patroness of missionaries and in 1944 she was named, along with Jeanne d'Arc, patroness of France. The fact that Rome is presently considering declaring Thérèse a doctor of the Church only adds to the interest of determining to what extent Bernanos, the "greatest novelist of his time," according to André Malraux, was indebted to her for his own Christian thought.

The only son of a Catholic royalist family, Bernanos would indeed have been aware of the publicity surrounding the future saint who had lived in a small Norman town only a few hours distance from Paris. In reading Thérèse's <u>Histoire d'une âme</u>, the young Bernanos' discovery of someone else who, like him, had a hero worship for the saints and martyrs, a distaste for half-measures, and a desire to dedicate her life fully to God's service, seems echoed in one of his earliest articles, "La Malibran," published in 1913. A close examination of this pen portrait of the Parisian born Spanish singer, María Felicia García, reveals that certain characteristics of la Malibran admired by Bernanos much better mirror traits found in the French saint, than those of the better known Teresa of Avila.

Some twenty-five years later, with his literary career well established, Bernanos finally expressed with astonishing accuracy the true meaning of Thérèse's message in <u>Les Grands cimetières sous la lune</u>. He thereby surpasses many of his well-meaning Christian contemporaries who completely failed to grasp its significance.

Scholars have long spoken of the influence of Thérèse on Bernanos, yet her impact has been only randomly observed. In 1954 the noted German-Swiss theologian, Hans Urs von Balthasar, declared: "Sainte Thérèse est partout présente dans l'oeuvre de Bernanos." In his 1960 article comparing the author with the saint, Guy Gaucher, an authority on both Thérèse and Bernanos, stated: "Nous avons cité beaucoup de textes mais nous sommes certain qu'un travail exhaustif donnerait des résultats étonnants." It was such statements which prompted the writing of this dissertation on Bernanos' debt to Thérèse of Lisieux.

The dissertation therefore examines in chronological order Bernanos' entire work, fiction and non-fiction, in search of Thérèse's presence. It is divided into two unequal parts. Part one, representing a little over a quarter of the dissertation, points out explicit textual references to the saint, whether to her name, quotations from her works or to earlier studies done by scholars attempting to show her influence on the author. Part two traces Thérèse's implicit presence in Bernanos' fictional characters, whether they reveal parallel or reverse images of the saint.

This close analysis of Bernanos' debt to Thérèse of Lisieux does indeed open new perspectives. First of all, it is in "La Malibran," published in 1913, and not in "Madame Dargent," published in 1922, that the earliest indication of Thérèse's presence in Bernanos' work should be sought. Bernanos' use of Thérèse as a model can be applied to far more of his characters than the critics have pointed out. While parallel images of Thérèse's spirituality appear in Bernanos' "saints," reverse patterns of it flow through his "sinners." Indeed, when the saint's spirituality is traced through all the major characters, the consistency of the reverse image of her spirituality becomes all the more overwhelming. Such a discovery tends to indicate that for Bernanos it was Theresian qualities which marked the spiritual life. Yet, in spite of the many characters in Bernanos' fictional world who, to varying degrees, are negative images of Thérèse, none, including the notorious Monsieur Ouine, is ever entirely a reverse image of the saint.

Even more significant is the discovery that Thérèse's message seems in deep harmony with Bernanos' favourite themes. These we find in heroic childhood, the acceptance of weakness, the uniting of personal suffering with the Holy Agony, and the attitude of approaching God with a beggar's empty hands.

The author's work of the twenties and thirties was dominated by explicit references to the saint and culminated in the statement of her message in <u>Les Grands cimetières sous la lune</u>, published in 1938. At the beginning, moreover, the implicit references had always taken a second place to explicit references. In the thirties, however, implicit evidence of the saint's presence prevailed in the fictional works. <u>Journal d'un curé de campagne</u>, published in 1936, has only one explicit reference while <u>Nouvelle histoire de Mouchette</u>, published in 1937, has none. Nevertheless, both of these works affirm Thérèse's implicit presence as we see her spirituality lived on the supernatural level in the young curé of Ambricourt and on the natural level in the little Mouchette.

The works of the forties testify to a deepening of the saint's presence. The essay on "Frère Martin," published in 1943, reveals Martin Luther, like many of Bernanos' fictional characters, to be a reverse image of the saint of Lisieux. Moreover, Bernanos' own definition of sanctity as seen in his 1947 lecture, "Nos amis les saints," is purely Theresian. Finally, in <u>Dialogues des Carmélites,</u> Thérèse is so implicitly present on every page and in every character that one begins to wonder if the words on the printed page are the author's or the saint's.

One may therefore conclude that as Bernanos' work evolved and as Thérèse of Lisieux' message of childhood and acceptance of weakness had indeed become Bernanos' own, explicit references to the saint gradually gave way to yet more imposing implicit ones as in <u>Dialogues des Carmélites</u>. This dissertation not only attempts to answer Gaucher's request for an exhaustive examination of Thérèse's presence in Bernanos' work, but it also opens up other possibilities which could be pursued in the future such as the author's acquaintance with other saints. An examination of Bernanos' Christian sources could also reveal how the thought of other Christians, including Dominic Gusman, Francis of Assisi, Teresa of Avila, the curé d'Ars, Jeanne d'Arc, and Martin Luther, influenced the author and was transformed into the message he presents for our times.

NOTES

AUTHOR'S PREFACE

[1] Pius X's statement about Thérèse being the greatest saint of modern times appears in many works but its origin is somewhat obscure. The only source of this information is to be found in a small typed booklet entitled "Pie X et la Servante de Dieu Soeur Thérèse de l'Enfant-Jésus 1910-1914: Pie X et la Sainte Face du Carmel de Lisieux 1905-1907." The booklet, which is about the size of an ordinary exercise book, may be seen at the Centre de Documentation Thérésienne at the Lisieux Carmel. On page 12 one reads the following: "... Et montrant un jour, à un évêque missionnaire, le portrait de la Servante de Dieu, il dit 'VOICI LA PLUS GRANDE SAINTE DE NOTRE TEMPS.' (ou: des temps modernes)." Authorities at Carmel believe this statement to have been made between 1907 and 1913.

INTRODUCTION

THÉRÈSE, BERNANOS, AND THE CRITICS

INTRODUCTION

THÉRÈSE, BERNANOS, AND THE CRITICS

As early as 1954 the noted German Swiss theologian, Hans Urs von Balthasar, states in his work, <u>Le chrétien Bernanos</u>, that "Sainte Thérèse est partout présente dans l'oeuvre de Bernanos" (<u>von B</u> 289). In 1960 the well-known Carmelite scholar, Guy Gaucher, an authority on both Thérèse and Bernanos, comments: "Son nom figure dans presque tous les écrits de combat et on le retrouve dans quelques romans" ("BT" 229-230).

To what extent are these statements justified? Is it possible that this obscure little Carmelite really did have such an influence on a writer whom André Malraux called "le plus grand romancier de son temps"?[1]

Many other scholars have also pointed out either in a general or specific manner the impact of this tubercular young Carmelite, dead at the age of twenty-four, on the vision of Georges Bernanos.[2] Whether their comments involve textual and thematic comparisons or bring to light interesting, previously undiscovered facts, all are in agreement about this influence.

Possibly the earliest remark concerning Thérèse's influence on Bernanos is the claim made by Luc Estang in his 1949 article on <u>Dialogues des Carmélites</u>. In this work written in 1948 shortly before the author's death, Estang believes that "Constance et Blanche sont deux aspects de sainte Thérèse de Lisieux; deux aspects qui, en définitive, s'identifient dans ce que Bernanos aimait à nommer:'la douce pitié de Dieu.'"³ Unfortunately the critic does not elaborate on this highly significant observation.

In 1951, the influence of the saint on the writer's spirituality was mentioned by Don Paul Gordan in the second part of his article, "Bernanos au Brésil." He reveals that "Quant à la 'petite' Thérèse, dont les <u>Ultima Verba</u> ne quittaient guère sa table de chevet, Bernanos aimait en elle une soeur cadette de la Pucelle."⁴ It is not surprising, therefore, that quotes from Thérèse's last sayings are scattered throughout Bernanos' works.

One of the earlier scholars grasping the impact of Thérèse's message on Bernanos is Charles Moeller. In his 1953 work on twentieth century literature and Christianity, Moeller contends that Bernanos' thought concerning the Christian and Christ's Passion resembles the saint's: "C'est en assumant cette passion, qu'il rachète le monde et que, ensuite, il connaît la joie."⁵

But it is to von Balthasar in his above-mentioned work in 1954 that we owe the earliest major examination of Thérèse and Bernanos. Textual and thematic evidence concerning the influence of the saint on the writer are indeed revealed by this great scholar. He shows us that the short story, "Madame Dargent," published in 1922, contains the earliest explicit textual evidence of the saint's presence in the writer's works.

Von Balthasar also points out how Thérèse's spirit has been translated into Bernanos' works. The critic has thus noted the impact of the message contained in the sermon for the feast of Saint Thérèse that comprises some twenty pages of Bernanos' volume on the Spanish Civil War, <u>Les Grands Cimetières sous la lune</u>, written in 1937-1938. He claims that the author is criticizing the world for having watered down the saint's message (<u>von B</u> 289-291).

In addition, von Balthasar comments on how Bernanos' heroes and heroines are patterned on Thérèse. He proclaims, for example, that both Thérèse and Jeanne d'Arc serve as models for the author and that as such they offer an important message for our times (von B 286-287). Yet it is Thérèse who is seen as one of the main models for the theme of the spirit of childhood found in the author's works. Von Balthasar explores this particular theme, along with the virtue of hope, in the writer's personal correspondence and in his polemical and fictional works (von B 282-300).

According to this noted theologian, Thérèse serves too as a pattern for the numerous agony and death scenes in Bernanos' works. Among the first to touch on this aspect, von Balthasar comments that the thought of dying was a source of great anguish for the author who even from an early age knew "le cri de douleur de la petite Thérèse, qui, par delà tout art de mourir, n'est plus qu'une interrogation pleine d'angoisse . . ." (von B 426).

Finally, the Theresian influence penetrating La Joie published in 1929 and Journal d'un curé de campagne published in 1936 is very evident to von Balthasar who shows how Thérèse is the prototype for both Chantal de Clergerie and the young parish priest of Ambricourt. This scholar discloses how in La Joie the author constantly employs images and expressions mirroring those of Thérèse. Then, pointing out how several traits of the priest-hero parallel those of Thérèse, he concludes that the curé of Ambricourt is "une sorte d'adaptation en profondeur du message thérésien, non plus, comme dans La joie par l'emprunt des détails caractéristiques, mais par une libre transposition des intuitions centrales, élevées du plan terrestre au plan de l'esprit" (von B 289). This highly provocative observation however has never been pursued any further.

In his 1959 work, Le sens de l'amour dans les romans de Bernanos, Michel Estève also perceives Thérèse's spirit in Journal d'un curé de campagne. He contends that love is the central theme of Bernanos' works and that Thérèse is the example par excellence of how human love can reach perfection. Aware that Bernanos has borrowed the saint's words, "tout est grâce" (DE 41), Estève, in the wake of von Balthasar, declares that: "Les dernières paroles prononcées par le petit curé de campagne traduisent de façon saisissante la pensée directrice de toute l'oeuvre romanesque bernanosienne."⁶

In the same year, in her comparative study entitled "Bernanos et l'esprit d'enfance," Soeur Raymond-Marie goes further still in demonstrating the proof of these ties. Analyzing the parallels between Thérèse and the novelist's characters, and in particular, Chantal de Clergerie and the curé of Ambricourt ("R-M" 292-317), she offers a detailed comparison of Thérèse's and Chantal's vocations of love and suffering showing how both experience a call to save others. Their extraordinary confidence in God is based on the reality of their insignificance and their faith in God's all-merciful love. Commenting on <u>Journal d'un curé de campagne</u>, Soeur Raymond-Marie points out that Bernanos' saints, following in the steps of Thérèse, do not die in transports of joy ("R-M" 309-312).

This critic's keen observations have thus greatly advanced our understanding of Bernanos' debt to Thérèse of Lisieux as has the work of Guy Gaucher who, in his 1960 article, "Bernanos et Ste Thérèse de l'Enfant-Jésus," also establishes a close parallel between the saint and the writer. Gaucher notes similarities in their character such as their desire for glory, their dislike of half measures, their childhood love of stories of heroes and saints, their special devotion to Jeanne d'Arc, their warrior-like attitude with regard to the spiritual life, and their love for truth ("BT" 239-243). Going further and beyond Bernanos' writing to his biography, Gaucher describes how even in death there was a similarity between the saint and the writer in the expression of serenity and the hint of a smile on their faces ("BT" 268). Moreover, drawing upon Bernanos' letters, Gaucher traces the evolution of the author's spirituality and detects that he, like Thérèse, offers a message of hope to the world ("BT" 266-267). He also affirms that in <u>Les Grands Cimetières sous la lune</u> Bernanos deems Thérèse to be a sign for our times ("BT" 234-235).

Like von Balthasar and Soeur Raymond-Marie, Gaucher also takes very seriously the many Theresian parallels to be found in Chantal de Clergerie and her spiritual director, the abbé Chevance. A major portion of his excellent article even presents a series of parallel texts proving this similarity not only in character, attitudes, vocabulary, and use of imagery, but also in their spirituality, trials, temptations, and even in their respective agonies. Indeed the Carmelite scholar seems amply justified in concluding that: "Les analogies sont trop frappantes pour qu'on ne décèle pas une influence de la sainte sur le romancier" ("BT" 247). We shall examine this evidence in our first chapter.

Gaucher also considers the role of Thérèse in Bernanos' essay, "Jeanne, relapse et sainte," published in 1929. He points out quite astutely that the author felt that Jeanne's trial resembled the way the world questions Thérèse's doctrine of spiritual childhood ("BT" 241), before concluding that Bernanos' spiritual testament, Dialogues des Carmélites, is "l'occasion d'un suprême hommage à la sainte" ("BT" 238).

It is hardly surprising then that two years after this article appeared, Gaucher, in his spiritual biography of Bernanos, Georges Bernanos ou l'invincible espérance, affirms that not only the writer's own spirituality but also that of his fictional characters is impregnated by Thérèse's teaching (IE 115). Then, adding weight to von Balthasar's thesis that Thérèse is present in the many agony and death scenes in Bernanos' works, Gaucher indicates how the little Carmelite's use of the expression "On ne tombe qu'en Dieu"[7] became a part of Bernanos' own philosophy on death (IE 147).

Also in 1962, William Bush pointed out the affinity between Thérèse and Bernanos in the writer's first novel, Sous le soleil de Satan. In his volume, Souffrance et expiation dans la pensée de Bernanos, Bush carefully draws our attention to the contrast between Thérèse, Donissan, and Chantal de Clergerie in connection with their feeling of impotence. Unlike Thérèse, Donissan did not accept his helplessness and offer it to God. Herein lies the secret of his self-hatred (SE 133-141, 150).

In her 1963 publication, Bernanos fidèle à l'enfant, Marie-Agnès Fragnière elaborates on how Bernanos recognized the urgency of Thérèse's teaching on the spirit of childhood. She concludes her study by stating that the author stressed the importance of the young Carmelite's message, "un message de l'enfance à l'enfance et à tous ceux qui sont aptes à le recevoir."[8]

In his volume published in 1966, L'esprit d'enfance dans l'oeuvre romanesque de Georges Bernanos, Yves Bridel not only recognizes the now established impact of Thérèse's spirituality on Bernanos, but also brings to our attention another facet of the curé of Ambricourt's spirituality which resembles that of the Carmelite's. The young priest, Bridel points out, seems to beg love from those to whom he ministers as a sign of their reconciliation with their neighbour and ultimately with God. Viewing this as essentially Thérèse of Lisieux' concept of the Divine Beggar's love of mankind, Bridel concludes that "le curé imite ainsi l'amour tel que le pratique le Christ, dans la conception qu'en a sainte Thérèse, de beaucoup plus près que Chantal" (EE 179). This scholar thus views the curé of Ambricourt as one of the most significant "Theresian" characters in Bernanos' works.

Bridel also proclaims Thérèse's influence on the novelist in Nouvelle histoire de Mouchette. According to the Swiss critic, the young heroine's total misery calls forth God's merciful love and, for this reason, he believes that "Bernanos n'a jamais été plus proche qu'ici de la voie d'enfance spirituelle de sainte Thérèse . . ." (EE 197). It is in deliberately making oneself little, as did the saint of Lisieux, that one satisfies God's desire to give Himself to those who are the least and most abandoned. "Mais Mouchette ne se fait pas petite, elle l'est. Elle n'a jamais perdu son esprit d'enfance, au contraire" (EE 197). The heroine's search for truth, purity, and love in contrast with the extreme poverty of her condition are thus viewed by Bridel as being an incarnation of Thérèse's doctrine of spiritual childhood as it would appear in a world without the presence of God.

In his critical analysis of the writer's works, Georges Bernanos, first published in 1967, Max Milner affirms that Bernanos' encounter with "la vraie figure de sainte Thérèse de l'Enfant-Jésus"[9] oriented the author's spirituality in a different direction from that indicated in <u>Sous le soleil de Satan</u>. According to Milner, we don't know if Bernanos read the <u>Histoire d'une âme</u>, published in 1898,[10] "mais, c'est un fait qu'il ne commence à citer sainte Thérèse qu'à partir de 1927" (<u>M</u> 144). Since the earliest edition of her last sayings, the <u>Novissima Verba</u>, was not published until 1926, this critic assumes that "c'est la lecture de cette oeuvre qui révéla à Bernanos la forme de sainteté particulière à la petite carmélite de Lisieux" (<u>M</u> 144).

Milner seems to be unaware of the facts. Von Balthasar as early as 1954 indicated a reference to Thérèse's words in "Madame Dargent," published in 1922. Michael Tobin, in 1985, has definitively demonstrated the impact of the <u>Histoire d'une âme</u> on <u>Sous le soleil de Satan</u>, completed in 1925. Thus one can only conclude that Bernanos had read the <u>Histoire d'une âme</u> well before the 1925 canonization of the young Carmelite.

An article going further than anything heretofore regarding the influence of Thérèse on Bernanos in <u>Dialogues des Carmélites</u>, was published by Gaucher in 1972. It illustrates as it were Luc Estang's 1949 statement that Blanche and Constance are two aspects of Thérèse. In it Gaucher reminds us of the saint's full name - Thérèse de l'Enfant-Jésus et de la Sainte-Face and directs our attention to the fact that Bernanos based the chaplain's sermon on the Suffering Servant passage from Isaiah 53, that same passage from which Thérèse derived her devotion to the Holy Face. Gaucher, who is at once both a Theresian and a Bernanosian scholar, observes that Bernanos' saints are in total conformity with Thérèse for whom the spirit of childhood cannot be separated from the redemption. Seeing Constance and Blanche together offering their lives to God, he proclaims that "Constance est Thérèse de l'Enfant-Jésus et Blanche de l'Agonie du Christ Thérèse de la Sainte-Face."[11]

In 1972 we find both Bridel and Bush returning to the question of the author's fusion of Thérèse and Jeanne d'Arc. In an article on Bernanos and Jeanne d'Arc, Brdel, examining passages where the writer unites the two saints, declares it is evident that Bernanos believed Jeanne d'Arc to have lived according to Thérèse's concept of the spirit of childhood and concludes, in agreement with von Balthasar, that these two young women have a similar message for the world.[12]

Bush, for his part, clarifies Bernanos' fusion of Thérèse and Jeanne d'Arc in his article on the composition and themes of <u>Les Grands Cimetières sous la lune</u>. By uniting honour and childhood, Bernanos is able to join together his two favorite saints: "Jeanne d'Arc qui incarnait l'honneur, et Thérèse de Lisieux qui incarnait l'esprit de l'enfance . . ."[13] Furthermore, Bush considers that the sermon for the feast of Saint Thérèse contains the essence of Bernanos' own spirituality ("HED" 11).

In the same year Pierrette Renard re-examines how Thérèse is a prototype for Bernanos' heroes and heroines and adds the name of Teresa of Avila to that of Thérèse of Lisieux and Jeanne d'Arc as models chosen by Bernanos for his heroines. Through the gift of their love they give life to others.[14]

The next critic to make a significant contribution to the question of Thérèse's influence on Bernanos is Michael Tobin who in his 1985 study of Thérèse and <u>Sous le soleil de Satan</u> supports Bush's theory of Donissan's rejection of his impotence. Tobin explains how the author's treatment of Donissan and Menou-Segrais with regard to the understanding of sanctity and vocation resembles certain aspects of Thérèse's life. In addition, through pointing out the presence of Theresian vocabulary and imagery in the scene where Bernanos describes Mouchette as being the plaything of Satan, Tobin perceives the unfortunate young woman as having been created by Bernanos as an infernal reflection of Thérèse ("T" 85-89). Tobin thus definitively corrects Milner's thesis that Thérèse is not cited in Bernanos' works before 1927.

In 1986, Jean-Loup Bernanos' biography confirms for us his father's great affection for Thérèse,[15] and in an article published in the same year, Estève adds to his earlier thesis that love is the central theme of Bernanos' works, recalling that the Theresian words "tout est grâce" (<u>DE</u> 41) show that the attitude of both the little Carmelite and the young curé of Ambricourt towards human agony and death is essentially an act of love.[16]

The pertinent elements of Georges Bernanos' debt to Thérèse of Lisieux have been examined only randomly, however, in spite of the considerable progress that has been made. Certain critics have in fact called attention to the need for a more exhaustive treatment to be done on the rapport between the two authors.

René Laurentin, a Theresian scholar, has observed: "On n'a pas fini d'évaluer la part de Thérèse dans l'inspiration de Bernanos, et jusque dans ses formulations,"[17] whereas Gaucher, as we have already seen, has stated: "Nous avons cité beaucoup de textes mais nous sommes certain qu'un travail exhaustif donnerait des résultats étonnants" ("BT" 264). From this statement made by Gaucher three decades ago has come our decision to undertake such a "travail exhaustif."

NOTES

INTRODUCTION

[1] André Malraux, préface, Journal d'un curé de campagne, by Georges Bernanos (Paris: Plon, 1974) 9.

[2] Scholars other than those mentioned in the Introduction who have spoken of the influence of Thérèse of Lisieux on Georges Bernanos include the following: Hans Aaraas, "La conversion de Bernanos," Bernanos: continuités et ruptures, Actes du Colloque international organisé par le Groupe d'Informations et de Recherches sur Bernanos, Nancy-juin 1987, études réunies par Pierre Gille et Max Milner (Nancy: Presses Universitaires de Nancy, 1988) 18, 22-23; ---, Littérature et sacerdoce: essai sur "Journal d'un curé de campagne" de Bernanos (Paris: Lettres Modernes Minard, 1984) 101, 134. Ernest Beaumont, "Le sens christique de l'oeuvre romanesque de Bernanos," La Revue des Lettres Modernes 81-84 (1963) "Etudes bernanosiennes" 3-4: 89. P. Blanchard, "Georges Bernanos et l'Esprit d'enfance," Vie Thérésienne 14 (avril 1964): 60-74. Gerda Blumenthal, The Poetic Imagination of Georges Bernanos (Baltimore: The John Hopkins Press, 1965) 82-83. Pierre de Boisdeffre, Métamorphose de la littérature, tome 1, Barrès, Gide, Mauriac, Bernanos, Montherlant, Malraux (Verviers, Belgique: Gérard et Cie., 1974) 231-233. J. Boly, o.s.c., "Dialogues des Carmélites": étude et analyse (Paris: Editions de l'Ecole, 1960) 45. Bernard Bro, o.p., The Little Way: The Spirituality of Thérèse of Lisieux, trans. Alan Neame (Westminster, Maryland: Christian Classics, 1980) 26, 52, 83, 101-102. R.-L. Brückberger, o.p., Bernanos vivant (Paris: Albin Michel, 1988) 62-64, 68, 174. John E. Cooke, Georges Bernanos: A Study of Christian Commitment (Amersham, Buckinghamshire: Avebury Publishing Company, 1981) 106. Henri Debluë, Les romans de Georges Bernanos ou le défi du rêve (Neuchâtel: Editions de la Baconnière, 1965) 118-120, 135, 240, 249-251, 258. François Frison, "Le thème de la chevalerie et le mythe personnel de Bernanos," La Revue des Lettres Modernes 290-297 (1972) "Etudes bernanosiennes" 13: 216. Jessie Lynn Gillespie, Le tragique dans l'oeuvre de Georges Bernanos (Genève: Librairie E. Droz; Paris: Librairie Minard, 1960) 59. Henri Guillemin, Regards sur Bernanos (Paris: Gallimard, 1976) 351. Bernard Halda, Bernanos ou la foi militante et déchirée (Paris: Téqui, 1980) 16-17, 79-82, 160, 165. Peter Hebblethewaite, s.j., Bernanos: An Introduction (New York: Hilary House Publishers Ltd., 1965) 85. Philippe Le Touzé, Le mystère du réel dans les romans de Bernanos (Paris: Librairie A.-G. Nizet, 1979) 37-38, 109, 116, 146, 251, 268, 291. Sister Marie-Céleste, Bernanos et son optique de la vie chrétienne (Paris: A.-G. Nizet, 1967) 10, 51, 125-135. Monique Michaud, "Les Grands Cimetières sous la lune revisités," Paradoxes et permanence de la pensée bernanosienne, études publiées sous la direction de Joël Pottier (Paris: Aux Animateurs de livres, 1989) 85. Meredith Murray, o.p., La genèse de "Dialogues des Carmélites" (Paris: Editions du Seuil, 1963) 25, 126, 132-133, 140, 147. Eithne M. O'Sharkey, "Portraits of the Clergy in Bernanos' 'Diary of a Country Priest,'" The Dublin Review 504 (Summer 1965) 190; ---, The Role of the Priest in the Novels of Georges Bernanos (New York: Vantage Press, 1983) 44, 49, 97, 106. Joël Pottier, "Un jugement de Gertrud von le Fort sur 'Jeanne, relapse et sainte' de Georges Bernanos," Paradoxes et permanence de la pensée bernanosienne, études publiées sous la direction de Joël Pottier (Paris: Aux Animateurs de livres, 1989) 184. Emile Rideau, Thérèse de Lisieux: la nature et la grâce (Paris: Fayard, 1973) 318-321. Yvon Rivard, L'imaginaire et le quotidien: essai sur les romans de Georges Bernanos (Paris: Lettres Modernes Minard, 1978, "Bibliothèque des lettres modernes" No 21) 220. John Saward, "Faithful to the Child I Used To Be: Bernanos and the Spirit of Childhood," The Chesterton Review XV-XVI. 4-1 (1988-1989): 468-469, 472, 478.

Jean-François Six, La véritable enfance de Thérèse de Lisieux: névrose et sainteté (Paris: Editions du Seuil, 1972) 8, 18; ---, Thérèse de Lisieux au Carmel (Paris: Editions du Seuil, 1973) 351. Robert Speaight, Georges Bernanos: A Study of the Man and the Writer (London: Collins and Harvill Press, 1973) 266-267. Max Vilain, "Bernanos et les Novissima Verba," Vie Thérésienne (janvier 1974): 57-65. Nicole Winter, "Conception bernanosienne du sacerdoce à partir du Journal d'un curé de campagne," La Revue des Lettres Modernes 67-68 (1961-1962) "Etudes bernanosiennes" 2: 76.

³ Luc Estang, "Les Dialogues des Carmélites," Bulletin de la société des amis de Georges Bernanos 1 (1949): 14.

⁴ Dom Paul Gordan, "Bernanos au Brésil," (suite), Bulletin de la société des amis de Georges Bernanos 6 (1951): 5.

⁵ Charles Moeller, Littérature du XXe siècle et christianisme, tome 1, Silence de Dieu (Paris: Castermann, 1953) 425.

⁶ Michel Estève, Le sens de l'amour dans les romans de Bernanos (Paris: Minard Lettres Modernes, 1959, "Thèmes et Mythes" No 7) 11.

⁷ Monique Gosselin [Monique Gosselin, L'écriture du surnaturel dans l'oeuvre romanesque de Georges Bernanos, 2 tomes (Lille: Atelier Reproduction des thèses Université de Lille III; Paris: Librairie Honoré Champion, 1979) 461-462] points out that the words, "On ne tombe qu'en Dieu," are attributed to Thérèse of Lisieux whereas in actual fact, they were the words of Mme Jourdain, one of the foundresses of the French Carmelites. Henri Brémond relates Mme Jourdain's description of the difficulties encountered in the crossing of the numerous precipices of the Pyrenees when on her way to Spain to meet the Spanish Carmelites who were to found the first French monastery: "- Au bord de ces abîmes béants, Mme Jourdain disait avec allégresse: 'Je ne saurais tomber qu'en Dieu!'"
[Histoire littéraire du sentiment religieux en France depuis la fin des guerres de religion jusqu'à nos jours, tome II, L'invasion mystique (Paris: Bloud et Gay, 1930) 295].
Though the above words are not really hers, Thérèse of Lisieux delighted in applying them to the events of her own life.

⁸ Marie-Agnès Fragnière, Bernanos fidèle à l'enfant (Fribourg: Editions Universitaires, 1963) 116.

⁹ Max Milner, Georges Bernanos (Paris: Librairie Séguier, 1989) 144. Cited hereafter as M.

¹⁰ Judging from the rapid spread of devotion to Thérèse which took place immediately following the publication of her manuscripts, it is hard to conceive that Bernanos did not read the Histoire d'une âme long before the saint's canonization. In Rohrbach's The Search for Saint Thérèse, we read regarding the demand for her autobiography: "Between 1898 and 1915, over two hundred thousand copies of the French edition were published, and seven hundred thousand copies of the abridged French edition."
Rohrbach points out further that the volume of letters arriving at the Carmel of Lisieux grew from approximately fifty per day in 1911 to as many as five hundred per day after 1914. He also mentions numerous reports of favors obtained through Thérèse's intervention and how she became known as "the darling of the troops in the French trenches" as well as of Irish, American, and Canadian soldiers.

Peter-Thomas Rohrbach, o.c.d., The Search for Saint Thérèse (Garden City, New York: Hanover House, 1961) 218-219.
Considering the author's Catholic background, it seems inconceivable that Bernanos was not familiar with Thérèse's autobiography before 1927.

[11] Guy Gaucher, o.c.d., "L'appel de Bernanos," Courrier Georges Bernanos 2-3-4 (1971): 100.

[12] Yves Bridel, "Jeanne d'Arc et Bernanos," Bernanos, Centre culturel de Cerisy-la-Salle 10 au 19 juillet 1969, ed. Max Milner (Paris: Plon, 1972) 289-302.

[13] William Bush, "Honneur, enfance et désincarnation: composition et thèmes des 'Grands cimetières sous la lune,'" La Revue des Lettres Modernes 290-297 (1972) "Etudes bernanosiennes" 13: 13. Cited hereafter as "HED."

[14] Pierrette Renard, "La femme dans l'oeuvre de Bernanos," Bernanos. Centre culturel de Cerisy-la-Salle 10 au 19 juillet, 1969, ed. Max Milner (Paris: Plon, 1972) 280.

[15] Jean-Loup Bernanos, Georges Bernanos à la merci des passants (Paris: Plon, 1986) 20.

[16] Michel Estève, "La nuit de Gethsémani," La Revue des Lettres Modernes 771-776 (1986) "Etudes bernanosiennes" 18: 10.

[17] René Laurentin, Thérèse de Lisieux: mythes et réalité (Paris: Editions Beauchesne, 1972) 44.

PART I

EXPLICIT EVIDENCE OF THÉRÈSE OF LISIEUX' PRESENCE IN BERNANOS' WORK

CHAPTER I

FIRST EXPLICIT EVIDENCE (1905-1930)

In his work, <u>Littérature du XXe siècle et christianisme</u>, Charles Moeller explains that in the early part of the century most people were ignorant of Thérèse of Lisieux' real message and tended to confuse it with religious sentimentality. He claims that it was only in the late 1940's with the studies of the abbé Combes that one began to understand that Thérèse's true spirituality is based on suffering, abandonment, and agony.[1]

Long before that date however there is explicit evidence that Bernanos had already grasped the meaning of the saint's message. Whether we weigh references to her name and quotations from her works found in Bernanos' own work, or whether we take as equally conclusive explicit evidence the numerous previous studies done by critics on establishing her influence on the author, Bernanos' understanding of the Carmelite's significance was a profound one long before 1940.

Explicit Evidence prior to <u>L'Imposture</u> (1927)

As Guy Gaucher has indicated ("BT" 232), the first indisputable reference to Thérèse of Lisieux by name appears in L'Imposture, Bernanos' second novel, published in 1927, in which the author depicts the abbé Cénabre as a distinguished scholar engaged in writing an article refuting a recently published work on "la Bienheureuse Thérèse de l'Enfant-Jésus, dont le sourire céleste, tentation des niais faciles, restera toujours la rose la plus sanglante et la mieux défendue des jardins du paradis" (OE,I 358). Nevertheless, some scholars have observed explicit textual evidence of the Carmelite's presence in the short story, "Madame Dargent," published in 1922, and in Bernanos' first novel, Sous le soleil de Satan, begun in 1919 but not actually published until 1926.

Hans Urs von Balthasar is the first critic to detect an explicit textual reference to Thérèse of Lisieux in "Madame Dargent." Her words: "je ne peux pas mourir!... Je ne saurais jamais mourir!" (DE 188) are repeated by Bernanos' heroine on her deathbed: "je n'en finirai jamais de mourir" and "Je ne peux pas mourir . . ." (OE,I 6), as von Balthasar points out (von B 289).

As for the Carmelite's influence on Sous le soleil de Satan, it was in Souffrance et expiation dans la pensée de Bernanos that William Bush first examined that question. Pointing out that the chief cause of suffering in Bernanos' saints is the consciousness of their impotence before evil in the world, as is also found in Thérèse of Lisieux, Bush insists that the Carmelite found a means of overcoming her weakness by adopting a childlike attitude of simplicity and confidence towards God (SE 133-134). It was her desire for sanctity which led her to abandon herself to merciful love and, according to this critic, the words of her "Acte d'offrande à l'Amour miséricordieux": "je désire être Sainte, mais je sens mon impuissance et je vous demande, ô mon Dieu! d'être vous-même ma Sainteté" (HA 316) testify to the confident abandonment of her impotence to God. Bush points out that, similar to Thérèse's situation, the interior suffering of Donissan, the priest-hero of Sous le soleil de Satan, consists in his impotence before the power of Satan (SE 139). Certainly Bernanos describes Donissan in terms of his weakness. "Il a souffert longtemps de l'impuissance à exprimer ce qu'il sent . . ." (OE,I 138), he states, and then, "La Sainteté! [. . .] La certitude de son impuissance à égaler un tel destin bloquait jusqu'à la prière sur ses lèvres" (OE,I 142). But in contrast to Thérèse, Donissan refuses to accept his weakness and to abandon himself to God, and so we find Bernanos speculating on what would have become of his priest-hero had he abandoned himself to merciful love: "Fût-il devenu l'un de ces saints dont l'histoire ressemble à un conte, de ces doux qui possèdent la terre, avec un sourire d'enfant-roi?..." (OE,I 147).

But Donissan persists in revolting against his impotence and so he fails to raise the dead child to life. Instead of placing his weakness in God's hands, he relies on his own power, demanding God to perform a miracle in the name of justice rather than of love (SE 138-139) and at the same time desiring to know if God has accepted the offering of his life in exchange for the miracle. As Bush states: "La 'ruse divine' de Thérèse de Lisieux ne se trouve pas chez Donissan" (SE 141). Bush points out further that in contrast to Donissan, Menou-Segrais, the older priest, parallels Thérèse in his way of offering everything to God and thus overcoming his impotence (SE 144-145).

A further search for evidence of Thérèse's presence in Bernanos' first novel has been carried out by Michael Tobin who reveals therein Bernanos' use of Theresian imagery. Donissan's description of Mouchette, "Vous êtes comme un jouet, vous êtes comme la petite balle d'un enfant, entre les mains de Satan," (OE,I 200) is an echo of the Carmelite's offering of herself in love ("T" 85): "Depuis quelque temps je m'étais offerte à l'Enfant Jésus pour être son petit jouet . . ." (HA 158).

Tobin also highlights Theresian elements found in the conversation that takes place on Christmas night between Donissan and Menou-Segrais, who functions here as Donissan's spiritual director. At the beginning of their conversation, the older priest rebukes the younger one for his childish attitude: "Ne faites pas l'enfant!" (OE,I 127), an expression recalling that Thérèse too was childish, overly-sensitive, fearful, and readily given to tears before receiving the grace of that special Christmas night in her life at the age of thirteen ("T" 87-89). Similarly fearful and frustrated by his sense of impotence, Donissan believes that he would be better suited to monastic life. Menou-Segrais, however, warns him against this illusion: "Un couvent! Ce n'est pas un lieu de repos, un asile, une infirmerie!" (OE,I 127). But, contrary to regarding monastic isolation as an escape from the world, Thérèse confesses that she had no misconceptions about religious life: "Les illusions, le bon Dieu m'a fait la grâce de n'en avoir AUCUNE en entrant au Carmel" (HA 172).

There is also a key image of the Carmelite's humility and spiritual poverty found in her description of herself as appearing before God with empty hands. Her words: "Au soir de cette vie, je paraîtrai devant vous les mains vides" (HA 317-318), taken from her "Acte d'offrande à l'Amour miséricordieux," are echoed in Menou-Segrais' humble declaration of his spiritual inferiority to the younger priest: "J'arrive au port les mains vides..." (OE,I 133).

Tobin has discovered further parallels between the lives of Thérèse of Lisieux and Donissan, noting that suffering rather than joy dominates the spirituality of both ("T" 93). Thus he claims that Thérèse's statement: "Je n'ai point de capacité pour jouir, j'ai toujours été comme cela; mais j'en ai une très grande pour souffrir" (DE 99) parallels Donissan's "Je suis plutôt disposé par la nature à la tristesse qu'à la joie..." (OE,I 226). Tobin observes how both saint and hero experience a similar difficulty in prayer, a lack of spiritual consolation, and the temptation to despair which presents itself to each in a dream-like fashion ("T" 93-94). And so the demon ridicules Donissan's life of labour, fasting, penance, and fidelity. His efforts have all been in vain, for "tout n'est qu'un rêve, et l'ombre d'un rêve!" (OE,I 246). The demon's derision of the priest-hero is heard as an echo of his subtle temptation to Thérèse: "Tu rêves la lumière, une partie embaumée des plus suaves parfums, tu rêves la possession éternelle du Créateur de toutes ces merveilles . . ." (HA 243).

But explicit evidence of Thérèse's presence in Sous le soleil de Satan can also be detected in the contrast between the Carmelite and the priest-hero. In the course of the conversation between Donissan and Menou-Segrais, we discover two reverse images of the saint. From listening to Donissan's tale, Menou-Segrais detects that the younger priest has become Satan's toy: "Vous êtes (depuis combien de temps?...) la dupe, le jouet, le ridicule instrument de celui que vous redoutez le plus" (OE,I 224-225). This passage, similar to the one describing Mouchette as Satan's little ball, reflects in a contrasting manner the saint's description of herself as the Christ Child's ball.

A similar contrast between Thérèse and Donissan appears in another observation made by Menou-Segrais. Detecting the despair underlying the priest-hero's description of his strange encounters with the horse-dealer and Mouchette, the older priest asks: "Ai-je bien compris que vous blasphémiez en vous la divine miséricorde?" (OE,I 224). Thérèse, on the contrary, proclaims her confidence in divine mercy: "Je me sentais comme le publicain, une grande pécheresse. Je trouvais le bon Dieu si miséricordieux!" (DE 127) and "si j'avais commis tous les crimes possibles, j'aurais toujours la même confiance, je sens que toute cette multitude d'offenses serait comme une goutte d'eau jetée dans un brasier ardent" (DE 70).

Specific expressions borrowed from the Histoire d'une âme are also found in Menou-Segrais' attempt to reassure the young priest. "Mon petit, Notre-Seigneur n'est pas mécontent de vous" (OE,I 132) recalls, as Tobin remarks ("T" 89), the answer of Mère Anne de Jésus who appeared to Thérèse in a dream: "Le Bon Dieu ne demande rien autre chose de vous. Il est content, très content!..." (HA 218). We believe that Menou-Segrais' words of consolation also seem to echo those of Thérèse's retreat master, Père Alexis Prou: "Il me dit que mes fautes ne faisaient pas de peine au Bon Dieu, que tenant sa place, il me disait de sa part qu'Il était très content de moi" (HA 198). In Genèse et structures de "Sous le soleil de Satan," Bush points out that the original manuscript of Sous le soleil de Satan actually did contain Thérèse's exact words. He states: "Ces paroles pourtant ont été supprimées, biffées au stylo 302 au point d'être difficilement déchiffrables aujourd'hui."[2] Clearly the alteration of the passage distorts the saint's presence as we feel Bernanos had originally intended it to be in his first novel.

Bush also points out further modifications of other Theresian elements in the novel, such as the word "paternel" (OE,I 197) instead of "fraternel" (S* 179) to describe the look that Donissan gives Mouchette. The omission of the sentence: "Ainsi deux aurores monteraient d'un élan pareil, jusqu'à la cime, de deux points de l'horizon" (S* 179) also destroys not only the psychological and spiritual equilibrium established by Bernanos between the priest and the young woman, as Bush indicates, but we would maintain is yet another important evidence of Thérèse's influence on the novelist. These expressions stress the equality between "saint" and "sinner" and thus mirror Thérèse who, desirous to speak in the name of sinners, her brothers and sisters, sits down at the table with them: "ô Jésus, s'il faut que la table souillée par eux soit purifiée par une âme qui vous aime, je veux bien y manger seule le pain de l'épreuve jusqu'à ce qu'il vous plaise de m'introduire dans votre lumineux royaume" (HA 242). They also remind us of how Thérèse begged her sister, Pauline, to tell people the story of Paésie, a public sinner.[3] Although the saint herself had received adequate assurance that she had never committed a serious sin, she nevertheless identified herself with sinners and in particular with Paésie to whom God had shown such merciful love.

Explicit textual evidence of Thérèse's presence in Sous le soleil de Satan thus does exist and seems to strengthen Tobin's conclusion that "St Thérèse is indeed manifest in this first great novel and, though not yet in perfect focus, she is in view" ("T" 96).

L'Imposture and *La Joie* (1926-1929)

In his article, "Bernanos et Sainte Thérèse de l'Enfant-Jésus," Gaucher not only calls our attention to the allusion to the Carmelite by name in L'Imposture, but also proposes that this sentence constitutes in embryonic form the author's future statements regarding her message ("BT" 232-233). Bernanos' description of Thérèse therefore suggests the author's clear understanding that the saint's message is based not on cheap sentimentality but on suffering freely accepted out of love.

Although there is much implicit evidence that the spirituality of Chevance resembles that of Thérèse in L'Imposture, explicit evidence of her presence is to be found only in Chevance's spiritual daughter. This is Chantal de Clergerie, the young heroine of Bernanos' third novel and sequel to L'Imposture, La Joie. Textual comparisons of Theresian and Bernanosian texts reveal that La Joie, published in 1929, contains more explicit evidence of Thérèse of Lisieux' influence on Bernanos than any work prior to this date. Although many Bernanosian scholars have mentioned that the Carmelite saint serves as a model for Chantal, Soeur Raymond-Marie and Guy Gaucher have been the major contributors to our understanding of the explicit nature of those ties.

In her study, "Bernanos et l'esprit d'enfance," Soeur Raymond-Marie demonstrates how Bernanos' concept of spiritual childhood which we find in Chantal de Clergerie resembles that of the saint of Lisieux as described both in her "Lettre à Soeur Marie du Sacré-Coeur" which forms Manuscrit "B" of the Histoire d'une âme (HA 212-229) and in her explanation to Pauline in July, 1897 of the meaning of spiritual childhood: "Ma Mère, c'est la voie de l'enfance spirituelle, c'est le chemin de la confiance et du total abandon" (DE 223). Soeur Raymond-Marie shows how this particular definition along with a similar statement: "C'est reconnaître son néant, attendre tout du bon Dieu, comme un petit enfant attend tout de son père" (DE 119) are fulfilled in Bernanos' young heroine. Chantal's simplicity in the acceptance of her littleness is, as this critic claims, "comme une illustration parfaite du premier pas indiqué par Thérèse pour entrer dans sa 'Petite Voie', 'reconnaître son néant'" ("R-M" 293-294).

A parallel is then established between the saint and the heroine describing how both undergo a psychological and spiritual maturity at approximately the same age. Thérèse's awareness of her spiritual life, a direct result of her Christmas conversion, is reflected in Chantal who willingly assumes her responsibility as a baptized Christian in face of the evil surrounding her ("R-M" 295). Elaborating how Bernanos unites the spirit of childhood with the spirit of poverty in his works, Soeur Raymond-Marie contends that what is significant about the spirit of poverty found in Thérèse and Chantal is their awareness of their unworthiness and their total dependence on God's love. Specific examples from the saint's life find an answering echo in Chantal's attitude towards life in general and towards the responsibilities of her position as mistress of her father's house ("R-M" 297-299).

Bernanos portrays Chantal as recognizing that the spiritual gifts she possesses are for the benefit of others: "elle donnait, elle prodiguait, elle jetait à pleines mains, ainsi qu'une chose de rien, son espérance sublime" (OE,I 568). This description of the heroine closely parallels Thérèse's statement that being little implies that a person does not attribute his virtues to himself, but that he recognizes that "le bon Dieu pose ce trésor dans la main de son petit enfant pour qu'il s'en serve quand il en a besoin, mais c'est toujours le trésor du bon Dieu" (DE 119). Soeur Raymond-Marie is quick to point out, however, that this is not the only way in which Chantal resembles Thérèse. The young girl's mission to serve those in her immediate surroundings closely parallels Thérèse's vocation of offering herself as a victim of love for the salvation of sinners and for priests. For Soeur Raymond-Marie, the conversion of the criminal, Pranzini, which formed the point of departure for the saint's call to love, is reflected in the heroine's offering of her joy to the abbé Chevance as he is dying. In exchange,

Chantal takes upon herself the conversion of the abbé Cénabre who has lost his faith ("R-M" 300-301).

In addition, the heroine's solidarity with sinners is judged by this same critic to parallel the Carmelite's desire to eat at the table with sinners (HA 241-242). Soeur Raymond-Marie declares that this is not only the secret of Chantal's mystical experiences, but: "c'est à cette profondeur que l'héroïne de Bernanos nous semble suivre de plus près la 'Petite Voie'" ("R-M" 302).

Chantal's desire to assume the burden of the sins of those around her and her espousal of Christ's sufferings have, as this critic claims, a definite affinity with Thérèse's "Acte d'offrande à l'Amour miséricordieux." Both saint and heroine have the same desire for martyrdom ("R-M" 303). Soeur Raymond-Marie adds further that the saint's trial of faith is closely linked to her desire to save sinners and that as Thérèse died without knowing whether or not her suffering had saved Père Hyacinthe Loyson (a Carmelite priest who had left the Catholic Church and married a Protestant American widow) for whom she had offered her last communion, so too does Chantal die without knowing the spiritual fate of Cénabre ("R-M" 304-305).

In his highly significant article on Bernanos and Thérèse of Lisieux, Gaucher begins his examination of explicit textual evidence of the saint's influence on the characterization of Chantal by reporting Bernanos' words to a journalist in January, 1928: "vous connaissez la petite sainte Thérèse... Or, l'abbé Cénabre, cette âme stérile, abandonnée, hautaine, je la mettrai en présence d'une sainte . . . qui est toujours heureuse, se donne aussi entièrement que l'autre se refuse" (qtd. in "BT" 233). Thérèse's presence in this novel serves to confirm Gaucher's opinion that Bernanos had reflected deeply on the saint's message prior to writing L'Imposture ("BT" 233). After briefly stating that the subject of La Joie is the progressive discovery of evil and sin by an innocent being whose action is to offer herself for the salvation of others ("BT" 246), this scholar discusses the double nature of Thérèse's spirituality. He claims that many people do not understand that her message is one of suffering as well as one of joy, "que le mystère chrétien est indissolublement Mort et Résurrection" ("BT" 247). Gaucher asks: "où est la joie de la courte existence d'une obscure religieuse morte à vingt-quatre ans dans un carmel de province?" and "Pourquoi appeler La Joie ce roman obsédant qui se termine par la mort abominable d'une jeune fille toute simple?" ("BT" 247). Only a true understanding of the spirit of childhood which animates Thérèse and Chantal, the critic claims, resolves these paradoxes ("BT" 247).

To illustrate how closely Chantal lives the Carmelite's spirit of childhood, Gaucher then enumerates the diverse traits of the heroine's spiritual physiognomy. Under each of the following traits he lists parallels taken from passages in L'Imposture and La Joie and in Thérèse's writings. Gaucher examines, first of all, how Chantal's childlike manner resembles the saint's ("BT" 248). Various definitions of her spirit of childhood such as "L'âge n'est rien aux yeux du bon Dieu, et je m'arrangerai bien à rester petite enfant, même en vivant très longtemps" (DE 35) reappear in the heroine's remark to the abbé Cénabre that it is possible to act as an adult "et ne voir néanmoins les choses essentielles, élémentaires, la joie, la douleur et la mort, qu'avec le regard d'un enfant" (OE,I 600).

Gaucher then points out how Chantal possesses Thérèse's spirit of humility, poverty, and simplicity ("BT" 249-250). The heroine describes herself according to the saint's image of approaching God with open hands: "Alors, je me tiens sagement sous le porche de l'église, je tends la main au bon Dieu, je pense qu'il y mettra bien toujours deux sous..." (OE,I 498).

Chantal lives from day to day according to Thérèse's spirit of abandonment and confidence ("BT" 250). Her confident abandonment observed in such statements as "l'esprit, le rayonnant esprit de confiance et d'abandon" (OE,I 554) parallels the saint's attitude: "Je ne désire pas plus mourir que vivre . . . c'est le bon Dieu qui choisit pour moi, j'aime mieux ce qu'il veut. C'est ce qu'il fait que j'aime" (<u>DE</u> 35).

Like Thérèse, Chantal finds God's will in the accomplishment of little things ("BT" 251). The saint's discovery: "le moyen d'être <u>sainte</u> par la fidélité aux plus petites choses" (<u>HA</u> 87) becomes in the heroine's thoughts: "la certitude d'être née pour les travaux faciles qui rebutent les grandes âmes . . ." (<u>OE</u>,I 553).

Gaucher reveals how Thérèse's spirit of joy is reflected in Chantal's joy in knowing her weakness ("BT" 252). Her attitude concerning her impotence: "Il est bon d'être faible entre ses mains... Il est meilleur d'être faible" (<u>OE</u>,I 572) parallels Thérèse's recognition of her dependence on God: "Je ne suis qu'une enfant, impuissante et faible, cependant c'est ma faiblesse même qui me donne l'audace de m'offrir en <u>Victime à ton Amour, ô Jésus!</u> (<u>HA</u> 223). Furthermore, Bernanos' young heroine even rejoices in her imperfections as did Thérèse in hers ("BT" 252). The author's description of Chantal's acceptance of her faults: "Comme les âmes très pures, elle se résignait vite aux fautes commises, ne pensait qu'à en réparer de son mieux le dommage" (<u>OE</u>,I 597) reflects the saint's words: "maintenant je me résigne à me voir toujours imparfaite et j'y trouve ma joie..." (<u>HA</u> 182).

Both Chantal and Thérèse prove to be generous with God's gifts ("BT" 253). Chevance's words to his spiritual daughter: "Que vous êtes donc née prodigue, ma fille!" (<u>OE</u>,I 555) echo the Carmelite's words to her prioress: "Rien ne me tient aux mains. Tout ce que j'ai, tout ce que je gagne, c'est pour l'Eglise et les âmes. Que je vive jusqu'à 80 ans, je serai toujours aussi pauvre" (<u>DE</u> 72).

Detecting how both Thérèse and Chantal possess an invincible hope ("BT" 253-254), Gaucher points out how one of the saint's favourite sayings: "c'est dans les bras du bon Dieu que je tombe!" (<u>DE</u> 169) is used to describe Chantal: "Je ne puis tomber qu'en Dieu!" (<u>OE</u>,I 552).

Having shown how the various aspects of Chantal's psychological and spiritual nature mirror Thérèse's, Gaucher then presents explicit textual evidence showing how Bernanos has borrowed Theresian imagery and vocabulary to depict the spiritual adventure of his heroine. The first in this second list of parallel passages reveals how both the saint and the heroine use the image of a grain of sand or a speck of dust to describe their littleness ("BT" 255). Thus Thérèse's desire to remain "un petit grain de sable bien obscur, bien caché à tous les yeux, que Jésus seul puisse le voir" (LT 86) is echoed in Chantal's words as: "Je voudrais n'être qu'un petit grain de poussière impalpable, suspendue dans la volonté de Dieu' (OE,I 604). The image of a bird in flight is also used by the saint and the heroine to portray their littleness ("BT" 256). Thus Thérèse's childlike spirit is symbolized by the image of a bird in flight: "avec l'amour non seulement j'avance mais je vole..." (HA 198), while the description of a lark represents Chantal's littleness: "Une alouette, ce n'est qu'une touffe de plumes avec une chanson dedans . . . il y a le miracle de leur petitesse, de leur légèreté, et qu'elles ne sont pas utiles à grand-chose . . ." (OE,I 659). The weakness of a little bird caught in a storm symbolizes the interior suffering of both Chantal and her model ("3T" 256). The saint's comparison of herself to a "faible petit oiseau couvert seulement d'un léger duvet" (HA 226) appears in Bernanos' description of his young heroine as "un oiseau au creux de l'orage . . ." (OE,I 604). Thérèse's image of a drifting boat is similarly borrowed to describe Chantal's interior state ("BT" 257). Thus the heroine's statement: "Et je ne suis qu'un pauvre petit bateau vide qui va comme il peut" (OE,I 496) reminds us of Thérèse's words: 'le plus léger zéphyr ne faisait pas onduler les eaux tranquilles sur lesquelles voguait ma petite nacelle . . ." (HA 172).

Further evidence of Theresian imagery in La Joie apears in Chantal's comparison of herself to an article of no value that gives pleasure for a moment and then is cast away ("BT" 257-258). The saint, as we recall, longed to be the Christ Child's little toy, "une petite balle de nulle valeur qu'il pouvait jeter à terre, pousser du pied, percer, laisser dans un coin ou bien presser sur son coeur si cela Lui faisait plaisir . . ." (HA 159). In a similar fashion, Chantal is convinced that she is "une petite chose vaine et légère, faite pour un moment, pour la joie d'un seul moment, puis qu'on jette, sans regret . . ." (OE,I 678).

The striking analogy between Chantal's vocation of suffering and Thérèse's is the next parallel that Gaucher establishes. As this critic claims, "Or nous touchons là le coeur de la vocation de sainte Thérèse de Lisieux" ("BT" 259). The saint entered Carmel to save sinners and in particular to pray for priests. Bernanos has therefore modelled Chantal's interior trials and free offering of herself to save Cénabre on the Carmelite's trial of faith and her salvific mission to sinners and priests ("BT" 258-260). Like Thérèse, Chantal freely abandons herself to the Divine will and eventually experiences the silence of God, the temptation to despair, the dark night of the soul, and the fear of death ("BT" 260-263). Having led us through this examination of Theresian elements in Bernanos' young heroine, Gaucher concludes this perceptive study of La Joie by declaring that in abandoning everything to God, even the manner of her death, Chantal is doing exactly what Thérèse did ("BT" 263).

In his volume, Souffrance et expiation dans la pensée de Bernanos, William Bush also brings to light explicit textual evidence of Thérèse of Lisieux' presence in La Joie. He contends that the secret of Chantal's spirituality lies in her impotence: "Car à présent, l'idée, la certitude de son impuissance était devenue le centre éblouissant de sa joie, le noyau de l'astre en flammes" (OE,I 681). In her acceptance of her weakness, the heroine is judged to be a faithful reflection of the Carmelite saint. Bush thus reveals that the title of La Joie is explained by Bernanos' description of Chantal's abandonment to her impotence wherein she rediscovers that "joy" she felt she had lost, thereby echoing Thérèse's words in her "Acte d'offrande à l'Amour miséricordieux": "je désire être Sainte, mais je sens mon impuissance et je vous demande, ô mon Dieu! d'être vous-même ma Sainteté" (SE 147-150).

"Jeanne, relapse et sainte" (1929)

Written in the same year as <u>La Joie</u> as a tribute to Jeanne d'Arc in a special issue of a review devoted to that saint, the short biographical essay, "Jeanne, relapse et sainte," contains an explicit textual reference to the Carmelite saint. Noting this reference in which the author fuses Jeanne d'Arc and Thérèse of Lisieux, Gaucher declares that: "Desormais Bernanos ne séparera plus dans sa pensée ces deux filles de France" ("BT" 233).

In this essay Bernanos presents Jeanne d'Arc according to the Theresian concept of the spirit of childhood. Proclaiming that most saints are children, he lists several examples and concludes his study of the Maid of Orleans with an explicit reference to the Carmelite saint: "et la dernière venue, si étrange, si secrète, suppliciée par les entrepreneurs et les simoniaques, avec son incompréhensible sourire - Thérèse de l'Enfant-Jésus" (<u>OE</u>,II 40).

In April, 1934 when Plon Publishers were preparing to issue this little essay as a separate volume, Bernanos wrote a letter to his great friend, Robert Vallery-Radot, where he reveals his continuing desire to unite the two recently canonized French saints. "L'idée m'est venue," writes Bernanos, "de dédicacer ma <u>Jeanne d'Arc</u> à la petite Thérèse de l'Enfant-Jésus" (<u>Corr</u>.I 516). Because of the scandalous nature of this text, Bernanos asked Vallery-Radot to translate his dedication into Latin: "A la chère et auguste mémoire de celle qui fut, avec Jehanne la plus héroïque des saintes de notre race, un vrai petit chevalier français: Soeur Thérèse de l'Enfant-Jésus vendue par ses soeurs" (<u>Corr</u>.I 517). Unfortunately the proposed translation did not arrive in time to be published with the essay.

Explicit textual evidence of Thérèse of Lisieux' name, of images and vocabulary borrowed from her autobiography, as well as the establishing of parallels between her spiritual physiognomy and that of the author's "saints" thus already bear witness to her influence on Bernanos' works in the nineteen twenties.

NOTES

CHAPTER I

¹ Charles Moeller, <u>Littérature du XXe siècle et christianisme</u>, tome I, <u>Silence de Dieu</u> (Paris: Casterman, 1957) 426.

² William Bush, <u>Genèse et structures de "Sous le soleil de Satan"</u> (Paris: Archives des Lettres Modernes, 1988) 81.

³ Paésie was a common prostitute converted by one of the desert fathers. Touched by grace, the young woman followed the priest into the desert to live a life of penance. But instead of living a long life of penance, Paésie died during her first night in the desert and the priest, seeing her soul escorted to heaven by angels, heard a voice say that her short repentance, because it was without hesitation, had saved her, for her love and penance of only one day had been perfect. Paésie's story greatly impressed Thérèse and, for this reason, it has been recorded in both the <u>Histoire d'une âme</u> (<u>HA</u> 324-326) and in a shorter version in <u>J'entre dans la vie</u> (<u>DE</u> 70-71).

CHAPTER 2

EXPLICIT EVIDENCE IN THE SECOND PERIOD (1931-1938)

After publishing his personal tribute to Edouard Drumont with Grasset in 1931, La Grande peur des bien-pensants, the work which separates the first from the second period of his fiction, Bernanos would write, prior to his departure for Brazil in 1938, six major works: Un mauvais rêve (1931-1935), Monsieur Ouine (1931-1940), Un crime (1934-1935), Journal d'un curé de campagne (1934-1936), Nouvelle histoire de Mouchette (1936-1937), and Les Grands Cimetières sous la lune (1937-1938). Of these six, only two, Journal d'un curé de campagne and Les Grands Cimetières sous la lune, contain explicit textual references to Thérèse of Lisieux. In addition, the explicit references found in this period of the author's work are significantly different from those of the previous period. With but one exception, the borrowing of the saint's words, images, and biographical details that was so characteristic of her explicit presence in the fictional work of the twenties no longer appears in that of the thirties. The author turns instead to a new, more forceful manner of presenting Thérèse's message to the world.

The paucity of explicit textual references is important to note if we wish to evaluate the role the young Carmelite came to play in Bernanos' thought following his writing of La Joie. But at the same time we cannot afford to neglect the significance of the change in the explicit evidence of Thérèse's influence that seems to parallel the change Bernanos noted in his writing of the period. In at least three of his letters to Maurice Bourdel, the director of Plon Publishers, the author refers to this change in his writing between the years 1926 and 1934. In November, 1934 he stated that it was not until 1926, at the age of thirty-eight, that he was able to express his interior life in writing and that 1934 "marque une seconde transformation, voilà tout" (Corr.II 30).

As indicated in the previous chapter, Chantal de Clergerie represented a conscious attempt on the part of the novelist to incarnate Thérèse of Lisieux. In contrast to the works of the first period, those of the second period, as we shall soon see, testify to a deepening of Bernanos' awareness and understanding of Thérèse's message of childhood as a reply not only to his own individual spiritual needs, but also to the ever-increasing problem of the dechristianization of the modern world.

Although La Joie had been awarded the Prix Fémina in December, 1929, it seemed to Plon that following the writing of this novel, with no new novel appearing until Un crime in 1935, Bernanos had begun to lose his public. For this reason, the writer tried to reassure Bourdel in February, 1935 about the change that had occurred in his work: "Il me semble que mes trois romans font un tout. Après La Joie, on pouvait prévoir que je me recueillerais, pour livrer une autre bataille" (Corr.II 60). Five months later Bernanos wrote again to Bourdel regarding this change: "Je vous répète une fois de plus que j'ai commencé avec Un crime une nouvelle période de ma pauvre vie d'écrivain" (Corr.II 86). What caused this transformation in the author's work between 1926 and 1934? And why was 1934 in particular so important a year in his life?

The Crucible of Suffering

The answer to these questions can be found in a brief examination of the events that took place in Bernanos' life during these years where suffering came to play a major role in his daily life. As Thérèse commented about the change that took place in her own life after her mother's death: "une nouvelle période allait commencer pour mon âme, je devais passer par le creuset de l'épreuve et souffrir . . ." (HA 39). When we explore the evolution that took place in Bernanos' thought during this period in which he too would lose his mother, it does seem as if the experience of suffering deepened his identification with the Carmelite saint.

The great success of Sous le soleil de Satan in 1926 had encouraged Bernanos to resign his position as an insurance agent in order to devote himself more fully to his vocation as a writer. On September 5 of that same year, only months after the author's success, Pius XI had condemned the Action Française. Bernanos had been a member of the movement prior to World War I and letters written posterior to this event disclose the extent of his anguish in his attempt to see God's presence in this situation. He wrote to Henri Massis in October about how deeply hurt he was by "cette sorte de farce où Dieu est cependant, bien que nous ne puissions clairement le connaître . . ." (Corr.I 267).

Shortly thereafter the author was faced with his father's illness and death from cancer of the liver. In December, 1926, he expressed to his friend, Robert Vallery-Radot, his fears regarding his father's imminent death which would occur in January, 1927: "tant il est vrai que les choses obscures qu'on redoute, prennent, sitôt qu'on les nomme, une réalité abominable. Mais je sens la saleté de Mort dans ma maison" (Corr.I 284). The author's effort to have confidence in God in this new trial is also evident in a letter written at the end of the year to Henri Massis: "Il n'y a rien à espérer que du Bon Dieu" (Corr.I 285). The success of La Joie in 1929 had again been marked by a terrible personal trial, the death of his mother on March 8, 1930. This was followed shortly thereafter by that of a close friend of his, the abbé André Sudre, tragically killed in a mountain climbing accident on July 23.

Bernanos was sent to Divonne-les-Bains and Vésenex for a rest cure during the spring and summer of 1930. In a letter written during this summer, he described this distressful period to another friend of his, Jean Tenant: "J'ai été malade, c'est-à-dire exténué par un cruel hiver - deuil, maladies, crises aiguës d'impécuniosité, déceptions et trahisons d'amitié, rien ne m'a été épargné" (<u>Corr</u>.I 362). Although in October, 1934 the author confessed to Bourdel: "Les années 27, 28, 29 sont les plus sales de ma vie" (<u>Corr</u>.III 245), an examination of his correspondence indicates that the events of the early thirties were far worse than those of the late twenties.

The year 1931 was marked by three major literary happenings in Bernanos' life: the publication of <u>La Grande peur des bien-pensants</u>, the abortive beginning of <u>Un mauvais rêve</u>, quickly abandoned for the mysterious <u>Monsieur Ouine</u>, to be finished only in 1940, and his attempt to cope with finances by writing for <u>Le Figaro</u>. Robert Vallery-Radot, as literary editor of <u>Le Figaro</u>, opened the columns of that prestigious daily to Bernanos who projected a series of weekly articles. The author admired François Coty, the owner of <u>Le Figaro</u>, who, as a self-made man and rich perfume manufacturer was hated by the <u>Action Française</u>.

Little did Bernanos realize in November, 1931 that this venture would lead him to a bitter polemic and public break with Charles Maurras, head of the <u>Action Française</u>, who regarded Coty with his journalistic influence as his rival. When we recall the great admiration the young Bernanos had for Maurras and how he had supported him after the Vatican's condemnation of the Action Française movement in 1926, we begin to appreciate how deeply the author must have suffered in May, 1932 from his break with Maurras who had played such an important role in his life.[1] By taking sides in a political dispute between Coty and Maurras, Bernanos had become the object for a whole series of insults launched in the columns of the daily newspaper of the <u>Action Française</u>. Maurras labelled Bernanos both "imposter" and "hypocrite" because he had chosen to support a point of view different from his own. Both Léon Daudet, best man at Bernanos' wedding who had contributed to the success of <u>Sous le soleil de Satan</u>, and Maurice Pujo resorted to personal insults and slanderous attacks.

Pujo's slanderous remarks claimed Bernanos to be both "gluant et sinistre," and that "Il ne sent que plus mauvais lorsqu'il s'oint des parfums de son maître . . ." (<u>OE</u>,II 1286),[2] thus poking fun at the author for working for a perfume manufacturer. He accused Bernanos of being "feminine": "la conduite du pauvre garçon n'est pas seulement un jeu dont il resterait le maître: elle correspond à sa nature qui - chose bien fâcheuse chez un individu de notre sexe - est femelle" (<u>OE</u>,II 1293).[3] Then, as if to add insult to injury, he charged Bernanos with being a masochist: "Il y a dans son cas du masochisme, le goût du fouet et des crachats" (<u>OE</u>,II 1294).

That Bernanos was deeply hurt by insults such as these is understandable. We can judge the extent of his suffering from his article for <u>Le Figaro</u> on November 17, 1932 in which he confesses: "Certes, le coeur me lève un peu, je l'avoue, en voyant ma pauvre vie étalée sous ces sales mains expertes, notre maison familiale ouverte, et ces messieurs sur le seuil, avec leurs instruments" (<u>OE</u>,II 1283).[4]

Yet letters written to friends during this period indicate how his intense personal suffering seemed to enrich the interior life of the author. One such letter, written to Louis Brun in early January, 1933, when Bernanos was living in La Bayorre,[5] testifies to the deepening of the author's spirituality. In sending new year's greetings to his friend, Bernanos reflected that rather than waiting for happiness to come our way, it is God's mercy that is waiting to receive us: "Mais il y a la douce pitié de Dieu qui nous regarde, en attendant qu'elle nous reçoive" (<u>Corr</u>.I 463). Our powerlessness to assist our friends by any other means than by suffering with them is our greatest humiliation, Bernanos declared, but at the end of his letter he also added: "La prière n'est elle-même que la forme surnaturelle, la forme divine de la sympathie" (<u>Corr</u>.I 463). Although there are no explicit textual references to the saint's words in this letter, the author's attitude towards human weakness and the mercy of God is beginning to reflect Thérèse of Lisieux' concept of approaching God with empty hands and expecting all from God's merciful love as seen in her "Acte d'offrande à l'Amour miséricordieux" (HA 316-318).

Trust in God's mercy would certainly be important for Bernanos in 1933. His entire household was once again faced with more than its fair share of illness, and on July 31 of that year, the author himself was injured in a motorcycle accident and left permanently lame. Instead of easing the family's precarious finances, much of the money claimed for damages had to go to pay Bernanos' debts to Plon for long-overdue advances on his writing. Then, less than a year later, on May 3, 1934, a second car accident would complicate matters further by leaving the writer with an injured hand (Sp 135).

Letters written to Vallery-Radot during this time reveal Bernanos' despair over the writing of Monsieur Ouine. He wrote in March: "Mais quand j'ai raturé, déchiré, recopié, puis gratté chaque phrase au papier de verre, je compte que ma moyenne est d'une page et demie par jour. Je vous assure que je ne peux pas faire mieux, mon vieux" (Corr.I 465).

Added to the slow progress of Bernanos' work was his concern over the uncertain state of his finances. In a letter written to Jacques Marchand in June, 1938, the author summarized his financial negotiations with Plon Publishers over the years from 1926 to 1938. A major misunderstanding came about concerning the monthly cheques he received from Plon following the astounding success of Sous le soleil de Satan in 1926. According to Bernanos, Maurice Bourdel had assured him that Plon would willingly pay him 5,000 francs monthly, and that it was therefore unnecessary for him to consider returning to his former employment as an insurance agent. Bernanos however had not grasped that Plon was doing anything more than drawing from his large account built up from Sous le soleil de Satan When this was exhausted, the publishers continued to pay the same amount, saying nothing, while Bernanos' debt grew by the month. The author had mistakenly believed that his promise to give his work to Plon was all that was needed to guarantee him a regular allowance. He added further that the publishers' attitude was such as to confirm him in his error (<u>Corr</u>.III 327).

It was only after <u>La Joie</u>'s success and Bernanos' reception of the Prix Fémina in December, 1929 that Plon felt they could advise the author that his account was long since overdrawn and that the monthly advances would be discontinued. When the author questioned Bourdel as to why Plon had not warned him earlier, the reply was simply: "Nous vous laissons dans l'ignorance par <u>délicatesse</u>" (<u>Corr</u>.III 327).

Financial burdens thus led Bernanos to write articles on a regular basis for <u>Le Figaro</u> and, with the permission of Plon, to publish <u>La Grande peur des bien-pensants</u> with Grasset. He was also forced to sell the manuscript of <u>Sous le soleil de Satan</u> and to borrow money from Plon guaranteed on the compensation he expected to receive from his 1934 motorcycle accident.

It is not surprising therefore that the author began to lose faith in himself during this period, for the early thirties seem filled with nothing but frustration and suffering for him. The year 1934 in particular appears to have been a year of great mental and physical anguish. Bernanos wrote to Christiane Manificat in May of this year: "Bref, j'ai dû subir crise d'angoisse sur crise d'angoisse depuis onze jours" (<u>Corr</u>.I 525), and he confessed on July 4 to Pierre Belperron: "Tout croule autour de moi et ne pouvant dire l'exacte vérité à ma femme, je me sens réellement très seul et très abandonné" (<u>Corr</u>.III 237). And looking back on this same year, Bernanos was to declare some four years later in the above-mentioned letter to Marchand: "En 1934, souffrant encore de mon accident, je me trouvais absolument sans le sou" (<u>Corr</u>.III 328).

In order to survive with his family, Bernanos came up with the idea in 1934 of immediately writing a popular detective novel along the line of those written by Georges Simenon for which he would receive sixty francs per page of manuscript drawn as an advance on his future royalties.

Un crime, his first and last attempt at a detective novel, was thus begun in 1934 and finished the following year. It left Bernanos with the disappointing feeling that this type of literature was not for him. Finally, evicted from that large villa they occupied at La Bayorre for unpaid rent, their furniture and books seized to be sold at public auction, Bernanos, his wife and six children were forced to flee to Majorca in October, 1934 in search of a lower cost of living.

"Tout est grâce" (1934-1936)

But not all of Bernanos' 1934 correspondence is filled with despair and anxiety. Here and there are found hints of a transformation taking place within the writer himself. In a letter written in March-April of that year to Annie Jamet the little Carmelite's words, "tout est grâce" (DE 41), confirm for us the extent to which the spirituality of Thérèse of Lisieux was beginning to take hold of the author himself: "Je suis prête à tout accepter, disait soeur Thérèse (pas celle des 'châteaux de l'âme,' l'autre la plus vraie...) à tout accepter, même la mort sans sacrements. Qu'est-ce que cela fait? Tout est grâce" (Corr.I 520). Such a passage cannot help but pose certain questions regarding the author's life and spirituality. Why does Bernanos feel the need to clarify that it is Thérèse of Lisieux, and not Teresa of Avila, whose words he is borrowing? What is interesting is that he regards the French Carmelite as "plus vraie" than the Spanish Carmelite whose writings have caused her to be declared a doctor of the church.

Two years later, in Journal d'un curé de campagne, these same words of the little Carmelite, "tout est grâce" (DE 41), would be uttered by the curé of Ambricourt at the moment of his death. Realizing that he is about to die without receiving the last rites of the Church, the priest-hero attempting to console his friend, a defrocked priest who laments the delay of the parish priest with the sacraments, utters his last words: "Qu'est-ce que cela fait? Tout est grâce" (OE,I 1259).[6]

It would appear that Bernanos' interest in Thérèse of Lisieux following her canonization in 1925, joined to his own personal experience of passing through "l'hiver de l'épreuve" (HA 39), had led him to reflect so deeply on the saint's message that he began to incorporate it into both his personal correspondence and his professional writing.

In the above-mentioned letter to Annie Jamet it is not surprising to find Bernanos referring to his numerous trials. What is surprising is his attitude towards these trials. Instead of indulging in despair or anguish, as we might naturally expect of someone under such tremendous daily pressure, Bernanos displayed in his correspondence of 1934 an ever-growing attitude of acceptance. Perhaps the author had begun to discover in Thérèse's writings the saint's attitude of acceptance of her trials whereby he too might surmount the obstacles encountered in his own daily life.

We also find in a letter to Vallery-Radot written in this same year the author's renewed determination to serve God with what God had given him: "Je suis bien décidé à ne servir que le bon Dieu, et à ma manière - c'est-à-dire selon la nature qu'il m'a donnée, que je tiens de lui" (Corr.II 29).

A 1934 text quoted by Bridel discloses a further reference to Thérèse of Lisieux. Bringing together the Carmelite saint and the Maid of Orleans, Bernanos declares that both serve the same cause: "l'enfance héroïque, l'enfance sacrée qui reçoit la parole, referme ses mains pures sur le message de Dieu, et ne le rendra qu'à lui seul."[7] This passage illustrates how the author believed that the reply to the evangelical message of heroic childhood incarnate in both young women saints is to be rendered to God alone. Bernanos' thought in this text parallels his comment in the dedication written in the same year for the biographical essay, "Jeanne, relapse et sainte," that Thérèse of Lisieux, along with Jeanne d'Arc, is "la plus héroïque des saintes de notre race, un vrai petit chevalier français" (Corr.I 517). Both of these 1934 texts thus reaffirm Bernanos' earlier statement in the essay on Jeanne d'Arc that Thérèse and Jeanne offer the world a similar message of heroic childhood.

In "Jeanne, relapse et sainte," Bernanos points out that Jeanne's judges, the learned doctors and theologians, watered down the saint's heroism, a heroism which they failed to understand, to the point that all that remained of it was "la fade image d'une rosière inoffensive, à faire rêver les séminaires, un museau à confitures" (OE.II 30). In the above text quoted by Bridel, we find an echo of this passage. People either do not understand or are indifferent to the Carmelite's message. What is there about the message of a young, hitherto unknown Carmelite from a small monastery hidden away in an old Norman town that has roused Bernanos to make this accusation?

Thérèse's sister, Céline, believed her young sister's message to be so crucial that if she had had to choose between having Thérèse canonized or having her message officially recognized by the Church, she would have chosen the latter. Reacting to Benedict XV's official proclamation on August 14, 1921 of the heroic quality of Thérèse's virtues, Céline stated: "j'ai éprouvé plus de joie au Discours de Benoît XV qui exaltait "l'Enfance Spirituelle" qu'à la Béatification et la Canonisation de notre Sainte" (CSG 34).

In a letter written in September, 1896 to her sister, Marie, Thérèse explains the way to reach Divine love: "ce chemin c'est l'abandon du petit enfant qui s'endort sans crainte dans les bras de son Père" (LT 357).[8] Then, in answer to her sister Pauline's request to explain her "little way," the saint replied: "c'est la voie de l'enfance spirituelle, c'est le chemin de la confiance et du total abandon" (DE 223). On yet another occasion she explained to Pauline that being a child in the spiritual sense means that a person recognizes his nothingness and confidently expects God to provide him with whatever he needs just as a small child expects everything from his father. The person who follows the spirit of childhood also acknowledges that his virtues are but a part of God's treasure which He places "dans la main de son petit enfant pour qu'il s'en serve quand il en a besoin . . ." (DE 119). Thérèse concludes her explanation by stating that a person must not allow his failures to discourage him: "car les enfants tombent souvent, mais ils sont trop petits pour se faire beaucoup de mal" (DE 119).

What Thérèse has done, then, is simply take the good qualities of the relationship between a child and a parent and raise them to a supernatural level. There is, therefore, nothing childish about Thérèse's message of childhood; on the contrary, the practise of these virtues at the supernatural level demands heroic virtue and pure faith in God even when He seems most absent.

Contemporary Theresian scholars, such as François Jamart, have pointed out that amidst all the flowery devotion to the saint of Lisieux there were some people who "carefully examining Thérèse's words, recognized in them an echo of the Gospel and of the voice of God."[9] From his own emerging spirituality of confidence and abandonment as observed in his writings and from his consistently pointing out that people did not understand the message of Lisieux, Bernanos seems to have been such a one. This was to be clearly demonstrated in his polemical work on the Spanish Civil War, Les Grands Cimetières sous la lune. Before analyzing the very explicit impact of Thérèse on that work, where Bernanos would so clearly fuse the themes of childhood and sanctity through the Carmelite's example and teachings, we should note that the author had long viewed such a fusion as a sort of Christian ideal, even before explicitly associating it with the saint of Lisieux.

Bernanos' first novel, Sous le soleil de Satan, shows how the author has blended childhood and sanctity in the portrayal of his priest-hero. The abbé Donissan discovers that his memories of his childhood are somehow connected with the thought of God: "Mille souvenirs lui reviennent de son enfance si étrangement unie à Dieu . . ." (OE,I 142-143). The young priest's attempt at destroying the principle of evil within himself brings out a childlike response.

Having completed his self-imposed flagellation, Donissan is seen smiling "d'un sourire d'enfant" (OE,I 151). Then, after his unusual encounter with the horse dealer, it is in terms of childhood and sanctity that the priest-hero judges the character of Jean-Marie Boulainville, the carrier who helps him on his way. Thus Donissan wonders: "était-ce possible que cet ami de Dieu, ce pauvre entre les pauvres, se fût gardé dans la droiture et dans l'enfance . . ." (OE,I 189) and at the same time he sees in Boulainville "l'image d'un autre artisan, non moins obscur, non moins méconnu, le charpentier villageois, gardien de la reine des anges, le juste qui vit le Rédempteur face à face . . ." (OE,I 189).

The short biographical essay, "Saint Dominique," published in the same year as Sous le soleil de Satan, finds Dominique's sanctity tied in with his childhood. And so we discover Bernanos describing the saint's resolution to follow his vocation to evangelize as "si belle, si touchante, si pareille aux grands rêves de l'enfance!" (OE,II 9).

The sanctity of Bernanos' two "saints" of L'Imposture and La Joie is similarly fused with childhood images. If the abbé Chevance has the "âme d'enfant" (OE,I 337), he also possesses "une hardiesse dans les voies spirituelles, un sens extraordinaire de la grâce de Dieu" (OE,I 337). Chantal de Clergerie, his spiritual daughter, views her spirituality as connected with her childlike nature: "Au fond, je ne pensais qu'à Dieu, je n'étais simple et gaie que pour lui..., un enfant, un petit enfant... Mais les saints seuls sont des enfants!" (OE,I 670).

Chantal's thoughts are indeed similar to Bernanos' personal understanding of sanctity as witnessed in his biographical essay, "Jeanne, relapse et sainte," published in 1929. Sanctity and childhood are intertwined in his portrayal of Jeanne d'Arc as "une petite fille moqueuse et tendre" (OE,II 22), but nonetheless unafraid of shouting to her formidable judges: "Je m'en attends à mon Juge, c'est le roi du ciel et de la terre! Oui, je m'en attends à mon Créateur de tout! je l'aime de tout mon coeur!" (OE,II 28). Bernanos concludes this remarkable essay by discussing how the majority of saints belonging to the Church calendar possess the spirit of childhood.

But it is in <u>Journal d'un curé de campagne</u>, published in 1936, that Bernanos actually permits one of his "saints" to speak on the importance of the spirit of childhood. On more than one occasion the curé of Torcy discusses with the curé of Ambricourt the great treasure hidden in the Gospel message of spiritual childhood (<u>OE</u>,I 1045-1046, 1073).

Bernanos' portrayal of both historical and fictional saints thus reveals that he believed in the literal interpretation of the passage from Matthew's Gospel relating Christ's answer to his disciples' question about who is the greatest in the kingdom of heaven. Setting a little child in front of them, Christ proclaimed: "I tell you solemnly, unless you change and become like little children you will never enter the kingdom of heaven" (Matt. 18: 1-3).

Letters written during the period of <u>Journal d'un curé de campagne</u> and shortly after its publication also illustrate the gradual fusion of sanctity and childhood in the author's thought. To Marie Vallery-Radot, he stated in September, 1935: "Il n'y a qu'une seule enfance, la sainteté" (<u>Corr</u>.II 99). Writing to Marie's father in February, 1936 in reference to <u>Journal d'un curé de campagne</u>, Bernanos declared: "jamais, dans aucun de mes livres, je n'ai lâché tant d'enfants et de héros" (<u>Corr</u>.II 125-126). That a spiritual transformation had occurred in the author may be seen from a letter written in January, 1937 to his sister in which he remarked: "Pourquoi sommes-nous sortis de l'enfance! Et maintenant nous n'y pouvons plus rentrer qu'à la suite des saints, par un très grand effort. O Paradis perdu!" (<u>Corr</u>.II 166).

Finally, in the preface to <u>Les Grands Cimetières sous la lune</u>, Bernanos speaks of his desire to remain faithful to the heroes and traditions of his childhood days. He reflects that at the hour of death he will become a child once again: "c'est lui qui reprendra sa place à la tête de ma vie, rassemblera mes pauvres années jusqu'à la dernière, et comme un jeune chef ses vétérans, ralliant la troupe en désordre entrera le premier dans la Maison du Père" (OE,II 355).

This intertwining of the themes of childhood and death therefore is hardly exceptional in Bernanos' work. Having appeared even in the "Premiers essais romanesques," published in 1907 in Le Panache, there is no doubt, then, that the author had long idealized childhood.

Les Grands Cimetières sous la lune (1937-1938)

Published in the spring of 1938, Les Grands Cimetières sous la lune gives indisputably explicit evidence of how Thérèse of Lisieux confirmed for Bernanos this fusion of childhood and sanctity which he had so long espoused. The preface and first two parts of the work are particularly important in allowing us to determine the impact of Thérèse on Bernanos' thought. Part one recounts the author's personal reaction to the events of the Spanish Civil War which he witnessed in Majorca, while part two interprets these events in the light of the message of Lisieux. This second part features even the text of a very long "sermon" preached by a non-believer for the feast of Saint Thérèse.

As we have seen, Bernanos points out the importance of being faithful to the child we were in the preface to Les Grands Cimetières sous la lune. He claims that although we cannot speak in the name of childhood, for we are no longer children in the natural sense of the term, we must, nevertheless, continue to speak the language of childhood. The author then declares: "Et c'est ce langage oublié; ce langage que je cherche de livre en livre . . ." (OE,II 355).

But just what exactly is "ce langage oublié" of which the writer occasionally hears an echo? Does, perhaps, the Carmelite's message of childhood serve as an answering echo to Bernanos' interior longings for the purity and ideals of his childhood days? When the author claims that the only world which may yet be redeemed is the world of children, heroes and martyrs, is this not the sort of world to which Thérèse of Lisieux belongs?

Part one of <u>Les Grands Cimetières sous la lune</u> describes Bernanos' reaction to the events of the Spanish Civil War which he witnessed during the latter part of his two and a half year stay on the island of Majorca. As Michael Tobin has indicated in his thesis, "Incarnation and Desincarnation in the Thought of Bernanos," the witnessing of certain incidents that took place during the Civil War was for Bernanos "a pivotal event in his life, marking him deeply while adding clarity and depth to his Christian vision, as well as new precision in his expression of it."[10] In an effort to restore order to Spain upset by years of political and social unrest, the Church had willingly taken up forces with Franco. In doing so she had condoned mass executions of Catholics who did not adhere to the Church's precept of receiving the sacraments of Penance and the Eucharist during the Easter Season. Alarmed by the position that the Church seemed to be taking, Bernanos felt that as a Christian he had a duty to report the truth about what he saw. Deeply distressed by the numberless atrocities to which the Church had turned a blind eye, Bernanos let it be known that the scandal had wounded him "au vif de l'âme, à la racine même de l'espérance" (<u>OE</u>,II 426). He believed that the Church's role was not to condemn but, on the contrary, to love sinners whose care had been placed in her hands.

Thus did the Gospel message of fraternal love become a key element in this book. That the Church has faults is to be expected since she is a living organism, but if society were to be re-christianized, Bernanos felt that it had to begin with those who were its leaders and who were found so wanting in love for their neighbour. But how was this to come about?

It is in the second part of <u>Les Grands Cimetières sous la lune</u> that the author offers his readers Thérèse of Lisieux' message of God's love for us, His children, as a means of re-christianizing society. Bernanos points out, first of all, how the Carmelite's message is frequently misinterpreted by the many devout who make the pilgrimage to Lisieux. He claims that the pilgrimage is for many of the faithful little other than a visit to the huge basilica that stands on a hill overlooking the town, a visit to the Carmel chapel where the saint's relics are enclosed in a wax figure, and the purchase of a few touched up photos of the saint that can be bought by the dozens, if so desired, in one of the many souvenir shops that still line the streets leading up to the basilica. Speaking out against what he labels the fraud practised not only by those who promote devotion to Thérèse but by the faithful as well, the author declares: "Je n'attache aucune importance à cette supercherie" (OE,II 504).

Bernanos then begins setting down his thoughts on Thérèse, "cette fille mystérieuse" (OE,II 504), who, he asserts, has sown the seed of a message, "une graine dont rien n'arrêtera plus la germination" (OE,II 504). The saint's message is just beginning to take hold, he states, but rather than take it seriously "les pieux badauds" become emotional over it. To help us understand better the reaction of these curious onlookers, Bernanos imagines the conversation of two middle-aged women returning from a pilgrimage to Lisieux. For one of them, the spirit of childhood is nothing more than "une idée charmante, poétique, une idée de femme . . ." (OE,II 504). A bit of poetry is necessary, she believes, to balance the serious things in life.

Bernanos' pilgrim finds however that the promotion of a flowery, childish type of devotion to Saint Thérèse does not appeal to her daughter who looks on it as old-fashioned pious nonsense: "Lorsque j'en fais la remarque à ma fille, elle me répond qu'elle a soupé de la petite fleur bleue, qu'on ne la mange plus qu'en salade, et patati et patata" (OE,II 504).

For Bernanos, these typical pilgrims to Lisieux do not seem to have grasped that Thérèse, in the midst of terrible suffering, practised true heroic virtue based on the Gospel message that in order to enter the kingdom of God we must become like little children. In the midst of the trial of faith, she experienced what is commonly referred to by spiritual writers as the dark night of the soul where God seems to withdraw His presence. The soul is plunged into the temptation of doubting and despairing of the very existence of God and eternal salvation. Childlike abandonment is the only way to escape despair in such a case.

Hence for Bernanos the seriousness and urgency of Thérèse's message of childhood. He points out that the Carmelite's teaching on the spirit of childhood is the message sent by God for Christians of the twentieth century. He implies even that the modern world will be judged in the light of her message, even if the saint makes no such claim in her writings: "Le monde va être jugé par les enfants. L'esprit d'enfance va juger le monde. Evidemment, la sainte de Lisieux n'a rien écrit de pareil . . ." (OE,I 506). According to the author, Thérèse would never have imagined the tragic events of World War I: "'Je vais faire tomber une pluie de roses,' disait-elle vingt ans avant 1914. Elle ne savait pas quelles roses" (OE,II 507). Her promise of a shower of roses might be interpreted to mean not only her many miracles, but also, apocalyptically, the bombs of the war to end all wars.

Von Balthasar has well expressed this in Le chrétien Bernanos: "Le passage des fleurs de papier aux vraies fleurs, et de ces fleurs elles-mêmes aux bombes, est tout ensemble miraculeux et naturel, aussi miraculeux et aussi naturel que le passage, chez la sainte elle-même, d'une sainteté qui n'est qu'un jeu à la sainteté authentique" (von B 290). In any case the ferocity of the fighting in the Spanish Civil War indicated to the writer that the Christian world had not truly reflected on Thérèse's message.

Having thus proclaimed Thérèse of Lisieux to be the herald of a message for our times, Bernanos closes part two with a "sermon" given by a non-believer for the feast of Saint Thérèse. By this means, the author examines not only how faith seems to be of little importance in the lives of Christians today, but also how he believes Christians should react to the Carmelite's message.

The non-believer's "sermon" illustrates how modern society resembles that of Old Testament times, for instead of proclaiming Christ's message of hope and joy to the whole world, Christian society portrays hate and terror. The golden calf worshipped by to-day's society is that of money and power. The non-believer feels that Christian values have not influenced society as they should have if those who call themselves Christ's followers really believed in the Incarnation and Redemption.

Because their faith teaches that they participate in the divinity of Christ, as the liturgy of the Mass reminds them,[11] Christians have the duty to represent Christ to others. Michael Tobin remarks in his article, "The Christian Core: 'Ejus divinitatis esse consortes,'" that this prayer which is said at the Offertory "succintly summarizes the theology central to Bernanos' Christian vision: the divinization of man."[12] This type of Incarnation theology appears also at the heart of Thérèse's teaching on love. In a letter to Céline dated March 5, 1889, Thérèse speaks of how God's love for her sister and herself knows no bounds: "nous sommes plus grandes que l'univers entier, un jour nous aurons nous-mêmes une existence Divine..." (LT 135).

Like the Carmelite, Bernanos is not afraid to speak of the Christian's sharing in the divinity of Christ. For this reason, the non-believer states that it is up to Christians themselves to restore Christian values to society by being a living example of what they preach to others. Then boldly proposing to the members of his "congregation" Thérèse's message as the means of re-christianizing today's world, he makes several direct references to the saint of Lisieux.

The non-believer begins by rightly wondering what Christians have done with Christ's message and where they have hidden the joy that it should have produced. Indeed they seem to strike him as being indifferent to the teachings of Christianity and the message of the saints. He believes that Christians would show no emotion whatever if they were to hear that "'une petite carmélite tuberculeuse, par l'observation héroïque de devoirs aussi humbles qu'elle-même'" (OE,II 513) had converted thousands or had achieved the victory of 1918.

Bernanos' spokesman accuses Christians of living according to the principles of non-believers instead of practising heroic virtue and representing Christ to the world. His simple, childlike remarks in this regard would not, he affirms, be considered out of place as far as Thérèse of Lisieux is concerned. Indeed he proclaims quite confidently: "'Notre céleste amie ne m'en voudra pas de parler en enfant'" (OE,II 516).

And Thérèse would certainly not object to the non-believer's simplicity, for it is her message of the spirit of childhood, "ce langage oublié" of which he speaks in the preface, that Bernanos desires to communicate to Christians through the non-believer's words: "'Le seul parti qui vous reste à prendre est celui que vous propose la sainte: redevenez vous-mêmes des enfants, retrouvez l'esprit d'enfance'" (OE,II 516). The words, "'Redevenez donc enfants'" (OE,II 518), become a refrain throughout the "sermon" encouraging the non-believer's "congregation" to become children once again and acquire the heroic virtues of simplicity, honesty, and audacity. Through the mouth of his spokesman, Bernanos insists that contrary to betraying the Carmelite's message he is simply trying to apply it to the settlement of this world's affairs. A clear understanding of what Thérèse means by the spirit of childhood is, therefore, essential and so the non-believer warns Christians: "'L'esprit d'enfance peut le bien et le mal. Ce n'est pas un esprit d'acceptation de l'injustice. N'en faites pas un esprit de révolte. Il vous balaierait du monde'" (OE,II 518). In the words of the non-believer, Bernanos thus declares that Christians have a duty to interpret correctly and to transmit faithfully the message of the saints to the rest of the world.

Bernanos through his non-believer then proceeds to show how Thérèse's message of the spirit of childhood has little to do with the ways of the world. Stating that saints "sont à la fois des héros, des génies et des enfants" (OE,II 519), the non-believer then asks the members of his "congregation": "'Que voulez-vous que fassent d'une Thérèse de Lisieux nos politiques et nos moralistes?'" (OE,II 519). In their mouths, he claims, her message would lose its very meaning and effectiveness.

Since Christians cannot depend on to-day's politicians and moralists to transmit the Carmelite's message, the responsibility to do so rests in their hands. With the threat of atomic warfare in 1937 when <u>Les Grands Cimetières sous la lune</u> was written, her message becomes even more impelling, and so the non-believer proclaims: "'Une sainte, dont la foudroyante carrière montre assez le caractère tragiquement pressant du message qui lui est confié, vous invite à redevenir enfants'" (<u>OE</u>,II 520). And, indeed, Bernanos views its adoption as the world's last chance for salvation.

The non-believer's "sermon" reaches its climax in the union of Thérèse of Lisieux' message with that of Jeanne d'Arc: "'Chrétiens, l'avènement de Jeanne d'Arc au XXe siècle revêt le caractère d'un avertissement solennel. La prodigieuse fortune d'une obscure petite carmélite me paraît un signe plus grave encore'" (<u>OE</u>,II 522). The non-believer once again urges Christians to become children in the spiritual sense so that the rest of the world can quickly follow their example. By using someone who does not believe in Christ as his spokesman, Bernanos was able to present in a more convincing manner his own deep conviction that Thérèse of Lisieux' message of God's love for His creatures is a crucial one for the troubled times in which Christians find themselves. As both Guy Gaucher and William Bush have stated,[13] the pages containing the non-believer's "sermon" are apocalyptic. The political events which took place in Europe shortly after these words were written testify to Bernanos' prophetic vision.

Preface for <u>Louis le Cardonnel, pèlerin de l'invisible</u> (1938)

Shortly afterward Bernanos refers again to the urgency of Thérèse of Lisieux' message in a 1938 preface for Raymond Christoflour's volume, <u>Louis le Cardonnel, pèlerin de l'invisible</u>. In the beginning of this preface, Bernanos proclaims "la poésie" to be "l'éternelle exilée parmi les hommes" (<u>Cré</u> 117), and that it is to an honoured few, such as Louis le Cardonnel, who are worthy of the name of poet that poetry "ouvre les secrets de son coeur royal, de son coeur enfantin. A eux seuls elle laisse voir son visage d'enfant" (<u>Cré</u> 117). Poets, too, Bernanos declares, rank with children and saints.

Further on in the preface, Louis le Cardonnel is depicted as a "Prêtre-Poète" (<u>Cré</u> 118), who knew both solitude and misfortune. He suffered by the Church which, according to Bernanos, has no place for poets and which would soon no longer have any place for children if it were not for the saints who have sometimes begged the Church theologians and politicians to be quiet for a moment (<u>Cré</u> 119). This passage echoes the author's 1934 texts in which he shows how both Jeanne d'Arc and Thérèse of Lisieux give witness to heroic childhood, a message often misunderstood by the most learned of Church doctors and theologians. If it were left entirely to these latter individuals to interpret the Gospel message, it would not be long before there would not be any place left for children.

Bernanos' reference to Thérèse of Lisieux at the end of this preface serves as a fitting conclusion. He warns Christians here that the interpretation given to the Carmelite's message of childhood by Church theologians and politicians is a sentimental, watered-down version and that "S'il n'eût dépendu que de ces malheureux, la dévotion à la petite Soeur Thérèse ne serait plus aujourd'hui qu'une des mille recettes inoffensives de la confiserie dévote" (<u>Cré</u> 119).

And in these twentieth century Church politicians and theologians we are reminded once again of those to whom Bernanos referred in "Jeanne, relapse et sainte" as "ces renards scolastiques, ces rats" (<u>OE</u>, II 26) who condemned Jeanne d'Arc, an innocent young woman more in need of protection than anything else, to be burned at the stake for being a heretic. "<u>Notre Eglise est l'Eglise des</u>

saints" (OE,II 40), Bernanos proclaimed in his essay on Jeanne d'Arc, but he went on to add about the saints even then that "On voudrait qu'ils fussent des vieillards pleins d'expérience et de politique, et la plupart sont des enfants. Or l'enfance est seule contre tous" (OE,II 40).

The non-believer, too, in Les Grands Cimetières sous la lune, was able to tell us who the saints are: "'Je dirai qu'ils sont à la fois des héros, des génies et des enfants'" (OE,II 519). Bernanos' thought connects here with that of Thérèse of Lisieux who tells us that it is not always to the learned scholars that God reveals His secrets; in fact, the Carmelite believed that it was simply because she was a weak child that God Himself instructed her and that if Church theologians had come to question her "sans doute auraient-ils été étonnés de voir une enfant de quatorze ans comprendre les secrets de la perfection, secrets que toute leur science ne leur peut découvrir, puisque pour les posséder il faut être pauvre d'esprit!..." (HA 122).

With society becoming more and more materialistic and with the ever-increasing threat of godless totalitarianism taking over Europe, Bernanos, in his preface to Christoflour's volume, pleads once again with Christians to pay attention to the Carmelite's urgent message since "Le monde se meurt faute d'enfance, et c'est bien contre elle, en effet, que les demi-dieux totalitaires poussent leurs canons et leurs tanks" (Cré 119). The author remains convinced that Thérèse's means of making incarnate God's presence in us by our adoption of a childlike attitude towards God is one of the most important messages ever given mankind. His thought here concerning the totalitarian leaders of the twentieth century rejoins his declaration at the end of Les Grands Cimetières sous la lune. Successors of the fifteenth century theologians who condemned Jeanne d'Arc to the stake, political leaders who demand submission to the enemy offer the modern world no more hope of the re-birth of Christian society than did Jeanne d'Arc's judges offer her the hope of God's justice and mercy.

NOTES

CHAPTER 2

[1] Michel Estève, <u>Bernanos</u> (Paris: Gallimard, 1965) 26.

[2] Originally <u>Action Française</u>, November 18, 1932, reprinted in the <u>Bulletin de la société des amis de Georges Bernanos</u> 17-20 (Noël 1953): 45.

[3] Originally <u>Action Française</u>, November 20, 1932, reprinted in the <u>Bulletin de la société des amis de Georges Bernanos</u> 17-20 (Noël 1953): 52.

[4] <u>Bulletin de la société des amis de Georges Bernanos</u> 17-20 (Noël 1953): 43.

[5] This letter, written at La Bayorre, is listed as letter 278, page 463, volume I, and dated "début janvier 1933." One is surprised, therefore, to discover the same text listed as letter 182, page 247 of <u>Lettres retrouvées</u> and dated "La Bayorre, début janvier <u>1935</u>." Since Bernanos had been evicted from La Bayorre in October of 1934, and had settled with his family in Majorca that same month, returning to France only in March, 1937, it is clear that this letter was not written at La Bayorre in 1935.

[6] Thérèse was trying to console her sister, Pauline, in the event that she would find her dead some morning without having had the opportunity to receive the last rites of the church. The saint's exact words were: "Sans doute, c'est une grande grâce de recevoir les Sacrements; mais quand le bon Dieu ne le permet pas, c'est bien quand même, tout est grâce" (<u>DE</u> 41).

[7] Unidentified quote found in Yves Bridel, "Jeanne d'Arc et Bernanos," <u>Bernanos. Centre culturel de Cerisy-la-Salle 10 au 19 juillet 1969</u>, ed. Max Milner (Paris: Plon, 1972) 302.

[8] This same letter also appears in <u>Histoire d'une âme: manuscrits autobiographiques</u> 214.

[9] François Jamart, o.c.d., <u>Complete Spiritual Doctrine of St. Therese of Lisieux</u>, trans. Walter Van de Putte, c.s.sp. (New York: Alba House, 1961) 16.

[10] Michael Robinson Tobin, "Incarnation and Desincarnation in the Thought of Bernanos," Ph.D. diss., U of Western Ontario, 1985, 133.

[11] During the Liturgy of the Eucharist in the Catholic Church, at the preparation of the gifts of bread and wine, the priest proclaims: "By the mystery of this water and wine may we come to share in the divinity of Christ, who humbled himself to share in our humanity."

[12] Michael Tobin, "The Christian Core: 'Ejus divinitatis esse consortes,'" <u>Renascence</u> XLI.1-2 (Fall 1988 / Winter 1989): 92.

[13] William Bush, "Honneur, enfance et désincarnation: composition et thèmes des 'Grands Cimetières sous la lune,'" <u>La Revue des Lettres Modernes</u> 290-297 (1972) "Etudes bernanosiennes" 13: 13.

Guy Gaucher, o.c.d., "Bernanos et Sainte Thérèse de l'Enfant-Jésus," <u>La Revue des Lettres Modernes</u> 56-57 (1960) "Etudes bernanosiennes" 1: 235.

CHAPTER 3

EXPLICIT EVIDENCE IN THE LAST DECADE (1939-1948)

Both historical and personal circumstances played a key role in the third and final period of Bernanos' works. The critical state of events he observed taking place in Europe in the late nineteen thirties seems to have led the author to abandon permanently the writing of novels in favour of non-fictional works where he spoke of the meaning of freedom, truth, and justice.

Once he had published <u>Nouvelle histoire de Mouchette</u> in 1937, Bernanos would write no further fiction except the last chapter of <u>Monsieur Ouine</u> in 1940 during his Brazilian exile, plus, at the very end of his life, the dialogues for a film scenario which became <u>Dialogues des Carmélites</u>. These dialogues were completed but a few short months before his death from cancer of the liver on July 5, 1948.

Bernanos' non-fictional works between 1939 and 1948 reflect their author's anxiety and anguish over France's involvement in World War II and its aftermath. Compiled today in a number of volumes, they include political essays, lectures, and newspaper articles.

In four works of this period we find explicit textual references to the Carmelite of Lisieux: <u>Nous autres Français</u> where Bernanos explains what it is to be French (1939); <u>Le Chemin de la Croix-des-âmes</u>, newspaper articles from

Bernanos' Brazilian exile (1939-1945); Lettre aux Anglais where Bernanos exposes his admiration for the English and tries to explain the meaning of French honour (1942); and La liberté pour quoi faire?, postwar lectures in Europe and Tunisia (1946-1947).

The Brazilian "Exile" (July, 1938-June, 1945)

Bernanos' return to France from Majorca in March, 1937 was to be of short duration. In July, 1938 the author and his family left France for Paraguay where apparently he hoped to experience, with his wife and six children, that marvelous South American adventure of which he and a friend, Maxence de Coleville, had dreamed in the days of their youth. In addition there was also his growing disillusionment with what he determined to be France's abdication of her responsibilities as the eldest daughter of the Church. What the writer was really searching for in South America was, as André Rousseaux has stated, "toute aventure salvatrice où sa propre vie, s'engageant, réengageât la vie de la France."[1] The cost of living in Paraguay proved, however, to be far higher than in France. Bernanos finally decided to settle in Brazil where he and members of his family resided from the fall of 1938 until June of 1945.

The writer's works from 1939 to the end of World War II relate not only his reflections on the full scale catastrophe taking place on the European scene, but also the principal events of those seven years spent in Brazil during the war. Hoping to set up a cattle ranch in the remote area of Pirapora, Bernanos would listen with dismay each day as the radio broadcasts filtering into the remote Brazilian towns announced the débâcle of 1940: Hitler's advances into France in May; the French government's departure from Paris on June 10; Pétain's request on June 17 for an armistice; the formal signing of this document on June 22; the news that France was officially under German occupation on June 25.[2]

Bernanos viewed the collaboration of Pétain's government with the Nazis as spelling spiritual disaster for France, all the more so as the official Church hierarchy even urged French Catholics to accept the Nazis' occupation of their country.[3] The author's concept of France having a mission to promulgate Christianity in the world, which dated back to the medieval notion of Christian chivalry, caused him to view the destiny of the nation and the plan of God as one and the same thing. For Christians, man, redeemed by Christ, has become divinized. And from Christ's redemption of man have sprung up the traditional Christian values of honour, fidelity, and liberty.

The author believed that only through France's incarnation of these values, would she fulfill her historical role in offering hope to a despairing world. His political essays were thus an appeal to his nation to be faithful to that Christian vocation. This is shown clearly in an article written in July, 1943 and entitled "Le Général de Gaulle, chef et symbole de l'honneur français" in which Bernanos describes what he believes to be his country's tradition: "Comme l'a très bien compris Charles Péguy, la vocation de mon pays n'est pas de donner la grandeur ou la richesse au monde, c'est d'y maintenir l'espérance" (Che 610).

In his numerous articles and radio broadcasts during the war years, Bernanos took up the challenge to speak out courageously against what he saw to be France's dishonour and abdication of her historic mission. He declared in Rio de Janeiro's newspaper, O Jornal, on May 27, 1942 that "le premier devoir de la France était de demeurer fidèle à sa vocation spirituelle particulière, et de ne pas altérer le message historique que, victorieuse ou vaincue, honorée ou humiliée, elle a le devoir de transmettre, coûte que coûte . . ." (Che 379).[4]

i) *Heroic Childhood*

While encouraging French citizens throughout the world to respect their national heritage of honour, fidelity and freedom, Bernanos placed his hope for a regeneration of Christian principles in the young people of France. Once again, on July 12, 1942, the author wrote in <u>O Jornal</u>: "le devoir suprême de la France écrasée est de maintenir aujourd'hui, coûte que coûte, l'intégrité de sa pensée, de sa tradition, de son message, et de conserver toutes ces choses pour tous les hommes" (<u>Che</u> 388).[5] He found these qualities incarnate in Jeanne d'Arc, the ideal of the Christian knight of medieval times, and in Thérèse of Lisieux with her message of heroic childhood in modern times. Childhood and sanctity as embodied in the Maid of Orleans and the Carmelite of Lisieux thus were to become more and more important in Bernanos' thought as reflected in his writings during the war.

Thérèse, it would certainly appear, became a veritable companion to Bernanos in his "exile." In his article, "Bernanos au Brésil," Dom Gordan describes the effect that even the thought of Thérèse of Lisieux and Jeanne d'Arc had on the author whose voice would change whenever he spoke of his two favourite saints: "son langage tonitruant se fait doux comme une musique, lorsqu'il parle de l'humanité du Seigneur ou des saints qui eurent l'esprit d'enfance, Jeanne d'Arc, sainte Thérèse de l'Enfant-Jésus."[6]

It is in certain passages dealing with the theme of childhood, a major theme of much of Bernanos' polemical work of this period, that are found explicit references to the Carmelite saint. The first such reference occurs in <u>Nous autres Français</u>, begun in September, 1938 and completed in June, 1939.

Distressed over his fellow countrymen's attitudes of either pacifism or open sympathy for Nazis and Fascists, Bernanos judged the dishonour of France in spiritual terms. Since, in the author's opinion, the temporal salvation of France could not be separated from her spiritual salvation, honour was thus conceived on both the temporal and spiritual levels as a virtue that had to be restored to France. But who was to take on this responsibility? In urging collaboration the French ecclesiastical hierarchy had refused it in the name of "realism." Was it to be a "realist" such as Maurras who, refusing the risk that honour demanded, reneged on his former ideals of nationalism, and openly supported Mussolini's Fascism? Jacques Chabot points out in his "Notice" to the Pléiade edition of Nous autres Français that Bernanos was definitely against this type of imposture proposing instead "contre la bourgeoisie et les curés, de refaire une nation et une chrétienté françaises."[7]

The realists were those who turned a blind eye to the remilitarization of the Rhineland and the increasing aggression of Hitler, and, as Bernanos reassured his countrymen, realists can most certainly be proven wrong where grace is concerned. "La grâce est une inconnue, par quoi le calcul des réalistes est toujours faussé" (OE,II 714). Realists tend to reason as if everything depended on them, the author added, "Mais la grâce frappe, dans leur dos, qui lui plaît, doublant ainsi ce qu'on appelle le hasard d'un autre Hasard immense qui défie toutes les mathématiques" (OE,II 714). And so, because he can neither reckon with grace nor with those who possess simplicity and act with freedom of conscience, "Le plus expert réaliste du monde serait roulé par un petit enfant qui le regarderait droit dans les yeux. C'est bien pourquoi S.S. Pie XII a fait sagement d'élire Soeur Thérèse pour protectrice" (OE,II 744).[8]

In an interview given at Juiz de Fora on February 10, 1939, Bernanos condemned once again the modern world's betrayal of the traditional values of honour, liberty, and justice. The world is a failure; it is to be pitied, but its hypocrites and pharisees with their bombs and poisonous gases cannot destroy France's heritage of saints and heroes, "cet esprit d'enfance, cette jeunesse surnaturelle que vient d'incarner notre petite sainte Thérèse, pour l'épreuve et le scandale des fanatiques de toute espèce . . ." (Che 44-45).[9] Once again, therefore, the author warns the French nation that the Carmelite's message of joy and suffering is to be interpreted correctly. Through her saints and heroes France offers her people a hope that no one can destroy.

ii) Lettre aux Anglais (1940-1942)

At the beginning of November, 1940, Christopher Dawson, editor of the Dublin Review, asked Bernanos for an article "sur la guerre, Saint Louis, Jeanne d'Arc et l'honneur français."[10] The purpose of this article was to explain to the English-speaking world the meaning of Christian honour. Dawson's request turned out to be the point of departure for what was to become a series of seven "letters," dated between December, 1940 and November, 1941, which would eventually be published in Brazil in 1942 by Atlantica Editora under the title Lettre aux Anglais. The first five letters were addressed to the English, the sixth to the Americans, and the seventh to the Europeans; only the first "letter," however, was printed in the Dublin Review (Sp 202-203).

The first "letter" appeared in the April, 1941 edition of the Dublin Review under the title "A Letter to the English." Because it was dated "Christmas, 1940" it offered Bernanos the appropriate occasion to celebrate English childhood: "Je vous souhaite donc un joyeux Noël. Noël est la fête de l'enfance. Joyeuse enfance au peuple anglais! Hurrah pour l'enfance anglaise!" (Ang 17). The author reminds the English that if they are in the midst of writing one of the most glorious pages of history, a tale of heroes for children (Ang 18), it is, nevertheless, the French who are going to save the world: "le bon Dieu nous a choisis pour apporter la liberté, l'égalité, la fraternité à tous ces peuples dont nous ne savons même pas exactement la place sur l'atlas . . ." (Ang 22-23).

To the English who might wonder how the French could possibly save the world when their country was occupied by a foreign aggressor, Bernanos explains that suffering and impuissance only serve to strengthen the faith and hope learned by his fellow countrymen at their mothers' knees and at the hour of distress these are the qualities they rely on (Ang 27).

The author points out to the English that throughout history the French have always known how to make the best use of their national misfortunes. Their darkest hours can thus be their finest. He then puts forth Thérèse of Lisieux as an example of this: "'Oh! Mère, est-ce la fin? disait à sa prieure la petite sainte Thérèse de Lisieux à l'agonie. Comment vais-je faire pour mourir? Jamais je ne vais savoir mourir!...'" (Ang 28). It is at her weakest moment, her final agony, that she becomes for Bernanos the prototype of French heroism, a heroism within the grasp of the ordinary person, for "C'est à de telles paroles, et non à celles des héros de Plutarque, que frémiront toujours, d'âge en âge, les étendards de la patrie" (Ang 28).

Those who do not understand the concept of heroism that underlies this passage will never really know the French. The writer asks: "Qu'a donc à faire, dira-t-on, cette petite carmélite avec les étendards français?" (Ang 28). Christian heroism, in French terms, may be defined as an attitude of courage, dignity, and acceptance in the face of misfortune, even death. Bernanos reminds the English that the Chanson de Roland was the story of the defeat and the death of a young hero, his face turned to the enemy and his hand raised in allegiance to God (Ang 30).

Similarly, Jeanne d'Arc's finest hour was her death scene, and, like Thérèse of Lisieux, her acceptance of her death was heroic. Is it so surprising, therefore, to find Bernanos putting the Carmelite's words into the thoughts of the Maid of Orleans, that great archetype of French heroism: "'Comment vais-je faire pour mourir? Jamais je ne vais savoir mourir!' Ainsi devait penser Jeanne d'Arc le matin du 30 mai 1429" (Ang 29). What is significant for the writer is that Jeanne welcomes death "avec un scrupule de courtoisie, une espèce de timidité discrète, et comme la crainte de lui déplaire" (Ang 29).

Fused together more closely than ever before in Bernanos' works, we here find Thérèse of Lisieux and Jeanne d'Arc standing out as prototypes of the union of childhood, sanctity, and heroism. As such they testify to the author's faith in the Incarnation and Redemption, and more particularly to the Christian dogma that the Redeemer of mankind came to man in the guise of a little child, born of a virgin mother.

In another "letter" on the same topic, dated August, 1941, Bernanos reaffirms that Christianity has to be renewed. It is only through suffering that the strength of Christianity can be truly measured and it is suffering which places "les saints au premier rang" (Ang 131).

Towards the end of this letter to the English-speaking world, Bernanos renews his earlier attack on realist politicians: "Qui prétend utiliser l'Eglise à des fins réalistes, dans un esprit réaliste, sera toujours dupe du marché" (Ang 132). Realist politicians cannot found a Christian society, but they certainly expect Christians to support their non-Christian society. The author declares that those who were the natural guardians of the conscience of the French nation have failed in their duty to maintain a society based on Christian principles.

"Mon Eglise est l'Eglise des saints" (Ang 134), paralleling "Notre Eglise est l'Eglise des saints" in "Jeanne, relapse et sainte" (OE, II 40), becomes once again a refrain found in Bernanos' work as the author shows how, having formed a living tradition for the Church, the saints have surpassed the doctors of the Church in the teaching of the Gospel message. The letter reaches its climax in the last paragraph where the author, as in <u>Les Grands Cimetières sous la lune</u>, honours childhood into whose hands the care of the Church, with its doctors and theologians, has been entrusted. The letter then concludes with a thought provoking question concerning the timeliness of the twentieth century canonizations of Jeanne d'Arc and Thérèse of Lisieux (Ang 135). Is it not moving, asks Bernanos, to think that at a time when the Church of France "s'abandonne plus que jamais à toutes les froides spéculations de la prudence sénile, elle élève si haut deux jeunes filles, sainte Jeanne d'Arc et sainte Thérèse de Lisieux?" (Ang 135).

iii) *"Discours pour le baptême de l'avion brésilien 'Jeanne d'Arc'" (1943)*

Two years later, on September 24, 1943, Madame Bernanos (née Jehanne Talbert d'Arc and descended from a brother of the saint) was asked to christen a Brazilian airplane named "Jeanne d'Arc." Asked to speak at this event, Bernanos proclaimed once again to his Brazilian friends the significance of the canonizations of Jeanne d'Arc on May 9, 1920 and Thérèse of Lisieux on May 17, 1925: "ces deux saintes sont deux jeunes filles, on pourrait presque dire deux enfants - sainte Thérèse de l'Enfant-Jésus, que vous appelez dans votre langue si caressante Theresinha, et Jeanne d'Arc" (Che 651).[11] The writer specifies that he saw in the proximity of these two dates of canonization a symbol of the supernatural vocation of France. He thus reminded the Brazilians that he viewed these two young women saints as a sign from God confirming France's historic mission to establish a society based on Christian principles.

"The Final Years" (June, 1945-1948)

In early 1945, at the request of Général de Gaulle and after careful consideration, Bernanos came to the conclusion that he could best serve his country by returning to France, and so on June 2, he and his family left Brazil on a banana boat bound for Liverpool.

Following his return to France, the author eked out an existence the last three years of his life from various lectures (collected and published as <u>La Liberté pour quoi faire?</u>) and from writing articles for various newspapers and journals such as <u>La Bataille</u>, <u>Carrefour</u>, <u>L'Intransigeant</u>, <u>Le Figaro</u>, <u>Le Semeur</u>, <u>Combat</u>, <u>Témoignage Chrétien</u>, <u>La Plume</u>, and <u>Temps Présent</u> (collected and published as <u>Français, si vous saviez 1945-1948</u>).

In his spiritual biography of the author, <u>Georges Bernanos ou l'invincible</u>

espérance, Guy Gaucher claims that those last three years of Bernanos' life were among the most difficult. Although the writer had acquired some hope and serenity from his "exile" in Brazil, everything he had gained seemed to disintegrate upon returning to France and finding his native land torn apart by the very abuses he had been denouncing so vehemently (IE 128-129).

For what Bernanos discovered was a France liberated by the Allied Forces, but where no true Christian freedom was present. The principles of the Resistance movement seemed doomed to moral failure, with the country facing the enslavement of Communism on the one hand and the chains of Capitalism with its false gods of industrialization, technological efficiency, and money on the other. For this reason Rousseaux has stated that Bernanos' last years are the story of his struggle to save France from perdition, or "Au moins pour l'arracher au mensonge qui sert de masque abject à une vie décomposée" ("Rousseaux" 320).

The author's anxiety over his country's failure to take up the challenge of her vocation to show the presence of Christ in the world can be readily understood in the passionate appeals he makes for freedom in the last period of his work. The freedom he hails is that of the children of God, the freedom to choose to love, the freedom of spirit to which the life of Thérèse of Lisieux testifies.

Thus though specific textual references to the Carmelite saint and her words occur more rarely in the last three years of Bernanos' works, her teachings seem to have taken an even deeper hold on the author. His understanding of Christ's love for mankind now seems to parallel Thérèse's image of the Divine Beggar, "ce Dieu qui devient le mendiant de notre amour . . ." (LT 346). In an article written on October 2, 1946 for La Bataille, Bernanos makes a sharp contrast between the godlessness of modern technology, "cette Providence mécanique" (Fra 243), and the message of Christ, "le Divin Mendiant pendu à ses clous . . ." (Fra 243). That the image of Christ as the Divine Beggar was a meaningful one in Bernanos' own spiritual life can be seen from the January 19, 1948 entry recorded in his "Dernier agenda": "Il n'est pas venu en vainqueur, mais en suppliant. Il est comme réfugié en moi, sous ma garde; et je réponds de Lui devant son Père."[12]

i) "Nos amis les saints" and "Derniers appels" (1947)

The necessity of freedom to Christian love is seen finally in "Nos amis les saints," the last lecture delivered by Bernanos in Tunisia on April 4, 1947 to a group of women religious belonging to the order of Charles de Foucauld. For Bernanos, as for Thérèse of Lisieux, sanctity consists in the loving acceptance of God's will in the ordinary events of one's daily life. Thus, the poor man steeped in misery who renders thanks to God for having created him as a free being capable of loving, or the mother grieving over the death of her beloved child can become saints by accepting their sorrow (Lib 225).

In this same lecture Bernanos' familiar themes of sanctity and childhood become more closely linked than ever before. The writer reflects here that sanctity cannot be that difficult to learn. Children play "grownups" by imitating the actions of their elders and then, one day, they become like those they have imitated. So, Bernanos believes, does one become a saint by "playing saints." This gives him a chance to invoke once again Thérèse of Lisieux about whom "on pourrait dire qu'elle est devenue sainte en jouant aux saints avec l'Enfant Jésus . . ." (Lib 213). The originality of this analogy between a child's game and the acquisition of sanctity shows us the close rapport between nature and grace in the mind of Bernanos. The supernatural is built on the natural.

The last explicit reference to the Carmelite saint's words found in the author's polemical work is to that already well-known quotation "tout est grâce." Towards the end of 1947, in a text originally intended for the French edition of

Le Chemin de la Croix-des-Ames but published as "Derniers appels" in Le lendemain, c'est vous!, Bernanos again recalls this phrase. Speaking about how certain of his fellow countrymen were not acting as Frenchmen should, the author claims that they did not possess the French virtues of faith, hope, and charity, nor did they know the state of grace in which their ancestors lived unawares, "par une sorte de privilège mystérieux, car, dans l'ordre de la nature comme dans celui de la Surnature, tout est grâce" (Len 180-181).

ii) *Dialogues des Carmélites (1947-1948)*

Regarded as Bernanos' spiritual testament, Dialogues des Carmélites consists of dialogues written for a scenario by Père R.-L. Brückberger and Philippe Agostini based on Gertrud von le Fort's novelle, Die Letzte am Schafott. Bernanos' Dialogues were published by Albert Béguin in 1949, presented on the stage for the first time in German in 1951 in Zürich, produced as an opera by Francis Poulenc in 1957, and finally, with major changes to the text, appeared in a film version in 1960.[13]

A fictional play based on the guillotining of sixteen Carmelites of Compiègne during the Reign of Terror on July 17, 1794, Dialogues des Carmélites reflects the depth of Bernanos' interior life. The author's major themes - honour, fear of death, acceptance of death as the supreme gift of love, spiritual poverty, and spiritual childhood - are combined in such a way as to make Thérèse of Lisieux' presence highly felt.

The play however contains no specific textual references to the Carmelite saint. Yet Guy Gaucher views it as a supreme homage to her declaring that "A un niveau très profond, l'esprit thérésien est présent dans ce scénario" ("BT" 238). We have already commented on Luc Estang's highly significant observation made in 1948 that Soeur Constance and Soeur Blanche de l'Agonie du Christ, the two young heroines of the play, represent the two aspects of Thérèse of Lisieux' spirituality: her spirit of childhood and her vocation of suffering.[14] Finally Yves Bridel states that in <u>Dialogues des Carmélites</u> "nous sommes au coeur même de la spiritualité de sainte Thérèse de l'Enfant-Jésus . . . ." (<u>EE</u> 225).

Thus though a dearth of explicit textual references to the saint of Lisieux exists in <u>Dialogues des Carmélites</u>, it in no way indicates a lack of her influence. It is to be noted at every turn of the page, penetrating the whole atmosphere of the author's final work to such an extent that one can say that her message and spirituality had become his own. It is the process leading to this so complete assimilation in Bernanos' last work which we now propose to trace.

NOTES

CHAPTER 3

¹ André Rousseaux, "La démission de la France," <u>Georges Bernanos. Essais et témoignages</u>, ed. Albert Béguin (Paris: Editions du Seuil; Neuchâtel: Editions de la Baconnière, 1949) 318. Cited hereafter as "Rousseaux."

² H. R. Kedward, <u>Occupied France: Collaboration and Resistance 1940-1944</u> (Oxford: Basil Blackwell Ltd., 1985) 1-2.

³ Hubert Sarrazin, "On Being French and Catholic: 1938-1945," <u>Renascence</u> XLI.1-2 (Fall 1988/Winter 1989): 76-77.

⁴ This article was originally published in Portuguese in <u>O Jornal</u> as the first of a series of articles under the title "A Vocaçao espiritual da França." It was subsequently published in <u>Le Chemin de la Croix-des-âmes</u> (376-379) and also in Georges Bernanos, <u>La vocation spirituelle de la France</u>, inédits rassemblés et présentés par Jean-Loup Bernanos (Paris: Plon, 1975) 53-59.

⁵ This article was first published in Portuguese in <u>O Jornal</u> as the fourth in a series of articles under the title "A Vocaçao espiritual da França: IV. Para os homens livres, as palavras livres." It was subsequently published in <u>Le Chemin de la Croix-des-âmes</u> (385-389) and in <u>La vocation spirituelle de la France</u> 69-74.

⁶ Dom Paul Gordan, "Bernanos au Brésil," <u>Bulletin de la société des amis de Georges Bernanos</u> 5 (1950): 5. Dom Gordan remarked in this article on how Thérèse's <u>Ultima Verba</u>, the little book containing her last sayings to her sister, Pauline, were on the author's bedside table.
Thérèse's "presence" in Brazil appears also in a photo on page 121 of <u>Bernanos, iconographie recueil ie, choisie et présentée par Jean-Loup Bernanos</u> (Paris: Plon, 1988). A statue of the Carmelite of Lisieux is seen on the left hand side of the little altar where Bernanos used to read the mass to his family every Sunday.
During the colloquium on "Bernanos et l'interprétation" held in Amiens in May, 1990, Jean-Loup Bernanos stated to the author that at their house in Barbacena his father had kept a vigil light lit to the saint and that a pathway had been named in her honour. Jean-Loup Bernanos also confirmed the fact that his father had read the <u>Histoire d'une âme</u> and the <u>Novissima Verba</u>.

⁷ Jacques Chabot, "Notice," <u>Essais et écrits de combat</u>, tome I, textes présentés et annotés par Yves Bridel, Jacques Chabot et Joseph Jurt sous la direction de Michel Estève, by Georges Bernanos (Paris: Gallimard, "Bibliothèque de la Pléiade," 1971) 1541.

⁸ Jacques Chabot has made the following comment on this passage: "C'est le pape Pie XI qui avait fait de sainte Thérèse de Lisieux 'l'Etoile de son pontificat.' Pie XII a continué à se placer lui aussi sous le patronage de la petite Carmélite" (<u>OE</u>,II 1578).
The <u>Histoire d'une âme</u> contains the following information: "1923 29 avril: Béatification de soeur Thérèse de l'Enfant-Jésus par Pie XI. Le pape fait d'elle 'l'étoile de son pontificat'" (<u>HA</u> 335); "1927 . . . 14 décembre: Pie XI proclame sainte Thérèse de l'Enfant-Jésus patronne principale, à l'égal de saint François-Xavier, de tous les missionnaires, hommes et femmes, et des missions existant dans tout l' univers" (<u>HA</u> 336); "1944 3 mai: Pie XII nomme sainte Thérèse

patronne secondaire de la France, à l'égal de sainte Jeanne d'Arc" (HA 336).

[9] This interview at Juiz de Fora was originally printed in O Jornal on February 10, 1939. It was subsequently published in Le Chemin de la Croix-des-âmes (42-45) and also in Georges Bernanos, La France contre les robots, suivi de Textes inédits, présentation et notes de Jean-Loup Bernanos (Paris: Plon, 1970) 161-166, under the title "Le monde moderne est un monde humilié."

[10] Hubert Sarrazin, L'oeuvre de Bernanos à l'époque de la seconde guerre mondiale, suite chronologique de 1938 à 1945 / texte et commentaire établis sur documents originaux (Weldon Library University of Western Ontario Special Collections: London, Ontario, 1984) IV, Section 49.

[11] This address was first published in Portuguese under the title "A França nao duvida mais da liberdade." The text of the manuscript was subsequently published under the title "Discours pour le baptême de l'avion brésilien 'Jeanne d'Arc'" in the Bulletin des amis de Georges Bernanos 24-25 (juin 1955), in Le Chemin de la Croix-des-âmes (647-654), and also in La France contre les robots (187-201).

[12] Albert Béguin, Bernanos par lui-même (Paris: Editions du Seuil, "Ecrivains de toujours," 1958) 146.

[13] William Bush, Georges Bernanos (New York: Twayne Publishers Inc., 1969) 117.

[14] Luc Estang, "Les Dialogues des Carmélites," Bulletin de la société des amis de Georges Bernanos 1 (1949): 14.

PART II

IMPLICIT EVIDENCE OF THÉRÈSE OF LISIEUX' PRESENCE IN BERNANOS' WORK

CHAPTER 4

A NATURAL AFFINITY: EARLY WRITING AND SHORT STORIES (1905-1930)

Explicit textual references to the Carmelite saint tend to occur more frequently in the earlier period of Bernanos' works. In the later period, however, Thérèse's influence had become so integrated as part of Bernanos' thought that it is present under many forms, some of them quite surprising when discovered in characters such as Monsieur Ouine or Simone Alfieri.

But should this really be surprising? Guy Gaucher pointed out in 1962 that with the exception of Donissan, the priest-hero of Sous le soleil de Satan,[1] who "malgré son humilité très réelle, s'apparente parfois plus au héros qu'au saint tel que Bernanos le concevra plus tard" (IE 114), all of Bernanos' "saints" share a common spirituality. Indeed Gaucher asserts that Thérèse of Lisieux' doctrine impregnates the author's own spirituality as well as that of his characters (IE 115-116). This comment leads to the rather obvious conclusion that Thérèse's presence can be seen <u>implicitly</u> as well as <u>explicitly</u> in Bernanos' fictional works.

In order for the saint's presence to appear implicitly in his works, Bernanos needed, however, not only to feel some sort of natural affinity with her spiritual adventure, but also to have sufficient time for reflecting on her message and assimilating it into his own spiritual and daily needs. Since there are strong indications that he was familiar with the Histoire d'une âme long before the 1925 canonization of its young author, it is important that before examining his works for implicit evidence of the Carmelite's influence, we examine the natural affinity which Georges Bernanos felt for the saint of Lisieux.

Early Correspondence (1905-1926)

In the author's correspondence prior to 1927 we find indications of a basic affinity between his own spiritual temperament and aspirations and Thérèse's. Letters written by the young Bernanos to the abbé Lagrange show resemblance between the author's adolescent concerns and those which occupied the heart of Thérèse as a young woman. A number of such resemblances are found in Bernanos' letter of March, 1905.

The author speaks in that letter, written when he was only seventeen, of his first communion as a grace-filled moment. The word "cadeau" becomes a key word in his description as it is in Thérèse's account of the joy that filled her heart on the day of her first communion and of her desire to enter the Carmelite monastery. For both saint and writer this "cadeau" is viewed in terms of their vocation, their commitment to the Person of Christ. Thérèse declares: "tous les cadeaux que j'avais reçus ne me remplissaient pas le coeur, il n'y avait que Jésus qui pût me contenter . . ." (HA 93), while Bernanos writes: "Et j'ai pensé à me faire missionnaire, et, dans mon action de grâces, à la fin de la messe de première communion, j'ai demandé cela au Père, comme unique cadeau" (Corr.I 75).

Aware, like Thérèse, of the special graces received on this solemn occasion and of the transitory nature of human existence, Bernanos adds that life, "même avec la gloire, qui est la plus belle chose humaine, est une chose vide et sans saveur quand on n'y mêle pas, toujours, absolument, Dieu" (Corr.I 76). His conclusion that happiness can be achieved only through living and dying for God becomes for him a remedy for his fear of death. The author thus gives us already at age seventeen a marvelous glimpse of his desire for glory as well as of his natural fear of death.

Similar thoughts appear in Thérèse's belief as a child that God had destined her for glory: "Il me fit comprendre aussi que ma gloire à moi ne paraîtrait pas aux yeux mortels, qu'elle consisterait à devenir une grande Sainte!!!..." (HA 85). Yet even though she longed to become a saint and to enjoy the presence of God in heaven, Thérèse also felt a natural fear of death. Having a premonition from childhood days that she would die young, it took her some time to arrive at the conclusion that what mattered most was not the length of her life but, as she explained in a letter to the abbé Bellière in July, 1897, her loving acceptance of God's will: "C'est donc la seule pensée d'accomplir la volonté du Seigneur qui fait toute ma joie" (LT 444).

During the long, pain-filled months preceding her death, Thérèse revealed to her sister, Pauline, her concern about how to die: "Je me demande comment je ferai pour mourir. Je voudrais pourtant m'en tirer 'avec honneur'!" (DE 42). When asked by Pauline if she were afraid to die, Thérèse replied: "Ah! de moins en moins!" (DE 59) and two days later, in answer to the same question: "...Pourquoi serais-je plus à l'abri qu'une autre d'avoir peur de la mort?" (DE 66).

Similarly, in the above-mentioned letter to the abbé Lagrange, Bernanos tells of how poor health during his childhood had made him fear death. He confesses: "La plus petite indisposition me semble le prélude de cette dernière maladie, dont j'ai si peur" (Corr.I 75). But he also adds that one of the graces of his first communion was the realization that "ce n'était pas surtout la vie qu'il fallait s'attacher à rendre heureuse et bonne, mais la mort, qui est la clôture de tout" (Corr.I 75). Though this is a rather profound reflection for a seventeen-year-old boy, it is certainly in line with the thought of Thérèse of Lisieux.

In addition to similar thoughts on death, both the saint and the author understood self-sacrifice in terms of the dedication of their lives to God and to His Church. In 1888, barely a few weeks before entering Carmel, Thérèse wrote to Pauline of her intention to devote her life entirely to Christ: "quand Jésus m'aura déposée sur le rivage béni du Carmel je veux me donner tout entière à lui, je ne veux plus vivre que pour lui" (LT 72). Then, two months before her death, she declared: "C'est par la prière et le sacrifice que nous pouvons seulement être utiles à l'Eglise" (DE 64). In a letter dated May 31, 1905, Bernanos told the abbé Lagrange that the works of Ernest Hello had taught him that we can make life meaningful only "par le sacrifice et l'oubli total de soi au profit de Dieu et de sa cause . . ." (Corr.I 79)

This same letter reveals that similar to Thérèse, who spoke quite openly about her imperfections and difficulties in prayer, Bernanos was able to admit his own shortcomings and spiritual trials. The Christmas message of peace which fostered in the author the desire to be "un homme de bonne volonté" (Corr.I 79-80) reminds us somewhat of Thérèse's admission of her own weakness and the account of her Christmas conversion. Unable to overcome her childishness through her own efforts, the saint records why on this particular night when Christ came to mankind as a helpless infant God gave her the strength to overcome her weakness: "En un instant l'ouvrage que je n'avais pu faire en 10 ans, Jésus le fit se contentant de ma bonne volonté qui jamais ne me fit défaut" (HA 114). Filled with the spirit of good will, both the adolescent Bernanos and the young Thérèse discovered in the Incarnation a message of courage and hope.

Further parallels with Thérèse appear in certain phrases in the author's correspondence which reflect the Carmelite's vocabulary. In a letter written to the abbé Lagrange in December, 1905 Bernanos employs images such as "un peu de brouillard" and a "petit trou noir où je serai quelque jour" (Corr.I 85) to describe his interior suffering. These metaphors recall Thérèse's description of her trial of faith as "un pays environné d'un épais brouillard" (<u>HA</u> 241) and her attempt to convey to Pauline her spiritual suffering: "Tenez, voyez-vous là-bas le trou noir (sous les marronniers près du cimetière) où l'on ne distingue plus rien; c'est dans un trou comme cela que je suis pour l'âme et pour le corps" (<u>DE</u> 153).

Like Thérèse, Bernanos also employs combat imagery to depict the trials of earthly existence. Thus "les armes à la main" is an expression found in the writings of both. With prayer and suffering as her weapons Thérèse proclaimed: "Je mourrai les armes à la main" (<u>DE</u> 123), while Bernanos wrote to Jean-Marie Maître in September, 1918 that God in His divine mercy captures souls, "les armes à la main" (<u>Corr</u>.I 154).

More significant, however, are certain letters to his wife which suggest that Bernanos' reflection on his combat experiences led him to an even deeper faith and understanding of the Carmelite's spirituality. These letters show that, like Thérèse, Bernanos also felt difficulty in prayer and the lack of divine consolation. He confided to his fiancée in 1916: "Il a plu à Dieu de me retirer l'une après l'autre mes consolations. Que veut-il donc de moi?" (<u>Corr</u>.I 108) and, in 1917, upon learning that his future parents-in-law wanted to postpone their marriage, he wrote again to his fiancée: "Tout me manque et je ne puis même plus prier" (<u>Corr</u>.I 123). Passages such as these echo several found in the <u>Histoire d'une âme</u> as, for example, the one in which Thérèse speaks of her retreat before profession: "elle fut loin de m'apporter des consolations, l'aridité la plus absolue et presque l'abandon furent mon partage" (<u>HA</u> 187).

Letters from this same period also reveal that Bernanos treasured the Lamennais translation of the <u>Imitation of Christ</u> from which Thérèse drew much spiritual profit, claiming in her autobiography: "c'était le seul livre qui me fît du bien, car je n'avais pas encore trouvé les trésors cachés dans l'Evangile" (<u>HA</u> 118). In a letter to his fiancée in 1917, Bernanos begged her to send him a copy of that translation (<u>Corr</u>.III 89-90). That the author received a copy of the Imitation of Christ and made good use of it is indicated in subsequent letters to his wife. It is significant to note that in one such letter Bernanos refers to a passage which helped him recognize his weakness and need of God during his trial of the absence of God: "C'est mon humiliation et mon espérance de me sentir aussi pauvre, si faible, dès que cette voix se tait dans mon coeur. Je ne puis plus me passer de Dieu un seul moment, et il le sait" (Corr.I 155-156).

From their writings we can also determine that both Bernanos and Thérèse possessed a common understanding and appreciation of the mystery of the Redemption. From reflecting on Christ's Passion and Death, they discovered that suffering, trials, fear of death, and the silence of God were simply means of sharing the Redemption. Both thus understood that, though He was divine, Christ truly felt His suffering and death in His humanity. Thérèse points out that Christ experienced a real agony: "Notre Seigneur au Jardin des Oliviers jouissait de toutes les délices de la Trinité, et pourtant son agonie n'en était pas moins cruelle" (DE 58) and "Notre Seigneur est mort sur la Croix, dans les angoisses, et voilà pourtant la plus belle mort d'amour" (DE 56). A letter to Jean-Marie Maître written in August, 1919 reveals how Bernanos' thoughts on Christ's Agony resemble Thérèse's. The statement "Du Jardin au Calvaire, sache que Notre-Seigneur a connu et exprimé par avance toutes les agonies, même les plus humbles, les plus désolées" (Corr.I 169) reveals Bernanos' understanding of the true nature of Christ's suffering on behalf of mankind. His comparison of Christ with Marie-Antoinette in this same letter: "ce n'est pas un Dieu qui joue l'homme comme Marie-Antoinette jouait, à Trianon, la paysanne" (Corr.I 169) points out that Christ was not simply playing a role, but that He truly experienced the depths of human agony.

Gratitude to God for His many graces is also a characteristic of the spirituality professed by both the saint and the author in their adulthood and mentioned in their writings. Thérèse's words to Pauline describing her deep gratitude (DE 127) are reflected in Bernanos' letter to his wife in May, 1918 in which he sates that God can never be thanked enough for all the graces He bestowed on him (Corr.III 96).

Two or three letters written in the early nineteen twenties illustrate further the possible impact of the Carmelite saint on the writer's spirituality. One such letter written to Cosmao Dumanoir in June, 1924 contains the rather astonishing comment that Bernanos is not at all surprised that by simply washing dishes a servant can perform an act of perfect love "dont vacille la voûte des cieux, sans qu'une de ses casseroles en soit seulement ébranlée..." (Corr.III 118). Where did Bernanos discover this practical, down-to-earth type of spirituality where perfect love can be achieved through the accomplishment of daily tasks?[2] We believe he found it in the Histoire d'une âme whose author describes herself as "une très petite âme qui ne peut offrir au bon Dieu que de très petites choses . . ." (HA 286).

Letters written during this same period disclose further similarity between Bernanos and Thérèse in their understanding of the Incarnation and Redemption. Both stress the fact that this mystery is essentially a sacrifice of love on the part of God on behalf of sinful mankind. According to their thinking, God's love rather than His justice plays the leading role in this sacrifice on the part of God on behalf of sinful mankind. Their common vision of the Redemption, then, is one in which human suffering, freely accepted out of love, takes on infinite meaning.

Thérèse's offering of herself as a victim to merciful love formed a sharp contrast to the traditional spiritual background in which she was raised. We know historically that the nineteenth century presented "an understanding of God bound by images of fear and severe judgment,"[3] and so Thérèse's discovery of her special call to love was indeed a rare insight into the Gospel message. No doubt these words of hers would have inspired Bernanos: "Pour satisfaire la Justice Divine, il fallait des victimes parfaites, mais à la loi de crainte a succédé la loi d'Amour, et l'Amour m'a choisie pour holocauste, moi, faible et imparfaite créature..." (HA 223).

Reflection on God's love for mankind and mankind's share in the Redemption forms the basis of the Carmelite's little way as seen in her "Acte d'offrande à l'Amour miséricordieux" and in her correspondence. To her sister, Céline, Thérèse wrote in March, 1889: "L'amour ne se paie que par l'amour et les plaies de l'amour ne se guérissent que par l'amour" (LT 138). This passage finds a corresponding parallel in a letter written in June, 1926 to Frédéric Lefèvre in which Bernanos states: "au crime contre l'Amour, l'Amour répond à sa manière et selon son essence: par un don total, infini" (Corr.III 141). Thérèse's concept of God's love for mankind is presented primarily in terms of God as a loving Father who gives His children the graces they need. According to the saint, we must not, therefore, become discouraged because of our weaknesses, "car les enfants tombent souvent, mais ils sont trop petits pour se faire beaucoup de mal" (DE 119). This understanding of God's merciful love clarifies for us another statement of Bernanos in the above letter: "Dieu nous surveille du haut des âges et sourit paternellement à des fautes dont il connaît la vanité" (Corr.III 140). The author's description of God as a loving Father who pays no attention to His children's imperfections is thus an application of Thérèse's thoughts on the spirit of childhood.

From the beginning then as Bernanos' correspondence from 1905 to 1926 reveals, the author had an affinity for the spirituality incarnate in the saint. Moreover, as he came to know her work, he began to assimilate Thérèse's words and make her message his own. We are not surprised then to find in the above-mentioned letter that Bernanos observes: "Car la soeur de charité, excellente à moucher les gosses, devient au Carmel, pour les uns une fanatique et, pour les plus indulgents, une fleur rare et décorative, un précieux bibelot humain..." (Corr.III 140). Is Bernanos referring here, perhaps, to the various saccharine interpretations given to the Carmelite's message?

"Ecrits de jeunesse": premiers essais romanesques (1907-1914)

"On passera!," "Pour préserver les lys," "La Pitié du chouan," "Le Geste du roi," "Ce qui ne meurt pas," "Les Deux Fils," and "Mademoiselle Triomphe" are Bernanos' earliest bits of fiction and appeared in the royalist publication Le Panache in 1907 when the author was nineteen. Six years later "Virginie ou le Plaisir des champs" was published by another royalist paper, Le Mail. In 1913-1914, while editor of L'Avant-garde de Normandie, Bernanos also published in that royalist weekly "La Muette," "La Tombe refermée," and "La Mort avantageuse du chevalier de Lorges." These short pieces deal already with a fusion of the themes of military life and childhood which would later prove so important in the author's fictional and polemical works.

Certainly Bernanos' stories of young men freely abandoning themselves to the will of an earthly king and dying heroically on a battlefield find parallels in Thérèse's description of the spiritual life as a field of combat. In a letter written in May, 1897 to Père Roulland, Thérèse portrays God as a king leading his army to victory under the standard of the Cross: "depuis qu'Il a levé l'étendard de la Croix, c'est à son ombre que tous doivent combattre et remporter la victoire . . ." (LT 407). And how could Bernanos not be attracted to a saint who spoke of herself in these terms: "Un soldat n'a pas peur du combat et je suis un soldat" and "Est-ce que je n'ai pas dit que je mourrai les armes à la main?" (DE 211).

Childhood, with its strength in weakness, is also exalted in these earlier writings where in "Le Geste du roi" a child-king is the brave hero urging his men on to victory, and, in "Mademoiselle Triomphe," a little girl, adopted by an entire regiment of soldiers, spurs them on to win the battle. And as for the child herself, "Elle dormait, inattentive aux vaines rumeurs des hommes, dédaigneuse naïvement de ces bruits de bataille et de guerre, rêvant à je ne sais quoi de puéril et de divin . . ." (OE,I 1756). Bernanos' description of the child peacefully asleep, quite confident in her safety, is, on the natural level, similar to an image used by the Carmelite saint to describe her way of spiritual childhood: "ce chemin c'est l'<u>abandon</u> du petit enfant qui s'endort sans crainte dans les bras de son Père..." (<u>HA</u> 214).

The spirit of self-sacrifice observed in some of Bernanos' earlier fictional heroes finds a spiritual parallel in Thérèse. The sublime courage and generosity of the old maréchal in "Les Deux Fils" who gives even his last son to the king and of d'Epernon in "La Muette" who declares: "hors du service je n'ai jamais rien su refuser..." (<u>OE</u>,I 1760) are echoed in Thérèse's declaration: "Il faudra que le bon Dieu fasse toutes mes volontés au Ciel, parce que je n'ai jamais fait ma volonté sur la terre" (<u>DE</u> 73).

From Bernanos' use of such themes and imagery in his early attempts at writing there seems but a step to the supernatural plane of Thérèse's message where the spiritual life becomes a battlefield and childhood imagery a vehicle for expressing one's relationship with God the Father.

"La Malibran" (1913)

The earliest implicit evidence of Thérèse of Lisieux' presence in the author's work seems to appear in a 1913 publication. In 1974 William Bush presented his discovery of a text of Bernanos entitled "La Malibran" and published on August 20, 1913 in <u>La Liberté</u>. It is in fact a second text bearing the same title as an article published on September 2, 1913 in the <u>Action Française</u> and brought out by Albert Béguin in <u>Le crépuscule des vieux</u> (177-181).[4]

"Malibran I," as Bush entitles this short text, recounts the tragic life of the Parisian born Spanish singer, María Felicia García, who died of tuberculosis at the early age of twenty-eight. In the first paragraph of his article, Bernanos views the young woman in the eyes of posterity as "ornée de l'auréole mystique, et comme une sainte Thérèse de l'art du chant" ("M" 8). Upon reading this our first thought is of Teresa of Avila, a belief not without justification, for the young musician was of Spanish origin and Thérèse of Lisieux could not, properly speaking, be called "sainte Thérèse" before her canonization in 1925. What then are the indications that Bernanos might have had the Carmelite of Lisieux in mind when writing his article?

Parallels such as youth, dedication, heroic courage, and an early death from tuberculosis which are parallels marking both la Malibran and the French Thérèse would be difficult to draw between the singer and the Spanish Teresa. Indeed at the very age when la Malibran was approaching the height of her musical career and Thérèse of Lisieux was composing her "Acte d'offrande à l'Amour miséricordieux," Teresa of Avila was only at the point of making her decision to enter religious life for reasons quite other than the love of God, even as she herself tells us in the Libro de su vida: "Y en este movimiento de tomar estado más me parece me movía un temor servil que amor."[5] It was not until Teresa was in her early forties that her true spiritual nature revealed itself and the saint began her life's work of reforming the Carmelite monasteries in Spain.

In contrast to Teresa of Avila, Bernanos presents his consumptive young heroine as having sacrificed her short life in its entirety for the love of what was her own god: her musical career. La Malibran's "jeune et faible corps que consume un feu sacré" ("M" 8) strangely parallels the physical suffering of the young French saint who died of the same illness after having sacrificed her even shorter life for the love of God.

Certain of the traits of la Malibran which Bernanos emphasizes also find a remarquable counterpart in the young saint of Lisieux. La Malibran's display of temper in her words and actions: "'Il faudra que cette voix sorte,' disait-elle en frappant du pied" ("M" 8) parallels the saint's description of a stormy scene that took place between a maid and herself during her early childhood: "je me mis à lui dire bien haut qu'elle était méchante, et sortant de ma douceur habituelle, je frappai du pied de toutes mes forces..." (HA 48).

In a similar fashion the writer depicts la Malibran's childlike spirit of cheerfulness: "A presque tous les instants - et même aux derniers - de sa vie, elle montre la même exubérance, une gaieté d'enfant, mais d'enfant robuste" ("M" 9). We cannot but be reminded here of Céline's description of the "aimable gaieté" of her sister who during her last illness kept her "manières enfantines et charmantes qui rendaient sa compagnie très agréable" (CSG 173). La Malibran's lively nature reveals itself still further in her correspondence which is found "pleine de traits imprévus, de gamineries, d'insolences légères et ailées" ("M" 9). Like la Malibran, Thérèse, too, had a marvelous sense of humour as seen in her amusing comment about the new cough medicine she had just been given: "Qu'est-ce que cela me fait de prendre du sirop de limaçon, pourvu que je ne voie pas les cornes!" (DE 43). And just as la Malibran almost always spoke of suffering "comme d'une inconnue: jamais de plainte, mais parfois de la dureté" ("M" 9), Thérèse rarely spoke of her intense suffering, but instead tried to appear light-hearted when either the doctor or any of the sisters visited her in the infirmary.

Continuing his description of the Spanish singer, Bernanos recounts how "Rien ne l'arrête, rien ne saurait la distraire du but qu'elle s'est imposé et vers lequel elle s'efforce avec violence, et aussi une espèce de bravade" ("M" 9), once again suggesting the image of Thérèse who in her final agony was willing to continue souffrir if God so desired: "Eh bien!... allons!... Allons!... Oh! je ne voudrais pas moins longtemps souffrir..." (DE 186).

Bernanos then points out that only through the publication of unedited documents which present the young musician "comme une poitrinaire, et qui pourtant, si l'on excepte le hasard d'une mort imprévue, offre plutôt le charme d'une fleur éclatante et vivace" ("M" 10) did the public begin to understand better the true nature of la Malibran's life. Similarly did the publication of the <u>Histoire d'une âme</u> spread devotion to the young Carmelite who also was previously unknown beyond the small circle of her family and the twenty or so religious with whom she lived for some nine years.

In sharp contrast we find that Teresa of Avila was well known by many church and civil authorities, including Philip II with whom she had interviews. Even during her lifetime her writings had begun to circulate to some extent.

In his next sentence, the writer reveals his admiration for further traits of la Malibran: "Elle séduit par sa spontanéité, son audace et, dans la passion, quelque chose de l'impatience et de la franchise virile" ("M" 10). This "impatience" and "franchise virile" were not lacking in Thérèse of Lisieux who even accused herself of impatience to her sister, Pauline: "Je n'ai pas encore eu une minute de patience" (<u>DE</u> 132).

Another trait of la Malibran which might be considered to be a parallel with Thérèse of Lisieux is revealed in the September 2, 1913 text of "La Malibran" in the heroine's words: "Je ne puis préméditer le repos dans ma tête," and "Il faut que j'use ma vie . . ." (<u>OE</u>,II 924) which recall the saint's words to her sister, Pauline, in July, 1897: "Je ne puis pas me faire une fête de jouir, je ne peux pas me reposer tant qu'il y aura des âmes à sauver" (<u>DE</u> 85). Her mission of saving souls is to continue until the end of time.

Although it may certainly be argued that many characteristics were shared by Teresa of Avila and Thérèse of Lisieux, one final hint that it was the future French saint that Bernanos had in mind should be mentioned even if she had not yet been canonized. Towards the end of his article he recounts an event in la Malibran's life recalling an incident in the saint's life. In a letter to her first husband, la Malibran makes a rather odd request: "Je voudrais avoir un petit lacrymatoire pour recevoir tes douces larmes . . ." ("M" 10). Why should such a short article include this seemingly ridiculous episode? Whatever the reason, it does remind us of an episode in Thérèse's life taking place after the death of

Mère Geneviève, the foundress of the Lisieux Carmel. Noticing a tear on the eyelid of the foundress during her final agony, Thérèse returned to the chapel later on, carefully wiped up the tear with a small piece of fine linen, and kept it as a relic. Referring to this incident in her autobiography, she states: "Depuis je l'ai toujours portée dans le petit sachet où mes voeux sont renfermés" (HA 194).

Finally, why, barely two weeks after the publication of "Malibran I," did a second article bearing the same title appear? "Malibran II," it is interesting to note, lacks the greater part of the above indications of Thérèse's presence, and in particular, the one describing la Malibran as "une sainte Thérèse de l'art du chant" ("M" 8). We are tempted therefore to conclude that although the process for the Carmelite's beatification had begun as early as 1910, Bernanos may have been advised not to call Thérèse "saint" before the Church's official recognition of her sainthood. And did this "advisor" recognize the hidden references to the saint's presence in the article? Whatever the case may be, la Malibran as seen in "Malibran I" seems to us to be a reflection of Thérèse of Lisieux rather than of Teresa of Avila.

"Madame Dargent" and "Dialogue d'ombres" (1922-1928)

Similarities in thought and attitude as discernible in Bernanos' correspondence prior to 1927 as well as in his "Ecrits de jeunesse" and "La Malibran," lead us to believe that the author would have welcomed Thérèse's message. Implicit references found in some of the short stories written between 1919 and 1928, however, also testify to a more specific influence on the author.

As previously mentioned, Hans Urs von Balthasar (von B 289) has pointed out that the first of Bernanos' short stories, "Madame Dargent," published in 1922, contains an explicit reference to Thérèse's words: "je ne peux pas mourir!... Je ne saurais jamais mourir!" (DE 188) in the heroine's words: "je n'en finirai jamais de mourir" and "Je ne peux pas mourir . . ." (<u>OE</u>,I 6). Von Balthasar neglects, however, to comment on the fact that once Bernanos had called to mind Thérèse of Lisieux he continued the allusion throughout the story through the use of what seems to be a negative parallel or a reverse image of the saint.

In fact, the contrast between the death of the saint and that of Madame Dargent becomes more evident as the story progresses. Well aware of the fact that she was dying, Thérèse remarked on the day of her death: "Mais c'est l'agonie toute pure, sans aucun mélange de consolation" (<u>DE</u> 183). Her agony and death, freely accepted are one with her life of suffering offered for the conversion of sinners. Indeed Thérèse interpreted the intensity of her agony as the result of her desire to save others (<u>DE</u> 185).

In comparison with the saint's death, Madame Dargent's death appears empty of meaning as we observe in Bernanos' statement: "En un mot, elle mourait sottement" (<u>OE</u>,I 5) and in the heroine's own words: "Oh! Charles, c'est bien plus affreux que je ne croyais! . . . - au-dedans et au-dehors, il n'y a que du vide - . . ."(<u>OE</u>,I 6).

Thérèse wonders what death is and so she asks: "Si c'est ça l'agonie, qu'est-ce que c'est que la mort?!..." (<u>DE</u> 184). Desirous of being prepared to die, she then begs her prioress: "Préparez-moi à bien mourir" (<u>DE</u> 185). Madame Dargent's attempt at self-deception and denial of her death: "J'essaie de me tromper moi-même, de rêver que je m'endors, que j'oublie, que je glisse... . . ." (<u>OE</u>,I 6) thus appears as a reverse image of the saint's lucidity and loving acceptance of God's will at the moment of death. For the first time, then, we feel that Bernanos employs reverse imagery to indicate Thérèse's presence in his work.

One of the two short stories published in 1928 ("Une nuit" in <u>La Revue hebdomadaire</u> and "Dialogue d'ombres" in the <u>Nouvelle revue française</u>) also implies the Carmelite's presence. This is in "Dialogue d'ombres" where Thérèse serves as a model for Bernanos' young heroine. Françoise is called by the saint's second name and possesses on the natural level the willingness to sacrifice herself for love which, on the supernatural level, raised Thérèse to the heights of sanctity. Françoise is ready to make a total gift of herself in love to Jacques, a man not entirely worthy of her, but who has become a sort of "god" in her eyes. Jacques, we must admit, recognizes her willingness to sacrifice herself entirely to him and so he tells her repeatedly: "Vous êtes une âme religieuse, Françoise" (OE,I 44). But when he says: "Vous êtes une petite sainte, seulement votre sainteté est sans objet" (OE,I 48), we begin to understand why Françoise wishes to destroy her desire for perfection. She seems to have no human goal that can match her high ideals. Her aspirations, though lofty on a purely natural level, remain empty because she cannot raise them above this level. And as the heroine herself confesses, she has no knowledge of God and does not want to have any. We cannot help but see the contrast between Françoise's feeling of emptiness and Thérèse's feeling of fulfilment as evidenced in her "Acte d'offrande à l'Amour miséricordieux" where she proclaims: "O mon Dieu! Trinité Bienheureuse, je désire vous <u>Aimer</u> et vous faire <u>Aimer</u> . . . je désire être Sainte, mais je sens mon impuissance et je vous demande, ô mon Dieu! d'être vous-même ma Sainteté" (HA 315).

The ending of "Dialogue d'ombres" contains two further hints of Thérèse's presence. Promising to wait for him to-morrow, Françoise tells Jacques: "et je n'emporterai rien d'ici, vous savez? rien de rien...les cheveux tondus des suppliantes, et les mains nues" (OE,I 53). This attitude of appearing before the beloved with empty hands recalls Thérèse's words: "Au soir de cette vie, je paraîtrai devant vous les mains vides . . ." (HA 317-318). The story closes with a sudden clearing of the sky which might be symbolic, as Yvonne Guers-Villate points out, of Bernanos' concept of grace,[6] as well as a reminder of the clearing of the sky at the moment of Thérèse's death.[7]

NOTES

CHAPTER 4

¹ Gaucher had probably not yet read William Bush's volume, <u>Souffrance et expiation dans la pensée de Bernanos</u>, which was also published in 1962. Bush points out quite clearly that Thérèse does appear in Donissan, for, like the saint, Bernanos' priest-hero also suffers from his impotence before the power of evil (<u>SE</u> 139).

² This type of spirituality is strongly reminiscent of that of the Carmelite, Brother Lawrence of the Resurrection, as described in the seventeenth century spiritual classic, <u>The Practice of the Presence of God</u>. In her introduction to this work, Dorothy Day notes the rapport between Brother Lawrence and Thérèse of Lisieux "in her practice of the 'little way,' . . ." [Dorothy Day, introduction, <u>The Practice of the Presence of God</u>, by Brother Lawrence of the Resurrection, o.c.d. (Springfield, Illinois: Templegate Publishers, 1974) 12].

³ John Russell, o.carm., "The Religious Plays of St Thérèse of Lisieux," <u>Carmelite Studies: Experiencing St Thérèse Today</u> (Washington, D.C.: ICS, 1990) 54.

⁴ William Bush, "Bernanos et la Malibran: commentaire et présentation d'un texte retrouvé," <u>Courrier Georges Bernanos</u> 15 (1974): 3. Cited hereafter as "M." The other text of "La Malibran," published two weeks later on September 2, 1913 in the <u>Action Française</u>, is found in the Pléiade edition of Bernanos' works (<u>OE</u>,II 923-926).

⁵ Teresa de Jesús, <u>Libro de su vida</u> (Garden City, New York: Doubleday and Company, Inc., 1961, "Colección Hispánica") 10.

⁶ Yvonne Guers-Villate, "Les premiers écrits de Bernanos," <u>La Revue des Lettres Modernes</u> 203-208 "Etudes bernanosiennes" 10 (1969): 129.

⁷ Guy Gaucher, o.c.d., <u>Histoire d'une vie: Thérèse Martin (1873-1897)</u> (Paris: Les Editions du Cerf, 1982) 219.

CHAPTER 5

PARALLEL AND REVERSE IMAGES OF THÉRÈSE IN <u>SOUS LE SOLEIL DE SATAN</u> (1919-1926)

Both William Bush and Michael Tobin have pointed out explicit evidence of Thérèse of Lisieux' presence in Bernanos' first novel, <u>Sous le soleil de Satan</u>. But there are also many implicit references to the saint that lend further support to the claims of these critics. Further parallel and reverse images of the Carmelite can be detected in both Mouchette, the teenage heroine, and Donissan, the priest-hero.

Mouchette

An examination of certain implicit references gives further proof to Michael Tobin's theory that Mouchette is "a sort of infernal reflection of St. Thérèse . . ." ("T" 85). The heroine's readiness to sacrifice herself to any man who comes her way negatively parallels the saint's readiness to sacrifice herself to sinners. Mouchette's words to Docteur Gallet reveal her inordinate desire for a host of lovers: "'Qu'importe l'amant! Qu'importe le lieu ou l'heure! . . . Pas une voix seulement m'appelle, tu sais! Mais des cents! des mille! Sont-ce là des hommes?'" (OE,I 98). The young girl's moral degeneration forms a direct contrast to the supernatural desire to save souls from eternal flames that Thérèse felt born in her the night of her Christmas conversion (HA 115).

Bernanos' use of reverse imagery prepares us for Mouchette's offering of herself to Satan, paralleling in a negative fashion Thérèse's gift of herself to God in her "Acte d'effrande à l'Amour miséricordieux." The description of Satan as "l'astre livide" (OE,I 212) along with the novel's title, <u>Sous le soleil de Satan</u>, emerge as reverse images of Thérèse's description of God as "Le divin Soleil," "L'astre divin" (LT 240) and "le Soleil de son <u>amour</u>" (LT 144).

The novelist directly opposes Mouchette's situation to Thérèse's life in the monastery: "Les plus grands saints ne sont pas toujours les saints à miracles, car le contemplatif vit et meurt le plus souvent ignoré. Or l'enfer aussi a ses cloîtres" (OE,I 213). Reverse images of the saint culminate in Bernanos' final image of his heroine as a servant of Satan in the cloisters of hell: "cette mystique ingénue, petite servante de Satan, sainte Brigitte du néant" (OE,I 213). And just as Thérèse's short life would have remained unknown had her autobiography not been published shortly after her death, so also is Mouchette's life a hidden one, "un secret entre elle et son maître, ou plutôt le seul secret de son maître" (OE,I 213).

In a similar manner, Bernanos' description of Satan's search for Mouchette among the weak and powerless of the world: "Il ne l'a pas cherchée parmi les puissants, leurs noces ont été consommées dans le silence" (OE,I 213) brings to mind the Carmelite's description of God's role in her own spiritual development: "parce que j'étais petite et faible il s'abaissait vers moi, il m'instruisait en secret des <u>choses</u> de son <u>amour</u>" (HA 122). It was, therefore, in the silence of the souls of these young women that Satan and God performed their actions. Reverse images such as these thus lend more support to Tobin's statement that Mouchette is an infernal reflection of Thérèse of Lisieux, yet it is also true that Bernanos' young heroine resembles the Carmelite saint in a positive manner.

To begin with, certain of Mouchette's characteristics, such as her confidence, determination, good sense, generosity, and readiness to sacrifice everything to the unknown can be witnessed in Thérèse at the same age. Bernanos portrays his heroine on the natural level as having "la confiance intrépide de celles qui jouent toute leur chance en un coup, affrontent un monde inconnu . . ." (OE,I 68). Mouchette's readiness to give herself entirely to Cadignan, a man who takes advantage of her innocence but in whom she places all her youthful dreams of love and happiness, recalls Thérèse's free offering of herself to God in her words to her sister, Pauline, in March, 1888: "je veux me donner tout entière à lui, je ne veux plus vivre que pour lui" (LT 72).

Also, like the saint, the heroine has few friends and rarely ventures beyond the confines of the family property. The young girl's fear of being looked at or spoken to which she describes later on in these terms: "Ah! jadis... que j'avais peur! - d'une parole... d'un regard... de rien," (OE,I 97) is a parallel image of Thérèse's description of her timidity after her mother's death: "je devins timide et douce, sensible à l'excès. Un regard suffisait pour me faire fondre en larmes . . ." (HA 43).

To describe the reality of Mouchette's anguish, Bernanos borrows Thérèse's image of a black hole and a small boat caught in a storm. Thus the passage: "La minute présente était toute angoisse. Le passé un trou noir. L'avenir un autre trou noir" (OE,I 212) recalls the Carmelite's portrayal of her trial of faith to her sister, Pauline: "Tenez, voyez-vous là-bas le trou noir (sous les marronniers près du cimetière) où l'on ne distingue plus rien; c'est dans un trou comme cela que je suis pour l'âme et pour le corps" (DE 153).

Bernanos' use of boat imagery to convey his heroine's experience of the dark night of the soul also calls to mind the Carmelite saint. And so the description: "A chaque image recherchée, suscitée, volontairement épuisée, elle sentait littéralement frémir ses sens et sa raison, ainsi qu'un frêle navire dans le vent . . ." (OE,I 211) can be seen as a parallel image of the saint's description of her trial of faith: "J'étais dans un triste désert ou plutôt mon âme était semblable au fragile esquif livré sans pilote à la merci des flots orageux..." (HA 127).

If, in contrast to Thérèse, Mouchette's suffering seems devoid of hope, the original manuscript reveals that there is one instant in which hope is offered to Bernanos' heroine. Tracing the sign of the cross on her forehead, Donissan sees the very hope and joy that he has refused rising in Mouchette: "une espérance inouïe, un délire d'espérance, comme une expansion de la vie faisait craquer toutes les jointures de cette âme forcenée" (S* 179). But Mouchette refuses to abandon herself to hope, preferring to remain in her state of hatred and fear. She is thus a reverse image of Thérèse who through confidently abandoning herself to merciful love destroyed her fear.

In his encounter with the young woman, Donissan fully recognizes the sad state of her soul: "Car plus haut qu'aucune voix humaine criait vers lui la douleur sans espérance, dont elle était consumée" (OE,I 193-194). Thérèse, on the contrary, felt that no matter how intense her suffering was, God would not abandon her. A month before her death she stated: "je crois que je ne suis pas au bout de mes peines; mais Il ne m'abandonnera pas" (DE 144). Images such as these certainly arouse our sympathy for Mouchette who, to a great extent, is an innocent victim of her surroundings.

Donissan

i) *Character Traits*

But it is in the novelist's portrayal of his priest-hero, Donissan, that we find even more implicit evidence of Thérèse of Lisieux in Sous le soleil de Satan.

Donissan's simplicity, docility, deference, submission to his superiors, and piety (OE,I 139) are all traits that stand out in the Carmelite saint. Both also seem to be more given to suffering in their daily lives than to joy. As William Bush has noted, the main cause of the priest's suffering is his sense of impotence or failure in everything he does (SE 138). Thérèse, at an early age, recognized her weakness to be the source of her suffering. Indeed she even accused herself of being "une enfant, impuissante et faible" (HA 223).

Several comparisons can be set up to show how in other ways Donissan is both a parallel and a reverse image of the Carmelite saint. Extremely timid, both saint and priest-hero have difficulty expressing themselves. Following her mother's death, Thérèse became so shy that she would burst into tears if someone just looked at her (HA 43). His eyes full of tears, Donissan shows similar signs of weakness and: "c'est à peine si l'abbé Menou-Segrais entendit les derniers mots, prononcés à voix basse. Le malheureux prêtre se reprochait avidement son timide appel à la pitié comme une faiblesse" (OE,I 131).

Thérèse's timidity in parlor finds an echo in Donissan about whom Bernanos writes: "Il a souffert longtemps de l'impuissance à exprimer ce qu'il sent . . ." (OE,I 138). Neither the saint nor the priest seemed capable of finding companionship among their peers. Boarding school life was a severe trial for Thérèse who had no real friend among either her fellow classmates or teachers. She tells us that Jesus was the only one in whom she could confide (HA 103). It is only during his strange encounter with the horse dealer that Bernanos' priest-hero seems to become aware of the fact that he has no one in whom he can confide: "L'abbé Donissan se souvient qu'il n'a pas d'ami" (OE,I 168).

Also, in spite of the fact that Thérèse knew entire chapters of the Imitation of Christ by heart, her statement: "j'avais de la peine à apprendre mot à mot . . ." (HA 96) is reflected to some extent in Donissan's complaint about his lack of memory: "Intelligence, mémoire, assiduité même, tout me manque..." (OE,I 130). Similarly, the young priest's criticism of himself as lacking experience recalls the saint's confession that she was not accustomed to doing household tasks or waiting on herself. Her sister, Pauline, tells of how at Carmel "on la trouvait lente, peu dévouée dans les emplois . . ." (DE 77). And if Thérèse's uncle found her "incapable et maladroite" (HA 97), Menou-Segrais seems to have the same opinion of Donissan: "Il a crotté mon pauvre vieux Smyrne, et failli briser les pieds de la chaise qu'il a choisie la plus précieuse et la plus fragile, avec son ordinaire à-propos..." (OE,I 117).

Both saint and priest-hero are also judged to be victims of emotional illnesses. Many critics, such as Jean-François Six, have determined not only Thérèse's strange illness as a child, but also her excessive tears, scruples, and frequent migraine headaches to be symptoms of neurosis.[1] As for Donissan, the medical report given on his condition following Mouchette's suicide declared him to be suffering from "une grave intoxication des cellules nerveuses, probablement d'origine intestinale" (OE,I 231).

ii) *A Special Call*

Further images of Thérèse are evoked in Donissan's understanding of his vocation. In the case of both the priest-hero and the saint, their Christmas night conversion led them to embark on their respective vocations, as Michael Tobin was the first to recognize ("T" 87-92). Following this night of special grace, each one experiences a growth in maturity. No longer timid, Thérèse becomes courageous enough during a visit to the Vatican to ask Leo XIII for permission to enter the Carmelite monastery of Lisieux at the age of fifteen, while Donissan, with his new-found courage, does a thorough job of parish visitation.

Like the saint, the young priest's interior struggle with his calling does not appear exteriorly, but, nevertheless, Menou-Segrais, his director, sees clearly the state of his soul and the true nature of his vocation. In metaphorical terms, the older priest explains how a person undergoing the trial of faith can reach out to God. His statement: "chacun de nous n'a qu'à étendre les bras pour monter d'un trait à la surface des ténèbres et jusqu'au soleil de Dieu" (OE,I 133) is but a sentence summary of Thérèse's allegorical account of herself as a little bird whom, God, the Divine Eagle, will one day carry up to the heart of love (HA 226-229).

Similar to Père Prou who, according to Thérèse, was the only director who really understood her true vocation: "Il me lança à pleines voiles sur les flots de la confiance et de l'amour qui m'attiraient si fort mais sur lesquels je n'osais avancer..." (HA 197-198), Menou-Segrais launches Donissan on his vocation to save sinners: "je vous remets dans votre route; je vous donne à ceux qui vous attendent, aux âmes dont vous serez la proie..." (OE,I 134). And just as earlier Père Pichon had warned Thérèse of the dangers of not following God's plan for her: "remerciez le Bon Dieu de ce qu'il fait pour vous, car s'il vous abandonnait, au lieu d'être un petit ange, vous deviendriez un petit démon" (HA 173), so too does the older priest warn his protégé that his salvation lies in following the path God has marked out for him: "Là où Dieu vous attend, il vous faudra monter, monter ou vous perdre" (OE,I 134).

The older priest is of further service to Donissan in his discovery of his vocation. After the suicide of Mouchette, the priest-hero is ordered by his superiors to make a prolonged retreat. During their final conversation, Menou-Segrais warns Donissan that the retreat imposed on him will be for his good but that it will also be a bitter trial: "La retraite qu'on vous imposera bientôt sera sans nul doute un temps d'épreuve et de déréliction très amère" (OE,I 222). Although the young priest's retreat was an imposed period of five years with the Trappists of Tortefontaine and the saint's retreat was a ten day preparation for the solemn moment of her profession of vows, Thérèse experienced this particular retreat as a period of spiritual suffering: "l'aridité la plus absolue et presque l'abandon furent mon partage" (HA 187). For both the saint and the priest-hero the aridity and lack of consolations during their retreats were but a foretaste of their interior suffering throughout their entire ministry to souls.

iii) Ministry to Others

Bernanos borrows Theresian images to describe his priest-hero setting out on his ministry to sinners to whom he has just offered himself "pour la première fois, dans les ténèbres et le silence, à l'homme pécheur, son maître, qui ne le lâchera plus vivant" (OE,I 140). Are we not reminded here of Thérèse's ardent desire to save sinners that followed upon her Christmas conversion? For it is precisely at the very moment when love enters her soul that the future Carmelite is led to discover her vocation to sinners: "Ce n'était pas encore les âmes de prêtres qui m'attiraient, mais celles des grands pécheurs, je brûlais du désir de les arracher aux flammes éternelles" (HA 115), and so she begins to pray earnestly for the conversion of Pranzini, a hardened criminal.

But it is at this very point that the image of Thérèse becomes a reverse one in Donissan. The conclusion that Menou-Segrais draws from his daily observation of the young priest signals this change: "Son extérieur est d'un saint, et quelque chose en lui, pourtant, repousse, met sur la défensive... Il lui manque la joie..." (OE,I 141). This key passage reveals Donissan to be a reverse image of Thérèse who found joy in suffering out of love. Did not the saint ask: "Car est-il une joie plus grande que celle de souffrir pour votre amour?..." (HA 244)? Donissan, on the contrary, mistakenly believes his feeling of joy to come from Satan and so he tries to destroy it: "Je ne veux pas de la gloire! Je ne veux pas de la joie! Je ne veux même plus de l'espérance!" (OE,I 154-155).

Nevertheless, in his desire to save sinners from eternal damnation, the young priest resembles the saint in declaring his willingness to sacrifice everything he possesses, including his own salvation: "Si je le pouvais, sans te haïr, je t'abandonnerais mon salut, je me damnerais pour ces âmes que tu m'as confiées par dérision, moi, misérable!" (OE,I 155). And then, immediately after his strange encounter with Mouchette, Donissan reveals to Menou-Segrais how his hatred of evil has led him to offer all for the salvation of sinners: "Pour leur salut, j'ai offert tout ce que j'avais ou posséderais jamais... ma vie d'abord - cela est si peu de chose!... - les consolations de l'Esprit-Saint..." and "Mon salut, si Dieu le veut!" (OE,I 227). The priest's words mirror to some extent the saint's desire to spend eternity in hell, if it were necessary, in order that God be loved and glorified everywhere (HA 130-131).

Thérèse's action of forgetting herself and going downstairs courageously and joyfully to meet her father on that Christmas night of 1886 heralds her vocation of joy in suffering for others. This same action of having to face an unknown situation at the "bottom of a staircase" also plays a role in Donissan's vocation. On the last day of his life, as he hears someone coming to summon him, the priest-hero wonders "Qu'est-ce qui l'attend, au bas de l'escalier . . . quel nouveau combat?" (OE,I 239). Like Thérèse, he courageously accepts the challenge of his vocation of suffering for others, but contrary to the saint who joyfully found again the strength of soul she formerly had (HA 114), Donissan is neither joyful nor does he gain peace of soul. "Car il emporte en lui cette chose qu'il ne peut nommer . . . son angoisse, Satan. Il n'a pas recouvré la paix, il le sait" (OE,I 239).

iv) *The Challenge of Suffering*

Both Thérèse and Donissan also undergo exceptional interior trials which they dare not reveal to anyone. These trials are often represented in terms of a combat. Bernanos describes his priest-hero "comme un soldat qui se sent touché, et se dresse d'instinct avant de retomber . . ." (OE,I 134), while the Carmelite imagines herself as "dans la souffrance, au sein du combat" (HA 284). Her acts of self-denial are frequently depicted as "combats" (HA 254-255), while each new challenge in his ministry presents itself to Donissan as a "nouveau combat" (OE,I 191, 239). His words concerning the ministry of priests: "Nous sommes au premier rang d'une lutte à mort et nos petits derrière nous" (OE,I 257) reflect Thérèse's image of her duties with the novices as "une guerre à mort" (HA 272). Finally, Menou-Segrais' advice to Donissan on how to handle his trials: "plus que jamais, quoi qu'il vous en coûte, vous devez leur tourner le dos, fuir, sans seulement un regard en arrière" (OE,I 220) resembles Thérèse's combat strategy of "desertion": 'mon dernier moyen de ne pas être vaincue dans les combats, c'est la désertion . . ." (HA 256).

Other reminders of the Carmelite's influence appear in the young priest's feeling of impotence in the fulfilment of his ministry. Thérèse records her initial reaction at being placed as second in charge of the novices: "je vis tout de suite que la tâche était au-dessus de mes forces . . ." (HA 271). Donissan experiences similar feelings when thinking of his ministry: "il est dur de penser qu'un pauvre prêtre tel que moi - si lâche - si aisément terrassé, n'en a pas moins la mission d'éclairer le prochain, de relever son courage..." (OE,I 171).

As pointed out by William Bush (SE 139), this awareness of their impotence is the main cause of suffering in both the saint and the priest-hero. But it is in the handling of his impotence that Donissan becomes a reverse image of Thérèse. In spite of the fact that she feels it beyond her strength to deal with the novices, the saint places her confidence in God, asking Him to fill her hands with what her novices need (HA 271). Her words to her sister, Marie, show not only how Thérèse perceives herself as a weak, helpless child, but also how she makes use of her weakness: "cependant c'est ma faiblesse même qui me donne l'audace de m'offrir en Victime à ton Amour, ô Jésus!" (HA 223). Confidently and joyfully accepting her weakness, Thérèse is therefore able to say with Saint Paul (2 Cor. 12,5): "je ne me fais pas de peine en voyant que je suis la faiblesse même, au contraire c'est en elle que je me glorifie et je m'attends chaque jour à découvrir en moi de nouvelles imperfections" (HA 257).

Overwhelmed with despair even in the latter part of his life, Donissan is, nevertheless, able to bring peace to others. Bernanos depicts his priest-hero according to the Carmelite's idea of God filling our empty hands with gifts needed for others: "C'est ainsi qu'il donnait à pleines mains cette paix dont il était vide" (OE,I 243). In a letter to Frédéric Lefèvre dated June, 1926, the novelist explains how Donissan's despair is not in vain: "Mais il est dans l'ordre que Dieu fasse servir cette faute à ses desseins. Ne l'ai-je pas dit? Ne l'ai-je pas écrit? Ce désespéré jette l'espérance à pleines mains" (Corr.III 142). Contrary to Thérèse and Chantal de Clergerie, Donissan is portrayed throughout the novel as engulfed by his fearfulness and impotence. "La certitude de son impuissance à égaler un tel destin bloquait jusqu'à la prière sur ses lèvres. Cette volonté de Dieu sur sa pauvre âme l'accablait d'une fatigue surhumaine" (OE,I 142). Indeed, the poor priest finds himself "craintif, ridicule, lié à jamais par la contrainte d'une dévotion étroite . . ." (OE,I 142) because his spiritual life has failed to lead him to the discovery of God's merciful love. Once again Donissan proves to be a reverse image of the Carmelite saint in whom love dispelled fear. In a letter to the abbé Bellière three months before her death Thérèse confessed: "depuis qu'il m'a été donné de comprendre aussi l'amour du Coeur de Jésus, je vous avoue qu'il a chassé de mon coeur toute crainte" (LT 431). Her failures taught her to abandon her weakness to God's merciful love rather than rely on her own strength.

A passage deleted from the original manuscript reinforces this same contrast between the saint and the priest. Bernanos' description of Donissan: "Pourtant, prêtre indigne, serviteur ignorant, sa part n'était-elle point la crainte du Maître, et de ses jugements?" (S* 143) parallels, in a negative manner, Thérèse's statement: "le Seigneur est si bon pour moi qu'Il m'est impossible de le craindre . . ." (HA 286).

Even on the last day of his life we find Donissan still overwhelmed by his feeling of weakness. In his struggle against Satan to bring the dead boy back to life, the priest is unable to place his confidence in God. Refusing to abandon his weakness to God, he relies only on his own strength and, in the name of justice rather than love, he demands God to perform a miracle: "Non, non! il n'implore pas ce miracle, il l'exige. Dieu lui doit, Dieu lui donnera, ou tout n'est qu'un songe . . . Mais Dieu ne se donne qu'à l'amour" (OE,I 268).

Donissan's attitude contrasts sharply with Thérèse's perception of God's justice as indicated in a letter to Père Roulland: "le Seigneur est infiniment Juste et c'est cette justice qui effraye tant d'âmes qui fait le sujet de ma joie et de ma confiance" (LT 408). Since justice includes rewarding the virtuous as well as punishing the guilty, the saint felt confident in declaring: "J'espère autant de la justice du Bon Dieu que de sa miséricorde" (LT 408). Thérèse's understanding of God's justice is much broader than Donissan's, for it does encompass love and compassion, thus excluding fear. Being drawn to God more by this aspect of love than by fear of eternal punishment, the saint chose to offer herself as a victim of holocaust to God's merciful love rather than to His justice: "Pour satisfaire la Justice Divine, il fallait des victimes parfaites, mais à la loi de crainte a succédé la loi d'Amour, et l'Amour m'a choisie pour holocauste, moi, faible et imparfaite créature..." (HA 223).

The words by which the author comments on Donissan's blasphemous demand, "Mais Dieu ne se donne qu'à l'amour" (OE,I 268), show that Bernanos is aware that Donissan has failed to grasp that the Incarnation and Redemption were motivated by God's love for the human race rather than by his hatred of evil. Thérèse on the other hand did understand that without love "toutes les oeuvres ne sont que néant, même les plus éclatantes, comme de ressusciter les morts ou de convertir les peuples..." (HA 199).

Implicit evidence of the Carmelite's presence can also be detected even in the last moments of Donissan's life. Parallel images of the saint of Lisieux writing her autobiography in spite of being in the advanced stages of tuberculosis seem reflected in the priest-hero, who, in spite of the intense pain of angina, hurriedly pens the confession of his blasphemous demand before rushing off to hear the confessions of the throng of penitents, anxiously awaiting him in the church.

Bernanos closes his first novel in terms that could apply to both the Carmelite saint and the priest-hero: "Nous ne sommes point ces saints vermeils à barbe blonde que les bonnes gens voient peints, et dont les philosophes eux-mêmes envieraient l'éloquence et la bonne santé . . . Toute belle vie, Seigneur, témoigne pour vous; mais le témoignage du saint est comme arraché par le fer" (OE,I 308).

NOTES

CHAPTER 5

[1] Jean-François Six, <u>La véritable enfance de Thérèse de Lisieux: névrose et sainteté</u> (Paris: Editions du Seuil, 1972) 215.

CHAPTER 6

TOWARDS AN INCARNATION OF THÉRÈSE (1926-1930)

"Saint Dominique" (1926)

In addition to the two major novels, L'Imposture and La Joie, written immediately after Sous le soleil de Satan, Bernanos published two biographical essays between 1926 and 1929 which took saints as their subject: "Saint Dominique" published in the Revue universelle in December, 1926 and "Jeanne, relapse et sainte" first published in 1929 as an article in a special number of La Revue hebdomadaire devoted to Jeanne d'Arc.

Despite the fact that no explicit textual evidence of Thérèse of Lisieux can be found in the essay "Saint Dominique," the Carmelite's presence seems implicit in the portrayal of Dominique where the spirit of childhood and sanctity are intertwined. Bernanos introduces his study of Dominique by reminding us that sanctity is a paradox in itself: possessing no formulas, it possesses all. The saint rediscovers what other Christians seem to have lost: "Chaque vie de saint est comme une nouvelle floraison, l'effusion dans un monde rendu, par l'hérédité du péché, esclave de ses morts - d'une miraculeuse, d'une édénique ingénuité" (OE,II 5). Is this not how Thérèse's unique interpretation of the message of God's merciful love must have appeared to Bernanos in the early twenties?

The author imagines Dominique, first of all, as a little blonde-haired, blue-eyed boy, the descendant of military blood. He compares Dominique's reaction to heresy to that of a warrior attacking an enemy: "... nous voyons Dominique, ainsi qu'un chef de guerre, chercher le contact, non pour tâter l'adversaire, mais pour le battre" (OE,II 12). Images come to mind of another blonde-haired, blue-eyed child who centuries later would express her spiritual life in terms of combat imagery. Thérèse speaks about how happy she would have been to have taken part in a Crusade: "Avec quel bonheur, par exemple au temps des croisades, je serais partie pour combattre les hérétiques" (DE 113).

Discussing the development of Dominique's special call within the Church, the author stresses the similarity that exists in the call of every saint to love and serve others. The cross, symbol of the Redemption, is central to the vocations of both Dominique and Thérèse. Bernanos thus pictures the scholar Dominique opening himself up to merciful love "dans sa petite cellule, aux pieds du Crucifix ..." (OE,II 8). Dominique's reflection on his vocation to serve others parallels Thérèse's understanding of her vocation to love: "je résolus de me tenir en esprit au pied de la Croix pour recevoir la Divine rosée qui en découlait, comprenant qu'il me faudrait ensuite la répandre sur les âmes..." (HA 115).

For Bernanos, Dominique's many trials, especially those of solitude, despair, and the sensation of being stripped of everything, indicated God's presence in his soul and heralded the commencement of his real mission. "L'illusion que tout nous manque à la fois, ce sentiment de complète dépossession est le signe divin qu'au contraire tout commence" (OE,II 9) reminds us of Thérèse's comment regarding her complete spiritual poverty at the end of her life: "Mais cette pauvreté a été pour moi une vraie lumière, une vraie grâce. ... On éprouve une si grande paix d'être absolument pauvre, de ne compter que sur le bon Dieu" (DE 117). In spite of her spiritual solitude, Thérèse also remained conscious of God's presence, believing that her real mission would begin only in heaven. It would seem that her witness helped Bernanos understand that it is only through the acknowledgment of impotence and total dependence on God that the Christian begins to share fully in Christ's redemptive mission.

It is thus of special interest to note that the author portrayed Dominique as living according to Thérèse of Lisieux' spirit of childhood. The spirit of poverty, solitude, interior liberty, a readiness to give all, and complete abandonment to God's will, virtues readily seen in the Carmelite saint are also associated with the great preacher.

Even during their death agonies, both saints are seen as willing to continue living and suffering if God so desires. Thus Thérèse's acceptance of life or death: "je suis bien abandonnée pour vivre, pour mourir, pour guérir, et pour aller en Cochinchine, si le bon Dieu le veut" (DE 31) is reflected in Bernanos' characterization of Dominique: "il a gardé ses gros souliers. Il est prêt, si Dieu le suscite de nouveau" (OE,II 16). Certainly Dominique's brothers gathered around his bedside to catch the last words of the dying saint do remind us of Thérèse's sisters, Pauline especially, who spent hours at the saint's bedside writing down her last thoughts. But more significant, however, is the image of Thérèse's spirit of childhood that Dominique offers at the moment of death: "il entre néanmoins dans la mort, ainsi qu'il a surmonté la vie, du même élan sans retour, avec le regard de l'enfance" (OE,II 16). How not here recall Pauline's description of Thérèse's appearance at the moment of her death: "Son visage avait repris le teint de lys qu'il avait en pleine santé, ses yeux étaient fixés en haut brillants de paix et de joie" (DE 187).

"Jeanne, relapse et sainte" (1929)

Implicit evidence of the young Carmelite's influence can also be detected in Bernanos' second biographical essay, "Jeanne, relapse et sainte." In her work, <u>Joan of Arc: The Image of Female Heroism,</u> Marina Warner elaborates on how nineteenth and early twentieth century French authors were able to make Jeanne d'Arc a patriotic symbol through the stressing of her natural virtue. For Warner, Bernanos is the writer who has best captured the central image of the Maid of Orleans by equating her innocence with childlikeness.[1]

Yves Bridel, going a step further than Warner, notes how Bernanos unites childhood and sanctity in Jeanne d'Arc and so does not hesitate to affirm: "Que pour Bernanos Jeanne d'Arc ait vécu selon l'esprit d'enfance thérésien, cela nous paraît évident."[2] Yet Bernanos is not the first person to identify Jeanne d'Arc with Thérèse.

From reading the Histoire d'une âme the author would certainly have been aware of Thérèse's devotion to Jeanne d'Arc and how she connected her vocation with Jeanne's in her statement: "comme Jeanne d'Arc, ma soeur chérie, je voudrais sur le bûcher murmurer ton nom, O JÉSUS..." (HA 221). Moreover, in 1894 and 1895 Thérèse actually composed two recreational plays on the Maid of Orleans: "La Mission de Jeanne d'Arc" and "Jeanne d'Arc accomplissant sa mission." Fragments of both plays were published in the 1898 version of the Histoire d'une âme and in the April and May, 1929 issues of the Annales de Sainte Thérèse de Lisieux.

What is unusual about the Carmelite's interpretation of Jeanne d'Arc in these plays is that "tout montre que Thérèse s'exprime elle-même et s'identifie à Jeanne."[3] Images of the childhood, sanctity and suffering of Jeanne d'Arc stand out in the writings of both Thérèse and Bernanos. In "La Mission de Jeanne d'Arc," Thérèse presents her heroine as a timid young shepherdess who, upon hearing God's call, protests: "Je ne suis qu'une enfant faible et timide" (RP,I 66). Key passages in Bernanos' essay also bring out Jeanne's youth and weakness: "on voudrait que Jeanne d'Arc n'appartînt plus qu'aux enfants" (OE,II 21), "l'on voit entrer une petite fille moqueuse et tendre" (OE,II 22), "ce mot d'enfance éternelle" (OE,II 30), and "La voilà entre vos mains prisonnière, plus faible qu'un petit enfant, avec ses folles pensées, son vain honneur, le rêve brisé de sa jeunesse . . ." (OE,II 38).

The Maid of Orleans is similarly portrayed by both the saint and the author as being courageous in the face of death, confident that God will provide what is best for her. In a scene in her first play, Thérèse has Jeanne encouraging her young sister: "il faut abandonner l'avenir entre les mains du Bon Dieu . . ." (RP,I 79), while Bernanos envisages Jeanne as living like the soldiers "qui viennent manger leur pain de chaque jour dans la main de Dieu" (OE,II 35). From their treatment of Jeanne's childlikeness and dependence on God, we can certainly observe how Thérèse has projected her own sentiments onto Jeanne and how Bernanos has injected Thérèse's spirit of childhood into his interpretation of the Maid of Orleans.

Bernanos and Thérèse also highlight how Jeanne remained steadfast and confident throughout her trial despite the fact that her judges tried to intimidate and trick her. Pointing out how they literally stole her soul, Bernanos then borrows Theresian toy imagery to tell what they did with Jeanne afterwards: they threw into the fire "le jouet brisé" (OE,II 39). And in these words Thérèse's image of herself as a ball in the Hands of the Christ Child comes to mind: "s'il veut briser son jouet, il est bien libre . . ." (LT 64).

La Grande peur des bien-pensants (1931)

In a third biographical essay of this period, a lengthy volume devoted to Edouard Drumont entitled La Grande peur des bien-pensants and published in 1931, it would be surprising if implicit reference to Thérèse of Lisieux were to be found. It should nonetheless be mentioned before passing over this work that Bernanos' denunciation of Léo Taxil and his fictitious companion, Diana Vaughan, in La Grande peur des bien-pensants does have ties with the saint.

Noted for his anti-clericalism, Léo Taxil was supposed to have been converted and have spoken out against freemasonry. In the early 1890's he announced his attempt to convert to Catholicism Diana Vaughan, a young woman of French and American descent who was devoted to the cult of Lucifer. Articles begging French Catholics to pray to Jeanne d'Arc for her conversion appeared in prominent Catholic newspapers. The conversion supposedly took place in 1895 and there was even question of Diana entering a monastery.

Word of this miraculous conversion reached the Carmelite monastery in Lisieux where Thérèse was talked into writing to Diana and sending her a picture of herself dressed as Jeanne d'Arc in prison. Moreover, Diana Vaughan's conversion was sometimes a topic of conversation during the Carmelites' recreation hours. In 1896 Thérèse composed a short play, entitled "Le triomphe de l'humilité," based on Diana's supposed conversion and presented to the Carmelites during one of their recreations.

The strange thing was that all during this time no one had ever seen Diana. Finally, after much coaxing, Taxil agreed to introduce her to the public. When everyone arrived for the scheduled meeting in April, 1897, the truth was discovered: Diana was none other than Taxil himself who then proceeded to entertain his audience with a projected image of Thérèse of Lisieux as Jeanne d'Arc in prison Perhaps Bernanos was unaware of Thérèse's suffering occasioned by the deceit of this affair,[4] but <u>La Grande peur des bien-pensants</u> certainly indicates the writer's contempt for Taxil's fraud.

<u>*L'Imposture*</u> and <u>*La Joie*</u> *(1926-1929)*

Regarding the composition of <u>L'Imposture</u> and <u>La Joie</u>, Bernanos wrote to Henri Massis in a letter dated August, 1927: "Je vis avec deux saints délicieux, deux vrais saints, que j'invente à mesure" (<u>Corr</u>.I 311). In both of these novels, Bernanos emphasizes love and joyful confidence in God which had lacked in <u>Sous</u>

le soleil de Satan. Through their joyful acceptance of their suffering, both the abbé Chevance in L'Imposture and his spiritual daughter, Chantal de Clergerie, heroine of La Joie, testify to the transforming power of love in the world. Thérèse of Lisieux' spirituality is therefore incarnate in these "deux saints délicieux."

Chevance

The abbé Chevance appears as a parallel image of the Carmelite saint whom he resembles in his humility (OE,I 343, 484, 490) and his love of poverty and simplicity (OE,I 343, 485, 487, 493, 494). Bernanos also portrays his priest-hero as having the soul of a child (OE,I 337) and as a "fleur sauvage dérobée au jardin du Paradis" (OE,I 494), thus recalling Thérèse's spirit of childhood and her use of flower imagery to describe herself. As in Thérèse whose spiritual maturity lay hidden beneath her timidity so, too, Chevance's excessive timidity "masquait aux yeux de tous une hardiesse dans les voies spirituelles, un sens extraordinaire de la grâce de Dieu" (OE,I 337). His simplicity and confidence are mindful of Thérèse's image of appearing empty-handed before God. The priest-hero is thus able to beg Cénabre, who no longer has the gift of faith, to give him his blessing: "Vous pouvez, sans sacrilège, appeler sur un frère à peine moins misérable que vous cette grâce dont vous êtes à présent vide" (OE,I 347).

Parallel images of Thérèse are also observed in Chevance's agony and death. Madame de la Follette, the caretaker of the building in which the dying priest lives, does not take his illness any more seriously than one of Thérèse's Carmelite sisters took hers seriously. Every night a certain sister used to come to the infirmary, stand at the foot of Thérèse's bed and laugh. The saint's humble acceptance of this display of insensitivity (DE 147) is reflected in Chevance's childlike attitude of simplicity and humility in the face of Madame de la Follette's lack of feeling for his sufferings (OE,I 482-491).

Bernanos enters realistically into the various physical and spiritual sufferings of his priest-hero whose tears, heavy perspiration, hemorrhages, weakness, and despair find parallels in Thérèse's sufferings as witnessed in J'entre dans la vie.[5] Chevance also models the Carmelite in his childlike acceptance of the humiliations of his final sufferings and death: "Ainsi qu'un enfant ouvre ses petits bras à la mort par un geste sacré, il s'était livré du premier coup . . ." (OE I 492). His resignation "à souffrir petitement, bassement, lâchement, et à scandaliser le prochain" (OE,I 492) thus reflects Thérèse's thoughts on her suffering: "Le bon Dieu veut que je m'abandonne comme un tout petit enfant qui ne s'inquiète pas de ce que l'on fera de lui" (DE 48). It is worth noting that joy has no role to play in the early stages of either the priest's or the saint's suffering. Although Thérèse longed for suffering from her childhood days, it was only towards the end of her life that she experienced joy in suffering (DE 105).

Like Thérèse who recognized the value of suffering (HA 206), Chevance, in his last agony, finds "une espèce de joie" (OE,I 509) in the thought that his suffering will help another person. In the midst of her agony the Carmelite saint offered her suffering "pour obtenir la lumière de la foi aux pauvres incrédules, pour tous ceux qui s'éloignent des croyances de l'Eglise" (DE 224). In a similar fashion, Chevance recognizes his suffering to be for someone more unfortunate and abandoned than he. Thus he willingly gives his last breath to save Cénabre, his brother-priest: "Le suprême secret du vieux prêtre était un secret d'amour" (OE,I 512). Chevance's act of love during his last agony forms a parallel image of Thérèse who offered her last communion for the conversion of Père Hyacinthe Loyson, a renegade Carmelite priest (HA 305; DE 137), whom, in a letter to her sister, Céline, she called "notre frère" (LT 210).

To represent in visual terms his priest-hero's intense spiritual anguish, Bernanos again employs Theresian images of "le trou noir" (DE 153), "un épais brouillard" (HA 241), and "un mur qui s'élève jusqu'aux cieux et couvre le firmament étoilé..." (HA 244). In his delirium Chevance imagines "des trous noirs où sombrait d'un seul coup l'angoisse glacée . . ." (OE,I 506) and "comme dans un brouillard épais l'arête d'un toit, l'angle d'un mur . . ." (OE,I 507).

Chantal de Clergerie

Though Chevance reflects Thérèse so faithfully, he is allowed to die at the end of L'Imposture, for Bernanos had found a better representative of Thérèse of Lisieux in the young Chantal de Clergerie, Chevance's spiritual daughter and the heroine of his third novel. Chantal appears for the first time at the end of L'Imposture during Chevance's agony. Even more perfectly than Chevance she was to reflect the Carmelite saint's spirituality in her description of herself: "Je suis très, très simple, voilà tout" (OE,I 497). Many of her personality traits as well as her attitude towards her suffering are reminiscent of Thérèse.

If, for example, Chantal's father were to tell her that they were going to Canada or to India she would receive the news with the same happy smile with which Thérèse would have accepted being sent to the Carmelite monastery in Indochina (OE,I 497). And, like the saint, Chantal too believes herself to be a little soul, entirely dependent on God rather than on her own resources. Her happiness is derived from a certainty of her weakness and her childlike dependence on God: "cette certitude de n'être bonne à rien, et aussi l'espoir d'être au dernier jour jugée, comme telle . . ." (OE,I 498). Chantal's joy in her spiritual poverty reminds us of Thérèse's words: "Quand même j'aurais accompli toutes les oeuvres de St Paul, je me croirais encore 'serviteur inutile' mais c'est justement ce qui fait ma joie, car n'ayant rien, je recevrai tout du bon Dieu" (DE 50).

When Bernanos' heroine declares: "Moi, ma vocation est de recevoir. Il me faut si peu de vivre! Alors, je me tiens sagement sous le porche de l'église, je tends la main au bon Dieu, je pense qu'il y mettra bien toujours deux sous..." (OE,I 498) we are reminded of certain passages in the Histoire d'une âme where Thérèse speaks of approaching God with a beggar's empty hand: "on agit comme les pauvres qui tendent la main afin de recevoir ce qui leur est nécessaire . . ." (HA 259) and "Il nous enseigne qu'il suffit de frapper pour qu'on ouvre, de chercher pour trouver et de tendre humblement la main pour recevoir ce que l'on demande..." (HA 295).

Thérèse of Lisieux' spirit of childhood is therefore already in focus in Chantal de Clergerie as we see her in L'Imposture. Suffering and the dark night of the soul enter her life for the first time with the death of her spiritual director. Arriving at the dying priest's bedside shortly before his death, Chantal asks Chevance to give her his last blessing. In exchange, she generously offers him her joy which had pleased him so much and which, as she believes, she no longer needs (OE,I 527).

At the same time the heroine realizes that she has never taken the thought of death very seriously and that it is now time for her to reflect on what death is all about. Willing, therefore, to receive death from his hands, Chantal begs Chevance to accept the gift of her joy in exchange: "Après Dieu, c'est à vous que je devais ma joie, vous dis-je. Reprenez-la" (OE,I 528). But it is only after asking his spiritual daughter to bring Cénabre to him that Chevance is able to accept her gift. At the moment of his acceptance of her joy, Chantal becomes aware that she is trembling all over. Without understanding as yet what is happening to her, Bernanos' young heroine willingly accepts the burden of suffering for Cénabre that God has lifted from Chevance's shoulders and placed on her frail ones. ". . . et sans un mot, elle reçut innocemment, elle fit sienne, elle épousa pour l'éternité la mystérieuse humiliation d'une telle mort" (OE,I 530).

This mysterious exchange of gifts whereby Chevance dies a peaceful death and Chantal will later on suffer an ignominious one at the hands of Fiodor, the family's Russian chauffeur, prefigures Madame de Croissy's substitution of her death for that of Blanche de la Force in Dialogues des Carmélites. This loving acceptance of the suffering of another is reflected in Thérèse's desire: "Oh! que je serais heureuse, si en allant en purgatoire, je pouvais délivrer d'autres âmes, souffrir à leur place . . ." (DE 64). The dying priest's gift of suffering to his spiritual daughter parallels to a certain extent the gift of joy that at her death Mère Geneviève, the foundress of the Lisieux Carmel, gave to Thérèse, her spiritual daughter. The young Carmelite reveals what took place in her soul at this moment: "ma disposition intérieure a changé, en un clin d'oeil je me suis sentie remplie d'une joie et d'une ferveur indicibles . . ." (HA 193). Until now Chantal has not experienced any interior suffering in her short life and so it is without understanding the transformation taking place in her soul that she takes on the humiliation of the priest-hero's death. Joy in suffering is something that Bernanos' young heroine, following in the footsteps of Thérèse, has to learn gradually. In contrast to the sorrow in suffering experienced in her childhood, the saint was able to state at the end of her life: "ce n'est plus ainsi que je souffre maintenant, c'est dans la joie et la paix, je suis véritablement heureuse de souffrir" (HA 239).

It is in La Joie that Bernanos will not only demonstrate a fictional incarnation of Theresian spirituality in Chantal, but will carry it to the heights of spiritual maturity and the suffering of martyrdom. In attempting to go still further in studying the rapport between Thérèse of Lisieux and Chantal de Clergerie, it is necessary to examine the Bernanosian incarnation of the saint under three general headings: Physical and Spiritual Physiognomy, The Vocation to Manifest God's Merciful Love, and The Oblation of Love.

i) *Physical and Spiritual Physiognomy*

Certainly Theresian elements can be detected in Chantal's physical and spiritual makeup. Bernanos' description of his young heroine with "ses cheveux cendrés, son regard lumineux" (OE,I 545) calls to mind photos of Thérèse as a young teenager as well as her beautiful golden curls sheared off on the day of her reception of the Carmelite habit and now on display in the monastery museum in Lisieux.

With regard to natural temperament, Chantal possesses the same type of sunny, outgoing nature that her model had. The saint's sisters tell of her sense of humour and ability to mimic others. Thérèse herself relates how at school she loved to amuse her classmates with story-telling (HA 96). Bernanos' heroine displays a corresponding ability to please others "car elle était si malicieuse et si vive qu'on l'écoutait volontiers" (OE,I 555).

In the case of both young girls, the death of a loved one brought about a change in their normally happy dispositions. Although Chantal suffered the loss of her mother in early childhood, as did Thérèse, it was the death of the abbé Chevance that had more of an affect on her, for if the death of Madame Martin proved to be a traumatic experience for her youngest daughter, so also was the death of Chevance for his spiritual daughter. Referring to the period following her mother's death as the most painful part of her life, Thérèse declares: "mon heureux caractère changea complètement . . ." (HA 43), while Bernanos states about Chantal that after the death of her spiritual father "l'étroit univers familier dans lequel elle était née, où elle avait vécu, prenait un aspect nouveau" (OE,I 562-563). Fear of being a victim of a nervous illness plagued both the saint and the heroine over a prolonged period of time. Chantal's fears and almost guilty feeling of having inherited her mother's nervous disorder have some affinity with the strange nervous illness from which the saint suffered as a child and which became for her a source of martyrdom as she believed for a long time that she had deliberately caused the illness (HA 73-81).

Thérèse and Chantal also hold in common various spiritual qualities. In their desire to remain unnoticed by others they experience a similar joy in the knowledge of their impotence. Thérèse confesses: "Il m'arrive bien aussi des faiblesses, mais je m'en réjouis" (DE 57), while Bernanos says of Chantal: "la certitude de son impuissance était devenue le centre éblouissant de sa joie, le noyau de l'astre en flammes" (OE,I 681). The heroine's joy in her weakness not only explains the title of the novel, as William Bush has demonstrated (SE 147-150), but also reveals the contrast in spirituality between Chantal and Donissan, the priest-hero of Bernanos' first novel, Sous le soleil de Satan, for whom "La certitude de son impuissance à égaler un tel destin bloquait jusqu'à la prière sur ses lèvres" (OE,I 142). This contrast in characterization testifies to the author's evolution in the understanding of the saint's message. Thérèse's delight in her weakness observed in statements such as: "C'est si doux de se sentir faible et petit!" (DE 57) and "mais maintenant je ne m'étonne plus de rien, je ne me fais pas de peine en voyant que je suis la faiblesse même, au contraire c'est en elle que je me glorifie . . ." (HA 257) finds further echoes in these descriptions of Chantal: "un sens exquis de sa propre faiblesse l'avait merveilleusement réconfortée et consolée, car il semblait qu'il fût en elle comme le signe ineffable de la présence de Dieu . . ." (OE,I 553) and "Il est bon d'être faible entre ses mains... Il est meilleur d'être faible. Et qui est plus faible que moi désormais?" (OE,I 572).

To depict his heroine's spirit of poverty Bernanos also employs expressions parallel to those of the Carmelite. Statements reflecting Thérèse's concept of spiritual poverty such as: "Quand même j'aurais accompli toutes les oeuvres de St Paul, je me croirais encore 'serviteur inutile' mais c'est justement ce qui fait ma joie, car n'ayant rien, je recevrai tout du bon Dieu" (DE 50), "on agit comme les pauvres qui tendent la main afin de recevoir ce qui leur est nécessaire" (HA 259), and "Rien ne me tient aux mains. Tout ce que j'ai, tout ce que je gagne, c'est pour l'Eglise et les âmes" (DE 72) are duplicated in statements by or about Chantal: "Il me semble que je n'ai plus rien du tout à sauver: je n'ai plus rien" (OE,I 698), "Je reçois chaque heure que Dieu me donne parce que je n'aurais même pas la force de refuser . . ." (OE,I 554), and "Si longtemps elle avait mis son soin et sa peine à ne rien garder, à dépenser au jour le jour l'aumône tombée du ciel . . ." (OE,I 555). Recognizing that by herself she possesses nothing, Chantal, like Thérèse, relies on God for the spiritual gifts she is to bestow on others. Bernanos describes his heroine in these terms: "lorsque plus pauvre et plus seule que jamais, parmi ces visages hostiles ou clos, elle donnait, elle prodiguait, elle jetait à pleines mains, ainsi qu'une chose de rien, son espérance sublime" (OE,I 568). Chantal thus borrows Thérèse's sentiment regarding her position as assistant mistress of novices: "Je jette à droite, à gauche, à mes petits oiseaux les bonnes graines que le bon Dieu met dans ma petite main" (DE 29).

Implicit evidence of Thérèse can also be recognized in the spiritual direction given to Chantal. Parallel situations are revealed in the words of the various priests who come in contact with both young women. Bernanos' heroine is regarded as a schoolgirl by the dean of Idouville (OE,I 560) just as Thérèse was considered a child by Père Pichon (HA 173, DE 56). Chantal's anxiety about whether or not she is serving God: "Je n'ai pas voulu offenser Dieu, j'ai désiré de le servir. L'ai-je servi ou non?" (OE,I 693) recalls the saint's concern about pleasing God as seen in her words to Pauline: "J'étais un peu triste ce soir, me demandant si le bon Dieu était vraiment content de moi" (DE 33-34) and in her happiness over Père Pichon's assurance that God was pleased with her (HA 173).

Both saint and heroine encountered difficulty in finding a director who understood their spirituality and when they did find one they seemed to be the only ones in their immediate surroundings who really appreciated his worth. Thérèse felt that she alone derived any real benefit from Père Prou's retreat (HA

197), while Chantal's director is the subject of gossip among her father's friends. The psychiatrist, La Pérouse, thus repeats to Monsieur de Clergerie the tales he has heard about the abbé Chevance: "confesseur des bonnes... D'ailleurs un maniaque exquis, une sorte de saint" (OE,I 644).

Chevance's understanding of God's action in Chantal's soul and his persuading her to remain as she is (OE,I 560) recall Père Prou's encouraging Thérèse to continue in the path of confidence and love in which God was leading her. Thérèse records: "Il me lança à pleines voiles sur les flots de la confiance et de l'amour qui m'attiraient si fort mais sur lesquels je n'osais avancer..." (HA 197-198). Père Prou's counsel is certainly reflected in Bernanos' description of how Chevance was able to reassure Chantal and "la remettre doucement en route, par un petit chemin sûr, discret, qui ne fait envie à personne!" (OE,I 570-571).

The spirit of confidence and abandonment to the will of God inherent in both young women is readily discerned in them by their competent directors. Similar to Père Prou who launched the Carmelite on her "little way" of confidence and abandonment, Chevance recognizes in his protégée "l'esprit, le rayonnant esprit de confiance et d'abandon" (OE,I 554). Abandoning herself to the will of God, Bernanos' heroine thus echoes Thérèse of Lisieux' sentiments: "c'est dans les bras du bon Dieu que je tombe!" (DE 169) when she proclaims: "Je ne puis tomber qu'en Dieu!" (OE,I 552).

But it is in the implicit evidence of Thérèse of Lisieux' presence found in Chantal's vocation that we recognize the depth to which the saint has influenced the author. As Soeur Raymond-Marie has aptly stated: "C'est que Chantal a reçu du romancier une 'vocation' étonnamment semblable à celle de la sainte qu'il lui a choisie pour modèle" ("R-M" 299). In Thérèse de Lisieux: mythes et réalité, René Laurentin discusses what Theresian scholars have determined to be the three poles of the Carmelite's "little way:" her discovery of divine mercy, an awareness of her nothingness combined with an unshakeable confidence in God, and the desire to communicate God's merciful love to others.[6] L'Imposture and La Joie depict Bernanos heroine as actually living out these three poles in her vocation.

ii) The Vocation to Manifest God's Merciful Love

Like Thérèse, Chantal wonders what her special role is in life: "je n'arriverais jamais à trouver ma route - mais il y en a une!" (OE,I 678) and comes to a gradual realization of her call to give God's merciful love to others. In her autobiography the saint tells of the amount of prayer and reflection that were necessary before she could proclaim: "ma vocation, enfin je l'ai trouvée, MA VOCATION, C'EST L'AMOUR!..." (HA 222).

Monsieur de Clergerie tries to convince his daughter that she belongs in a monastery, but his motives are all for the wrong reason. As William Bush points out, he is anxious to get rid of his daughter in order to have more freedom to further his own ambitions (SE 51). Chantal, however, has the same opinion about religious life as Thérèse, her model (HA 172). She realizes that it is not an "escape" from life and so she informs her father that she can accomplish the little tasks of daily life just as well outside the walls of a monastery (OE,I 590).

When La Joie opens, Chantal is already aware of her own nothingness and her need of God's merciful love. Her statement: "Au fond je ne pensais qu'à Dieu, je n'étais simple et gaie que pour lui..., un enfant, un petit enfant..." (OE,I 670) bespeaks her sharing in the joy and simplicity of the Theresian concept of spiritual childhood and forms a parallel to the saint's own statement: "Je suis donc restée toujours petite, n'ayant d'autre occupation que celle de cueillir des fleurs, les fleurs de l'amour et du sacrifice, et de les offrir au bon Dieu pour son plaisir" (DE 119).

In addition to Bernanos' use of Theresian images of littleness as pointed out by Guy Gaucher ("BT" 255-258), flower imagery used by Bernanos in La Joie also resembles that found in the Histoire d'une âme. In Thérèse's writings flower imagery serves a dual purpose: it depicts not only the saint's idea of her littleness and childhood, but it also indicates the presence of suffering in her life. While comparing herself to a little flower, Thérèse, at the same time, can use the metaphor to suggest the trials that are to come into her short life. "De même que les fleurs du printemps commencent à germer sous la neige et s'épanouissent aux premiers rayons du Soleil," states Thérèse, "ainsi la petite fleur dont j'écris les souvenirs a-t-elle dû passer par l'hiver de l'épreuve..." (HA 39). The image of summer flowers evoking Chantal's presence functions in a parallel manner: "La joie du jour, le jour en fleur, un matin d'août, avec son humeur et son éclat, tout luisant - et déjà, dans l'air trop lourd, les perfides aromates d'automne . . ." (OE,I 552). Thus a beautiful summer day that will soon turn into the decay of autumn intimates the suffering that will shortly enter Chantal's soul.

Aware of the childlike quality of her spirituality, Chevance warns Chantal of the suffering that will soon come upon her: "Dieu veuille que vous fleurissiez d'abord de toute votre floraison, ma fille! Il n'y a pas de fruits sans peine, cela viendra . . ." (OE,I 556). The priest's warning reminds us of certain passages in the Histoire d'une âme where Thérèse describes the joys of her childhood days: "notre âme dans toute sa fraîcheur s'épanouissait comme une fleur heureuse de recevoir la rosée du matin" (HA 68). But elsewhere in her autobiography Thérèse uses flower imagery to symbolize her suffering lovingly accepted: "en jetant mes fleurs, je chanterai . . . je chanterai, même lorsqu'il me faudra cueillir mes fleurs au milieu des épines . . ." (HA 225).

iii) The Oblation of Love

With the death of the abbé Chevance, suffering enters Chantal's life and replaces her joy. It is during this period of suffering that the young woman's desire to communicate God's merciful love to those around her comes to fruition.

Chevance dies shortly after having set his spiritual daughter on the Carmelite's way of confidence and abandonment. His death brings an unexpected development in Chantal's vocation that in many aspects resembles Thérèse's call to love through suffering. Elements of the saint's Christmas conversion again furnish Bernanos with images to show how his heroine breaks the chains of self-love and opens herself up to charity. Both Thérèse and Chantal felt trapped in a circle which they knew had to be broken if they were to experience spiritual growth. The saint felt herself freed by the grace of God from the circle within which she was confined: "En peu de temps le Bon Dieu avait su me faire sortir du cercle étroit où je tournais ne sachant comment en sortir" (HA 117). In a corresponding manner, the heroine, too, came to the realization that the circle holding her captive had to be broken and so she believed "qu'elle était perdue, si elle ne rompait aussitôt le cercle enchanté" (OE, I 572). As in the case of Thérèse, Chantal too could state: "'J'étais contente que Dieu eût pris la peine de me dépouiller lui-même avec tant de soin qu'il me fût devenu impossible d'être plus pauvre'" (OE, I 577). Having been released from the bonds of self-love, the Carmelite describes the birth of her desire to bring God's merciful love to sinners and to those around her: "Je sentis en un mot la charité entrer dans mon coeur, le besoin de m'oublier pour faire plaisir et depuis lors je fus heureuse!..." (HA 114-115).

As Thérèse felt love enter her heart and an ever-increasing desire to offer herself as a victim of love for the redemption of sinners, Chantal also begins to experience an opening out to love for others: "le monde, qui n'était jusqu'à ce moment pour elle qu'un mot mystérieux, se révélait, non à son expérience, mais à sa charité - par l'intuition, l'épanouissement, le rayonnement de la pitié" (OE, I 561). Chantal begins to understand, as did Thérèse, that if one truly loves, one does not simply resign oneself to suffering: "Je ne suis pas résignée! disait-elle jadis à son vieil ami. La résignation est triste. Comment se résigner à la volonté de Dieu? Est-ce qu'on se résigne à être aimée?" (OE, I 598). Chantal's words recall Thérèse's remark to Pauline describing how a statement made by Mme Swetchine[7] had helped her accept their father's illness a few years earlier: "'La résignation est encore distincte de la volonté du bon Dieu; il y a la même différence qu'entre l'union et l'unité. Dans l'union, on est encore deux, dans l'unité, on n'est plus qu'un'" (DE 90).

Chantal's eyes become opened to the suffering of the members of her household. Although her first contact with sin frightens her, she nevertheless feels pity for sinners. The young woman now sees her father as the weak individual he really is, but her love for him takes charge of the situation: "Elle ne songeait qu'à le servir, les servir tous, et d'abord les plus déshérités . . ." (OE,I 602).

Responding to the call to love, both the saint and the heroine offer themselves as victims for the salvation not only of sinners but especially of those who have lost the gift of faith. Part of their suffering consists of the trial of faith in which both experience extreme solitude and the silence of God. Thérèse endures "les angoisses de la mort... et avec cela aucune consolation!" (DE 41), while Chantal receives "aucune aide, aucune parole de consolation" (OE,I 678). Bernanos' image of his young "saint's" trial: "voilà qu'elle s'avançait maintenant à travers un pays inconnu, hors des frontières de son ancien paradis, seule" (OE,I 560) mirrors the Carmelite saint's attempt to portray her night of faith as "un pays environné d'un épais brouillard" (HA 241).

During their experience of the dark night of the soul both Thérèse and Chantal not only come to understand the true nature of sin, but also to include themselves with sinners. Thérèse declares herself willing, therefore, to eat the bread of suffering at the same table with sinners (HA 241-242). Recognizing the common bond of sin in humanity, Chantal tells her grandmother about her discovery: "'bah! nous n'échappons pas plus les uns aux autres que nous n'échappons à Dieu. Nous n'avons en commun que le péché'" (OE,I 616). What Bernanos' young heroine has just re-discovered is the mystery of Redemption, the "buying back" of sin through suffering. On his death-bed, the abbé Chevance had taught her the meaning of sin: "'Le péché, nous sommes tous dedans, les uns pour en jouir, d'autres pour en souffrir, mais à la fin du compte, c'est le même pain que nous rompons au bord de la fontaine . . .'" (OE,I 671).

Aware of the sublime role of suffering in the life of the Christian, the saint and the heroine freely and confidently abandon themselves to the will of God in their regard. Suffering and lack of spiritual consolation are thus joyfully accepted. Parallel statements witness to the similarity in their attitudes. The sentiment heard in Thérèse's assertion: "je veux bien y manger seule le pain de l'épreuve jusqu'à ce qu'il vous plaise de m'introduire dans votre lumineux royaume" (HA 242) is repeated in Chantal's: "Je ne bougerai pas d'un pouce jusqu'à ce que la lumière revienne . . ." (OE,I 678).

The intense suffering and humiliating death that Bernanos gives his heroine can be explained from examining Thérèse's thoughts and words during her final illness. A short time before her death the saint stated that she would never have believed it possible to suffer so much: "Je ne puis m'expliquer cela que par les désirs ardents que j'ai eus de sauver des âmes" (DE 185), "Enfin j'offre ces peines bien grandes pour obtenir la lumière de la foi aux pauvres incrédules, pour tous ceux qui s'éloignent des croyances de l'Eglise" (DE 224), and we know that she was thinking in particular of Père Loyson. And in a similar manner, shortly before her death Chantal welcomes into her heart the abbé Cénabre, "ce pécheur des pécheurs les bras tendus . . ." (OE,I 686).

Cénabre

What is particularly striking in both novels, however, is that we discover in the abbé Cénabre, hero of L'Imposture and one of the principal characters of La Joie, a reverse image of Thérèse, quite in contrast to Chevance and Chantal.

Cénabre's childhood experiences and character traits are almost the direct opposite of Thérèse's. Orphaned at an early age and abandoned by all (OE,I 364), Cénabre believed the priesthood to be the only opportunity open to him to make a name for himself. In contrast to Thérèse who desired to live a hidden life and whose vocation was, as she stated later to Pauline, "de faire aimer le bon Dieu comme je l'aime . . ." (DE 85), love and self-sacrifice played no role in Cénabre's decision to become a priest. He saw himself "non seulement condamné au sacerdoce, mais encore à s'y distinguer de ses rivaux plus heureux, plus favorisés" (OE,I 364). In opposition to the saint's constant search for truth, Cénabre's vocation was thus regulated by a lie from the very start.

Like the Carmelite saint, however, Bernanos' priest-historian lives a life of silence, solitude, and interior suffering. Similar to her also, Cénabre is scrupulously faithful to the daily tasks of his state in life and obedience to his superiors but, unlike Thérèse, his actions are full of empty zeal and sadness (OE,I 445).

Cénabre, the author of several scholarly works on saints and mysticism and member of the Académie française, shows that he does indeed possess an intellectual knowledge of Thérèse's little way: "Il n'y a pas de meilleur remède, ni plus simple que la paisible observation de nos devoirs, dans un esprit de confiance et d'abandon" (OE,I 350). His words do not deceive Chevance, however, who detects in them an insincerity, indeed a mockery of the saint's teaching. As a reverse image of the saint, Cénabre shows that Thérèse does not yield to an intellectual approach but only to love, for as the Carmelite herself declared: "c'est l'amour seul qui compte..." (DE 228).

Both priest and saint experience a trial of faith where they are tempted to doubt the very existence of God and eternal life. In his trial of faith, Cénabre's attitude of despair tinged with pride is a reverse image of Thérèse's confidence and abandonment to God in the midst of her dark night of the soul.

Boat imagery aptly conveys the interior struggle of each. Cénabre's despair is compared to a shipwreck: "Entre le néant et moi, se disait-il, il n'y a que cette vie hésitante, qu'un souffle peut abolir, la rupture d'un petit vaisseau" (OE,I 444). Boat imagery also portrays metaphorically Thérèse's sense of solitude and anguish as in her description of the state of her soul: "mon âme était semblable au fragile esquif livré sans pilote à la merci des flots orageux..." (HA 127), but, contrary to Cénabre, her little vessel does not end up in shipwreck. The saint remains confident that even though she cannot see Him, God is present in her soul and she soon discovers that He has just been asleep: "Jésus en se réveillant m'avait rendu la joie, le bruit des vagues s'était apaisé . . ." (HA 129).

Circular imagery reveals how both Thérèse and Cénabre feel enslaved by a sense of powerlessness and anguish which they seem incapable of overcoming on their own. The priest-hero's inability to escape from the circle in which he feels trapped: 'Prières, menaces, mensonges, cris de fureur ou de désespoir, il semblait que rien ne pût dépasser le cercle enchanté" (OE,I 346) forms a reverse image of the grace which the saint received on that special Christmas night: "En peu de temps le Bon Dieu avait su me faire sortir du cercle étroit où je tournais ne sachant comment en sortir" (HA 117).

Satan's power over Cénabre's soul, symbolized by the "cercle enchanté" in which the priest is held captive, is directly opposed to God's presence acting in Thérèse's soul to liberate her from the "cercle étroit" in which she is held prisoner. Bernanos leads us to believe here that Cénabre ought to have relied on God to take the initiative in his soul, for it was God alone who was able to break the circle in which the saint felt trapped. A letter to the abbé Bellière dated July 26, 1897 reveals Thérèse's insight into how a person can overcome temptations to faith. The saint writes: "Il est vrai que pour jouir de ces trésors, il faut s'humilier, reconnaître son néant, et voilà ce que beaucoup d'âmes ne veulent pas faire . . ." (LT 451).

Further contrasts appearing in the interior suffering of Thérèse and Cénabre disclose how, unlike the Carmelite saint, the priest-hero is afraid of abandoning himself to God. With his strongest feeling resembling hatred rather than love, he is a reverse image of Thérèse who freely abandoned herself to God's merciful love. Cénabre's abandonment to despair is opposed to Thérèse's acceptance of her physical and spiritual sufferings. The "joie terrible" (OE,I 348) that the priest feels arising within him is in complete contrast to the resultant peace and joy in suffering that the saint eventually discovers: "c'est une souffrance sans inquiétude. Je suis contente de souffrir puisque le bon Dieu le veut" (DE 154).

Like Thérèse, Cénabre was also tempted to commit suicide, but his several unsuccessful attempts to do away with himself form another reverse image of the saint's enduring faith in a similar trial (DE 142, 224).[8] The priest-hero struggles intellectually with his temptations and in his constant refusal to abandon himself to God and to accept the spiritual help of the sacrament of penance as suggested by Chevance, Cénabre seems consistently to be a reverse image of the saint of Lisieux.

But is salvation still possible for Cénabre? The night of Chantal's death finds the priest wrestling with the idea of God as a final obstacle to be overcome. At this moment he has the sensation of seeing a vague light. We are tempted to wonder, therefore, if the "lueur vague" that Cénabre experiences at what is, in all likelihood, the very moment of Chantal's agony and death, symbolizes a special grace that the young woman has merited for him through her immolation. Otherwise what is the source of this light? "Comment était-elle entrée dans sa poitrine? Par quelle brèche?" (OE,I 719).

So it is that on almost every page of La Joie there seems to be some sort of implicit evidence of the Carmelite's influence whether dealing with Chevance, Chantal, or Cénabre. In any case, there is no dispute that Chantal de Clergerie afforded Bernanos his most perfect incarnation of Thérèse of Lisieux' presence to date.

NOTES

CHAPTER 6

¹ Marina Warner, <u>Joan of Arc: The Image of Female Heroism</u> (London: Weidenfeld and Nicolson, 1981) 265-266.

² Yves Bridel, "Jeanne d'Arc et Bernanos," <u>Bernanos. Centre culturel de Cerisy-la-Salle 10 au 19 juillet 1959</u>, ed. Max Milner (Paris: Plon, 1972) 298.

³ Emile Rideau, <u>Thérèse de Lisieux: la nature et la grâce</u> (Paris: Fayard, 1973) 225.

⁴ Thérèse de l'Enfant-Jésus et de la Sainte-Face, <u>Le triomphe de l'humilité (RP,7)</u>, Thérèse mystifiée (1896-1897), l'affaire Léo Taxil et le Manuscript B (Paris: Editions du Cerf et Desclée de Brouwer, 1975) 75-88.

⁵ Known also by its other name, <u>Derniers entretiens</u>, this work is a collection of Thérèse of Lisieux' words as recorded by her sister, Pauline, from April 6, 1897 until her death on September 30, 1897. The saint's words, along with her sister's frequent explanatory remarks, reveal the intensity of her sufferings. Works written on Thérèse since the early seventies tend to give a more realistic treatment of her sufferings. Among the best of these works is Guy Gaucher's study, <u>La passion de Thérèse de Lisieux</u> (Paris: Editions du Cerf et Desclée de Brouwer, 1972).

⁶ René Laurentin, <u>Thérèse de Lisieux: mythes et réalité</u> (Paris: Beauchesne, 1972) 162-170.

⁷ Mme Swetchine (Anne Sophie Swetchine) was born in Moscow in 1782 and died in Paris in 1857. Russian Orthodox by birth, she converted to Catholicism. Widely read in history, philosophy, and theology, Mme Swetchine had a salon in Paris where she attracted intellectuals. She showed herself to be especially gifted in understanding and guiding others. ["Swetchine," <u>New Catholic Encyclopedia</u>, 1967 ed.]

⁸ Thérèse warned Pauline about leaving any strong medication within easy reach of seriously ill persons who, unaware of what they were really doing, could easily take an overdose. She added that if she had not had faith she would not have hesitated to commit suicide.

CHAPTER 7

REVERSE IMAGES OF THÉRÈSE IN <u>UN MAUVAIS RÊVE</u>, <u>UN CRIME</u> (1931-1935), AND <u>MONSIEUR OUINE</u> (1931-1940)

The nineteen thirties were the beginning of a new period in Bernanos' career as a writer. With the exception of <u>Les Grands Cimetières sous la lune</u>, the author devoted the years from 1931-1938 to the preparation of five novels which, in contrast to those of the twenties, prove more cognizant of problems of the modern world as well as of human suffering in general. Bernanos' personal experience of suffering, solitude, and anguish during the early thirties are perhaps not totally unrelated to a more accessible vision of the human condition incarnate in the characters found in these novels. Of these five novels, however, only <u>Journal d'un curé de campagne</u> contains explicit textual evidence of Thérèse of Lisieux' presence. Yet implicit evidence of her influence seems to abound in all of them.

Michael Tobin's statement that "Bernanos wished to create in Mouchette a sort of infernal reflection of St. Thérèse . . ." ("T" 85) is an observation which can be applied to other characters in the author's fictional world. Reverse images of the Carmelite saint appearing in those characters we label as "sinners" remind us in fact that Thérèse believed she had the potential to be either a saint or a sinner. We recall here how Père Pichon told her: "remerciez le Bon Dieu de ce qu'il fait pour vous, car s'il vous abandonnait, au lieu d'être un petit ange, vous deviendriez un petit démon" (HA 173). Perhaps Bernanos wondered what Thérèse's life would have been like had she not responded to God's grace.

The saint's love for sinners, her identification with them, and the offering of her suffering for them seems reflected in Bernanos' unmistakable pity for those of his "sinners" upon whom he bestows certain traits resembling those of the Carmelite saint. Thus, few of Bernanos' characters are excluded from our sympathy and their interior suffering is experienced by the reader every bit as keenly as that of his "saints."

Un mauvais rêve and *Un crime*

Although Bernanos began writing Un mauvais rêve in January, 1931, he abandoned it after a few short weeks to commence Monsieur Ouine. February of this same year finds the author explaining his action to his friend, Vallery-Radot: "Imaginez-vous que j'ai commencé un autre livre, le premier me dégoûtait" (Corr.I 390). Perhaps the suffering of the foundering middle-aged writer, Ganse, was too closely related to the author's own personal experience at that time. In Genèse et structures d'"Un Mauvais rêve" William Bush points out that Bernanos stopped working on Un mauvais rêve at the point of Simone's "cercle enchanté." He states: "Venant d'abord la question la plus fondamentale de son propre conflit intérieur, le goût a dû lui manquer pour aller plus loin dans l'approfondissement de ses problèmes personnels."[1] Completed only in 1935, Un mauvais rêve was to remain unpublished until 1950, two years after the author's death.

1935 also saw the publication of Un crime, Bernanos' first and last attempt at writing a detective novel. As Robert Speaight points out, Un crime "is less interesting for itself than for its close relationship to the much more important novel - Un Mauvais rêve - which was at the back of the author's mind all the time he was at work upon it" (Sp 137-138). Whereas in Un mauvais rêve the author leads his heroine, Simone Alfieri, up to the moment when she must choose between murdering the priest or repenting, without indicating what her final decision is, the heroine of Un crime, Evangeline, pursues the career of Simone Alfieri after she has actually murdered the priest. Because of the strong ties in Bernanos' imagination between these two principal female characters, we will discuss the two novels together.

Simone is a very Bernanosian "sinner." Even before she appears in the novel the author is careful to present her in terms made by other characters as possessing a sort of heroic sanctity. As for Evangeline, she actually puts on the cassock of the priest she has killed and assumes the role of a "false" priest. In both cases Bernanos shows how easily the qualities of a saint could be reversed into those of a sinner. He illustrates, moreover, how the living out of a lie can destroy innocent victims, something diametrically opposed to Thérèse's passion for truth and her desire to bestow God's merciful love on others. Whether it be the spirit of childhood, the call to give God's merciful love to others, or the experience of the trial of faith, reverse images of the threefold nature of Theresian spirituality can be detected in the heroines of Un mauvais rêve and Un crime.

i) *The Reverse Spirit of Childhood*

In both novels, reverse images of the saint often begin as parallel images. In Un mauvais rêve, for example, Olivier Mainville's description of Simone to his aunt suggests that his employer's secretary possesses certain traits of Thérèse's spirit of childhood, such as her simplicity: "Quel silence autour de cette personne jamais poudrée ni fardée, vêtue de noir . . . " (OE,I 876); her goodness:

"chacun de ses gestes enfin - semble exprimer une bonté profonde, discrète, une perpétuelle vigilance du coeur" (OE,I 876); her childlikeness: "le front toujours lisse, bombé comme celui d'un petit enfant" (OE,I 877); her spirit of poverty and desire to live a hidden life: "le dégoût d'un monde où elle a brillé jadis, pour son malheur, n'explique pas qu'elle ait choisi - car elle l'a choisie - cette besogne obscure, ingrate . . ." (OE,I 877); and finally, her attitude of abandonment and patience: "Ni regret, ni remords, aucune mémoire de l'obstacle surmonté, nul souci de l'obstacle à venir, rien qu'une patience infinie, une patience qui à elle seule . . . me semble une espèce de sainteté" (OE,I 877).

But even in what appear to be characteristics similar to those of Thérèse, subtle indications that Simone is in reality a reverse image of the Carmelite's spirituality are detected in remarks such as ". . . et cependant l'espèce de vénération qu'elle inspire ne va pas sans une certaine angoisse, perceptible à peine, comme une ride à la surface de l'eau. Est-elle heureuse? Ne l'est-elle pas?" (OE,I 876) and "Non! non, ce n'est sûrement pas la joie qui a modelé ce visage pathétique!" (OE,I 876). Similarly, Ganse, a has-been novelist, also recognizes the joyless nature of his secretary's sanctity: "Mais je ne suis pas éloigné de croire que Mme Alfieri soit une espèce de sainte - oh! sans miracles, naturellement! - une sainte triste" (OE,I 910). Statements such as these are in direct opposition to an essential quality of Thérèse's spirituality, namely her childlike joy in suffering.

Nevertheless, Simone's innate appreciation of the spirit of childhood is nonetheless present. When Ganse informs her of his desire to write a book revealing the secrets of his childhood, his secretary does not approve of the idea. For Simone, what remains of one's childhood should be kept as something precious and so she advises the novelist: "En tout cas, si cette chose existe encore en vous, gardez-la. Il est peu croyable qu'il en reste assez pour vous aider à vivre, mais ça vous servira sûrement pour mourir" (OE,I 919).

As a child Thérèse dreamed of performing heroic deeds such as those of the Maid of Orleans. She even declared: "Le Martyre, voilà le rêve de ma jeunesse, ce rêve il a grandi avec moi sous les cloîtres du Carmel..." (HA 220). But as she grew older, the saint adapted her "dream" to the reality of her life, thus coming to understand that her mission "n'était pas de faire couronner un roi mortel mais de faire aimer le Roi du Ciel, de lui soumettre le royaume des coeurs" (LT 403) and that her dream of accomplishing "heroic deeds" was to consist in the daily living out of the intense desire she experienced at the age of thirteen to save sinners from eternal flames. Simone's statement that "les mêmes rêves qui servaient à treize ans, qui continueront à servir jusqu'à la mort" (OE,I 920) seems to indicate that she shares Thérèse's belief that a young girl's "dream" can be prolonged into adulthood.

But the concept of dream espoused by Bernanos' heroine is the exact opposite of the saint's notion, for instead of being focused on the good of others, Simone's "dream" is aimed at the senseless destruction of others. Her interior life which in earlier days had the potential to be luminous is in reality completely dark due to her preoccupations with lying, drugs, and illicit relationships through which she has attempted to give meaning to what has become an otherwise meaningless existence. Led from one self-deception to another, the heroine's last attempt to turn her false dream into reality is to murder the aunt of her young lover so that he can inherit a rich estate. In no way does the idea of this crime disturb Simone for "C'était simplement une image monstreuse . . . qu'elle avait senti grouiller en elle dès l'enfance et qui remplissaient déjà ses rêves" (OE,I 985). Simone wrongly believes that she is saving Olivier, but at the same time she seems really to be saving herself when she says to him: "Si tu n'étais pas entré dans ma vie, je l'eusse donnée pour rien - le rêve m'aurait suffi - tous les rêves! Quoi! Devrait-on garder pour soi, pour soi seul, ce monde intérieur si riche!" (OE,I 968).

Certainly the heroine's understanding of how to give of herself to others runs counter to the saint's belief that spiritual gifts are not to be kept for oneself but are to be given for the spiritual life and well-being of those with whom one comes in contact. Since Simone's whole life is built on this type of dream or "mauvais rêve," the only kind of "gift" that she can give to others is one that destroys them both spiritually and physically.

But perhaps Evangeline, masquerading as the curé of Mégère, clarifies even better this type of false dream when she states quite plainly to André, the young altar boy: "Mais peu d'hommes savent rêver. Rêver, c'est se mentir à soi-même, et pour se mentir à soi-même il faut d'abord apprendre à mentir à tous" (OE,I 860). We can only note how far this statement seems to be from the saint's simple but highly significant declaration regarding her attitude to truth: "je ne puis me nourrir que de la vérité" (DE 114).

ii) The Reverse Experience of Love

But what caused Bernanos' two heroines to dream of doing evil rather than good? The key to the answer lies perhaps in how love was or was not experienced by both young women in their childhood. If the Carmelite saint dreamed of doing good it was because she knew love in her life, first of all, within the intimate circle of her family. But more especially, it was because she felt God's merciful love for her, a weak sinner, that Thérèse was able to respond to love in a positive manner. We recall her description of her Christmas grace: "Je sentis en un mot la charité entrer dans mon coeur, le besoin de m'oublier pour faire plaisir et depuis lors je fus heureuse!..." (HA 114-115). From this moment on the saint experienced a growth in love leading her finally to offer herself as a victim of holocaust to God's merciful love for the salvation of others.

Contrary to Thérèse, Simone, brought up by an uncle who showed her no affection, did not experience love in her childhood. The love of God was also absent in her catechism lessons as the type of religion she was taught was purely legalistic with no mention of God's merciful love for the human race. Furthermore, all but one of the priests with whom she was acquainted were mediocre and thus, unfortunately, led her away from God. The only priest who recognized that Simone had the potential for good and who was anxious to help her was forbidden to do so by his superiors. The heroine therefore never learned how to love and accept herself according to Christian teaching. It is no small wonder then that she enjoyed corrupting the mediocre priests in her surroundings.

Bernanos' description of mediocrity among the clergy does have a certain connection with Thérèse's vocation as a Carmelite. The opportunity of spending much time in the company of priests during her pilgrimage to Rome led the saint to understand why the Carmelite vocation is one of praying for priests. She recognized that although many of the priests she met were saintly, they were, nevertheless, subject to human weaknesses. In a letter dated July, 1889, the saint explained to her sister, Céline, why it is so important to pray for priests: "Hélas! combien de mauvais prêtres qui ne sont pas assez saints..." (LT 155) and in October, 1890 she again urged Céline to pray for priests: "Ah! prions pour les prêtres, chaque jour montre combien les amis de Jésus sont rares..." (LT 199).

The author's choice of Evangeline for the role of an impostor priest coincides with the saint's concept of a bad priest. Left in complete despair by the heroine whom he has so greatly admired and trusted, André, the young altar boy, commits suicide. His feeling of emptiness is a reverse image of Thérèse's image of "empty hands": "L'enfant venait de retirer sa main sans que le prêtre fît aucun effort pour la retenir. Il ne leva même pas les yeux. Il regardait ses paumes vides" (OE,I 860). Having placed his confidence in an unworthy "priest," André did not receive the spiritual gifts that he was entitled to receive from a minister of God. The image of his empty hands is the reverse of the saint's belief that God would fill her empty hands with the spiritual gifts needed for the novices in her charge.

Since they had never experienced the Christian meaning of love in their lives, Bernanos' heroines were both incapable of the gift of self in love. Neither one could have borrowed the saying of John of the Cross which Thérèse of Lisieux never grew tired of repeating: "L'amour ne se paie que par l'amour et les plaies de l'amour ne se guérissent que par l'amour" (LT 138). Simone's confession to Olivier: "je n'ai jamais aimé personne d'amour. Ni mon coeur ni mes sens, nulle force au monde ne m'arrachera à moi-même, ne me fera la chose d'un autre, heureuse et comblée" (OE,I 964) is a reversal of the Carmelite's self-offering to merciful love. Similarly, the heroine's statement to Ganse: "Notre vie privée ne regarde que nous. Portons notre fardeau côte à côte, mais n'en échangeons rier..." (OE,I 917) contrasts with Thérèse's desire to share the lot of sinners with whom she placed herself (HA 242). After having murdered Olivier's aunt, Simone comes to the sad realization that everything in her life has been a lie, an attempt to escape the truth that she has never truly loved anyone and that even more especially all her hatred has really been directed at herself.

Evangeline, too, has never experienced the true meaning of love in her life. The daughter of a priest and nun, Evangeline has spent most of her life running away from society. As Henri Debluë explains in <u>Les romans de Georges Bernanos ou le défi du rêve</u>, the heroine has become the unconscious accomplice of her mother's guilt and obsession with priests. Instead of coming to know what is meant by love at an early age, she learns how to live a life based on lies and imposture.[2] Evangeline senselessly murders the aunt of her lesbian lover in order to secure her own rather precarious future.

That she does not understand the Christian concept of love is revealed in a letter to her lover where she writes: "Vous m'avez crainte, mon amie. Il n'y a pas d'amour sans crainte" (OE,I 862). Her view of love thus forms a complete contrast with that of the Carmelite saint in which fear finds no place: "la crainte me fait reculer; avec l'<u>amour</u> non seulement j'avance mais je <u>vole</u>..." (HA 198). Thus the life-giving force of Thérèse's concept of love which banishes fear turns into a blind destructive force in the type of love seen in Simone and Evangeline.

Innocent beings become victims of their fury and hate, but the real victims are Simone and Evangeline themselves.

iii) *Hopeless Interior Suffering*

Caught up in a circle of self-hatred, the two heroines undergo an interior darkness which in its intensity is as real as the suffering of the trial of faith experienced by the little Carmelite who offered herself as a willing victim of holocaust to merciful love. Simone experiences a sense of solitude and emptiness as did Thérèse: "La nuit où elle allait entrer, d'un coeur résolu et calme, n'avait pas d'issue vers le jour" (OE,I 984). But the heroine's efforts to save herself from despair are entirely opposite those of the saint. Her "night" is filled with self-hatred, self-deception, drug-induced fantasies, and crime. Simone believes that there is no way out of the lie upon which her life is built. Her despair is in reality her fear of recognizing and accepting her weakness, and then abandoning herself to God's mercy.

Existential anguish, solitude, trials of faith, and the temptation to despair are all components of Thérèse's trial of faith. But unlike Bernanos' heroine, the saint discovered a way out of her suffering through accepting her weakness and abandoning herself to God's merciful love.

Although Bernanos does not permit us to enter into Evangeline's spiritual drama as much as into Simone's, it would appear that the heroine of Un crime does undergo an experience of interior darkness and abandonment. Evangeline's external appearance as well as her words to André speak of her interior suffering and solitude, thus encouraging us to believe that Thérèse's words: "Mon âme est exilée, le Ciel est fermé pour moi et du côté de la terre, c'est l'épreuve aussi" (DE 52) could easily have been on her lips.

Both the saint and the heroine were, in addition, tempted to commit suicide. Indeed, it was faith alone that kept Thérèse from so doing as she herself states: "Si je n'avais pas eu la foi, je me serais donné la mort sans hésiter un seul instant..." (DE 174). Evangeline, on the contrary, lacks faith. Because she sees no way out of the path of evil she has chosen for herself, she commits suicide.

To describe the trial of faith of his heroines, Bernanos uses boat imagery recalling Thérèse's use of similar metaphors to describe the state of her soul. But in Un mauvais rêve and Un crime the images of shipwreck or of a boat aimlessly adrift contrast sharply with the boat imagery used by the saint. Images such as "un navire échoué" (OE,I 1013) and "des épaves poussées par le flot" (OE,I 1016) depict Simone's false dreams which can only end up in despair. Evangeline describes in metaphorical terms the emptiness of her spiritual adventure: "pour un tel voyage il n'est pas besoin de boussole ni même de navire" (OE,I 860). The heroine's "journey" ends up in disillusionment "comme un navire sous un pavillon étranger" (OE,I 860) because her search for a meaningful existence had been wrongly directed right from the start.

These images are the reversal of those used by the saint who described her soul as being 'semblable au fragile esquif livré sans pilote à la merci des flots orageux..." (HA 127), but who confidently adds: "Je le sais, Jésus était là dormant sur ma nacelle, mais la nuit était si noire qu'il m'était impossible de le voir . . ." (HA 127). Her faith helped her to ride out the storm for she believed that God was ever present carefully steering her little boat into the harbour. In yet another boat image the saint tells of how she discerns in the distance the lighthouse that will lead her safely to port: "O Phare lumineux de l'amour, je sais comment arriver jusqu'à toi . . ." (HA 222-223).

Although Bernanos' heroines have unexpected encounters with priests, and thus presumably God's grace is offered to them, they seem for the moment unable to accept it. As reverse images of Thérèse, Simone and Evangeline refuse to accept their impotence and humbly admit their dependence on God. As the saint wrote to her cousin, Marie, in July, 1890: "car là seulement se trouve la paix et le repos du coeur, quand on se voit si misérable on ne veut plus se considérer et on ne regarde que l'unique Bien-Aimé!..." (LT 179).

At the end of both novels we do not really know what choice the heroines make. Does Simone flee the priest the second time she meets him? Does Evangeline, lying on the railroad tracks, repent at the very last moment as the train is bearing down upon her? Though Bernanos does not reveal this to us, we cannot help but recall at this point his frequent borrowing of the saint's words "tout est grâce" (DE 41). Charles Moeller has aptly remarked that these words "do not mean that ultimately the optimists are right, but that crimes and blasphemies are sometimes the road to God, for God came to save what was lost."[3] The seemingly "unfinished" endings of Un mauvais rêve and Un crime serve as a reminder that the final choice made by Bernanos' heroines is known to God alone.

Monsieur Ouine

Although Bernanos began Monsieur Ouine in 1931, he would not complete the final chapter until 1940. The first fifteen chapters of the novel were finished by April, 1934, but the author abandoned a first version of Chapter Sixteen in July of that year. He returned to Monsieur Ouine in April, 1936, rewrote Chapter Sixteen, as well as all of Chapters Seventeen and Eighteen. It was not until the early part of 1940, however, only a few short months after Great Britain and France declared war on Germany that the author, by that time in his Brazilian exile, was to complete the final chapter of Monsieur Ouine.[4]

A letter written to Robert Vallery-Radot in November of 1934, when the novel was seventy-five percent completed, reveals Bernanos' thoughts regarding Monsieur Ouine: "Monsieur Ouine est ce que j'ai fait de mieux, de plus complet" (Corr. II 33). What then prevented the author from completing his novel sooner?

We have already seen that the nineteen thirties were years during which Bernanos underwent great personal suffering combined with deep, soul-searching reflection on the European crisis. Returning from Majorca in March, 1937, the author found France in the midst of political and economic upheaval under its first Socialist government which had come to power on June 4, 1936. The Front Populaire was a newly formed coalition of parties of the Left under the leadership of Léon Blum. The aim of the Front Populaire was to bring about badly needed social and economic reforms, but the party's attempt at governing the country was for the most part a failure.[5]

Bernanos believed that the world was daily becoming more devoid of Christian values. A letter to Marie Vallery-Radot in February, 1934 in which he refers to <u>Monsieur Ouine</u>, is indicative of his thoughts on life during these years: "Mon livre me dégoûte, mais la vie me dégoûte encore bien plus" (<u>Corr</u>.I 511). Various details of Bernanos' anguish already discussed are a testimony to his difficulty in giving birth to <u>Monsieur Ouine</u>.

As the novel's original title, <u>La paroisse morte</u>, would seem to suggest, the novel itself depicts a society in which spiritual values no longer exist. For Hans Aaraas, the parish of Fenouille is "une image du monde, ou plus exactement une extériorisation de la tragédie spirituelle de notre temps telle que Bernanos l'a vécue."[6] In "Vision créatrice et tentation littéraire," William Bush tends to view Fenouille as "l image d'une paroisse à rebours,"[7] while, in her remarkable article on <u>Monsieur Ouine</u>, Claude-Edmonde Magny understands the world of the novel as one which can only be "décrit à l'envers, vu par l'envers, parce que c'est ainsi qu'il existe effectivement, parce que c'est un monde en creux et, non en relief."[8]

Madame Magny's understanding of the fictional world of <u>Monsieur Ouine</u> was acclaimed by the author himself who, in a letter of August 18, 1946 to the critic, stated that her interpretation of the novel had actually clarified for him what he had been trying to convey in <u>Monsieur Ouine</u>: "Vous l'éclairez, ce monde, vous le pénétrez de lumière, je le vois, je le reconnais, je découvre le chemin que j'ai fait jadis à tâtons" (Corr.II 674).

One of the elements of the novel that this same critic draws forth is Bernanos' unintentional use of paradox whereby something is rendered present through its absence. Magny points out that through the use of this principle "ainsi Bernanos fait-il paraître Dieu par son absence même . . ." ("MO" 22). If, as Magny claims, God is thus present in Monsieur Ouine through His absence, one could suggest Thérèse of Lisieux' presence is also a presence through her absence.

Certainly a first reading of Monsieur Ouine would give the impression that the Carmelite saint is nowhere to be found in the village of Fenouille. Initial impressions notwithstanding, a close examination of the novel reveals that Bernanos goes even further in this novel than in Un mauvais rêve and Un crime in his use of reverse images of Thérèse. What we are really confronting here, therefore, is her spirit of childhood as it might appear on the reverse side of a tapestry. In Un mauvais rêve and Un crime, as we have seen, reverse images are found particularly in regard to the two heroines, Simone and Evangeline. In Monsieur Ouine, apart from Guillaume and the curé of Fenouille who are passive reflections of Theresian ideas, reverse images of the saint abound in a number of the novel's characters. Prior to examining these more subtle, negative images, let us examine parallel images in both the young cripple, Guillaume, and, to a lesser extent, in the curé of Fenouille.

i) Guillaume

Although he is but a secondary character, Guillaume proves unique in regard to our concerns in the novel. Crippled grandson of De Vandomme and best friend and confidant of the novel's hero, Steeny, Guillaume provides us with true parallel images of Thérèse of Lisieux.

Through the acceptance of his own suffering and solitude, and his generous assuming of the sins of his friend and of his grandfather, the young boy mirrors in a positive manner the saint's offering of her suffering to save priests and sinners. Guillaume's desire to help Steeny through his suffering corresponds also with Thérèse's idea that through love suffering can be transformed into helping others who are also suffering.

The saint's "grand désir de travailler à la conversion des pécheurs" (HA 114) is moreover paralleled in Steeny's own recognition of Guillaume's role in their friendship: "Enfin tu es mon âme, fiche-moi la paix, notre salut c'est ton affaire..." (OE,I 1381). Thérèse's statement: "...Ah! je sais ce que c'est que la souffrance!" (DE 165) is reflected in Guillaume's words to Steeny: "J'en sais plus que vous maintenant, plus qu'aucun d'eux, j'ai trop souffert. Souffrir, voyez-vous, cela s'apprend" (OE ,I 1384).

As Thérèse, an innocent victim of holocaust, thought she was suffering her trial of faith for those who did not believe, so, too, does the young crippled boy feel that his friend's suffering is passing through him. Because his own childlike innocence is still intact, Guillaume clearly sees the danger inherent in Steeny's growing admiration for Monsieur Ouine. It is, as he realizes, a relationship without love, "un héroïsme à rebours" (OE,I 1389), which can only lead to the sacrifice of Steeny's childhood.

Innocent childhood is further portrayed as a victim in Guillaume through his suffering on behalf of his grandfather. For it is through his grandson that De Vandomme will finally be delivered from the ridiculous dream that his ancestors belonged to the nobility. It is as if the spirit of childhood and love were born again in the old man: "Une nouvelle, une miraculeuse jeunesse gonfle sa poitrine, sa gorge, jaillit tout à coup de ses yeux ainsi qu'un filet de sang tiède" (OE,I 1461). De Vandomme's refusal of love to his daughter and son-in-law, a common poacher whom he feared would bring dishonour on the family name, results in the senseless suicide of the young couple. His words to Guillaume: "je ne mangerai plus de leur pain" (OE,I 1458) are directly opposed to Thérèse's desire to eat at the table with sinners (HA 241-242). Viewed in Theresian terms, De Vandomme's "je ne mangerai plus de leur pain" highlights the problem underlying Monsieur Ouine's troubled characters: the refusal to accept the presence of evil in oneself and to show forth the merciful love of God to others.

ii) The Curé of Fenouille

Apart from Guillaume, the only other character in the novel who approaches Thérèse as a parallel image is the curé of Fenouille. Although he resembles the saint in his intense suffering and spirit of poverty, in many ways he proves an abortive attempt at portraying her spirituality.

The nature of the curé's problem is revealed in his conversation with Monsieur Ouine. He longs for someone to give him sympathy because he is afraid of the solitude he feels. The curé's action thus runs counter to Thérèse's acceptance of her inherent weakness and her abandonment to God. She had three older sisters in the monastery, but refused to look to them for consolation in her trials.

Contrary to the Carmelite, the young priest's actions do not always match his words. He admits to Monsieur Ouine that he accepts the presence of evil in the world: "Je ne me révolte pas contre le mal. Dieu ne s'est pas révolté contre lui, monsieur, il l'assume" (OE,I 1469). And in his sermon at the funeral of the little farm lad, he assures his parishioners that he loves them, even to the point of loving their sins (OE,I 1485). But we wonder if, as he claims he does, the curé really does accept the presence of evil and how far love really does enter into the prayer and suffering he offers for his parishioners. We know from her autobiography the extent to which love played a part in the Carmelite's suffering for others. Having discovered in the Letters of Saint Paul "que l'Eglise avait un

Coeur, et que ce Coeur était BRULANT d'AMOUR" (HA 222), Thérèse believed that her place in the church was to be this heart burning with love.

In contrast to the saint, the curé of Fenouille sees himself as "Un coeur qui bat hors du corps . . ." (OE,I 1485). He does not seem to have understood fully Saint Paul's teaching on the Mystical Body of Christ. In any case he does not truly possess Thérèse's concept of merciful love, for instead of turning to God and asking Him to fill his empty hands with what his parishioners need, the curé turns to them, begging their pity: "Je ne suis rien sans vous - moi - sans ma paroisse" (OE,I 1490). His refusal to bless the little corpse: "Que je bénisse aujourd'hui ce malheureux petit mort, à quoi ça pourrait bien vous servir? Il a été l'instrument innocent de votre perte et c'est votre péché à tous, je ne bénirai pas votre péché!" (OE,I 1490) can be interpreted by his parishioners as his refusal to admit that he, too, is a sinner in need of redemption. The priest is thus here a reverse image of Thérèse who admitted her need of God's mercy and placed herself in the ranks of sinners, stating: "Mais aussi ne peut-elle pas dire en son nom, au nom de ses frères: <u>Ayez pitié de nous Seigneur, car nous sommes de pauvres pécheurs!</u>..." (HA 242). The curé of Fenouille thus fails in his attempt to restore love among his parishioners because he does not provide them with a good role model of God's merciful love. Having nowhere to place their frustrated sense of guilt then, the parishioners project it onto the nearest scapegoat: Jambe-de-Laine will be sacrificed to their hate.

After the tragic killing of the chatelaine, the priest feels even more deeply his sense of solitude. He gives in to the temptation to wallow in self-pity and in doing so he recognizes "le germe de la révolte qui, de jour en jour, avait empoisonné son coeur" (OE,I 1514). Unlike Thérèse who, in a childlike fashion, accepted her weakness and abandoned herself to God, the curé of Fenouille persists in his refusal to accept his weakness. He thus remains enclosed in the circle of his solitude.

Indeed if we were to examine <u>Monsieur Ouine</u> from the reverse side of the tapestry, we would find the bright-coloured threads of Thérèse's spirit of childhood often replaced by the darker hues of the sacrifice of innocent childhood, the abuse of childhood by those whose own childhood was mistreated, and the longing of certain characters for a rebirth of the innocence of their childhood days. These reverse images of Thérèse's spirit of childhood are noted specifically in the three major characters: Steeny, Arsène, and Monsieur Ouine.

iii) Steeny

As one of Thérèse's principal virtues, her childlike simplicity shows itself in her desire for truth and her intrepidity in abandoning herself to God's merciful love. Reverse images of the confidence and abandonment so closely linked with the saint's simplicity are discovered in Steeny, the adolescent hero, who longs to break out of the bonds of childhood, to find out the truth about his father's disappearance, and to set forth on the adventure of life. In her autobiography, the saint describes how she longed to break out of her childhood bonds by correcting certain childish faults that she felt were preventing her from entering the Carmelite monastery. The young Thérèse abandoned herself to God, and on Christmas, 1886, she received the grace to leave behind the immaturity of childhood and set out on "une course de géant!..." (HA 113).

At the outset of his adventure, Steeny's thoughts are similarly fixed on "une vie toute neuve, toute brillante, intacte - intacte, immaculée - miraculeusement remise entre ses mains à son bon plaisir . . ." (OE,I 1409). The open road symbolizes his hope in the wonderful adventure leading to adulthood: "Qui n'a pas vu la route à l'aube, entre ces deux rangées d'arbres, toute fraîche, toute vivante, ne sait pas ce que c'est que l'espérance" (OE,I 1409). But contrary to the saint's "course de géant," the young hero's adventure leads him in the direction of evil as symbolized in the château, especially in Monsieur Ouine, its mysterious guest. Steeny's night spent with the former professor of languages might even be suggested as a negative parallel to the saint's Christmas conversion. But what has led the young man to set off on this type of adventure?

The adolescent hero longs to escape his unhappiness at home. His depression is the direct fruit of the suffering inflicted on him by the adults with whom he lives. Miss, Steeny's governess, an orphan, was sexually abused by an uncle with whom she had to live. Now she has found a haven in what seems to be a lesbian relationship with Michelle, Steeny's mother. Michelle, after the death of her father, spent her girlhood days with an overly protective mother who taught her not to trust men. Not knowing how to relate to the opposite sex, Michelle had an unhappy marriage with Steeny's father.

Toy imagery used by Bernanos to describe the painful relationship between the young boy's parents is reminiscent of Theresian imagery. Suffering from what she judges to have been her young husband's lack of true feeling for her, Michelle complains that he treated her like a toy he no longer wanted: "Il vous arrache de terre et cinq minutes après ne sait plus que faire de vous, cherche un coin sombre où déposer son jouet" (OE,I 1354). This image is a reversal of Thérèse's description of herself as the Christ Child's "petit jouet" (HA 158) and, in particular, "comme d'une petite balle de nulle valeur qu'il pouvait jeter à terre, pousser du pied, percer, laisser dans un coin ou bien presser sur son coeur si cela Lui faisait plaisir . . ." (HA 159).

Instead of accepting the truth about the whereabouts of her husband who refused to return to her after the war, Steeny's mother fortifies herself with lies. Her intimate relationship with her son's governess denies her son the affection that is rightly his. As Soeur Raymond-Marie notes: "La tristesse, l'angoisse même, que Steeny traîne d'une maison à l'autre, est celle du dégoût, parce que son enfance va de déception en déception."[9] The observation is accurate, for Steeny suffers an intense solitude and anguish that lead him to search for love in the wrong place.

Feeling excluded by the intimacy between his mother and his governess, Steeny longs to escape the unhappy atmosphere of his home which he describes to Guillaume as "une cage de brique avec deux jolies bêtes dedans, ce n'est pas une maison" (OE,I 1385). His mother withholds her affection since she fears in her son the image of her husband whose story she tries to conceal from the boy. Having the impression of being an outcast in his own home, Steeny declares to his governess: "Ici, Miss, c'est moi qui suis seul, vous le savez bien" (OE,I 1443). The adolescent boy is, as Soeur Raymond-Marie describes him, "exceptionnellement triste et seul parce qu'il a été trompé dans son droit à l'amour et à la vérité" ("Enf" 104).

It is no wonder, therefore, that at the age of fourteen, almost the same age as Thérèse was when she broke out of the "cercle étroit" (HA 117) keeping her from advancing to adulthood, Steeny also appears anxious to break out of his circle: "il continuait de tracer par habitude, autour de la maison sans âme, le même cercle chaque jour élargi. Pour le rompre, il n'a fallu que le signe d'une main étrangère . . ." (OE,I 1419). But in contrast to the saint who chose God to help her break out of her circle and launch her on her "course de géant," Steeny chooses Monsieur Ouine. The old professor will indeed help him break out of the circle of childhood but does so by setting him on the path of evil.

Confident in God from her earliest years, Thérèse felt certain that she was destined to become "une grande Sainte" (HA 85), but Steeny has doubts about Monsieur Ouine as a person. "C'est peut-être ce qu'ils appellent un saint?" (OE,I 1366), he wonders with a sort of comic terror, and, as Guillaume points out, his friend has no love for his new hero. The sense of fear that the very thought of the former professor of languages inspires in the young adolescent is thus a reverse image of the saint's statement: "Ah! le Seigneur est si bon pour moi qu'il m'est impossible de le craindre . . ." (HA 286). But Steeny remains indifferent to the integrity of the master whom he has just met: "Qu'importe la main, qu'importe le signe puisque l'attend quelque part une aventure faite pour lui, et un maître?" (OE,I 1419). The only thing of importance for the young boy is that his hero help him replace his unhappy childhood with some sort of adventure.

With his voice already beginning to resemble Monsieur Ouine's, Steeny gradually becomes aware of a certain bond built on mutual solitude between himself and the former professor. Pupil and master thus converse together "dans l'ombre, d'égal à égal, ainsi que deux vagabonds au détour d'une route inconnue, dans une solitude parfaite" (OE,I 1556). Their ambiguous union in solitude is in contrast to Thérèse of Lisieux' union with God based on love alone.

Under the tutelage of their masters, both pupils undergo an interior change. On the night of her conversion, Thérèse learned the meaning of merciful love, for God performed in an instant what she claimed that she herself had not been able to accomplish in ten years: "En un instant l'ouvrage que je n'avais pu faire en 10 ans, Jésus le fit se contentant de ma bonne volonté qui jamais ne me fit défaut" (HA 114-115). Thérèse learned from her Christmas conversion that love means an emptying of oneself for the other. Her encounter with compassionate love would lead her to offer herself as a victim of holocaust for the salvation of others.

As a reverse image of the saint, Steeny learns from Monsieur Ouine that "love" is a hollow word, that life itself is essentially meaningless. A short time later, we find the adolescent hero reciting the lesson he has just been taught: "Il n'y a pas que la justice, il y a la miséricorde, le pardon. Ou rien peut-être, absolument rien, pourquoi pas?" (OE,I 1557).

But does Steeny really believe this or is he simply imitating the old professor's cynicism? Whatever the case may be, the young boy's interior life is in danger of becoming empty, devoid of spiritual values, and, therefore, in absolute contrast to the richness of Thérèse's interior life. If Steeny is on the road to becoming another Monsieur Ouine through the sacrifice of his childhood, just what exactly is the mysterious bond that ties him to the old professor?

Since it is clear that there is no true love in their union, their relationship must be based entirely on self gratification. As William Bush indicates, Steeny and Monsieur Ouine are mutually useful: "M. Ouine se sert de Steeny comme le garçon se sert de son maître. En reconnaissant cette vérité, Steeny devient homme."[10] The adolescent hero's passage into adulthood has been purchased at the expense of the positive qualities of childhood. Love, the only thing which a child is really capable of giving, has been destroyed at its root.

iv) Arsène, the Mad Mayor of Fenouille

In spite of the fact that in Monsieur Ouine childhood is generally considered as a weakness to be eradicated as quickly as possible, two characters, Arsène, the mayor of Fenouille, and Monsieur Ouine, the eponymous hero, possess a certain nostalgia for the lost innocence of their childhood. When the body of the murdered farmboy is brought to the mayor's office, those investigating the crime treat the young victim's corpse with little respect. People's true attitude towards the spirit of childhood seems to emerge before what William Bush appropriately calls "la présence gênante du petit cadavre" (AM 60). Those who have long since lost their childhood innocence seem to regard the presence of a murdered child as some kind of reproach which they cannot face.

Considering it to be a humiliation to his position as mayor to have an unsolved murder on his hands, Arsène simply shrugs his shoulders in disgust and says to the doctor: "On appelle ça une victime. En un sens, docteur, je trouve ça peut-être plus répugnant à voir que le coupable. Un coupable, c'est pareil à vous, ça vient, ça va, ça respire, c'est vivant" (OE,I 1398). The mayor fears losing his position over the unsolved crime, but at the same time he is obsessed with his guilt as a womanizer.

Arsène's obsession is manifested through his frustrated attempts to regain his former innocence. Madame Marchal, Monsieur Ouine's nurse, expresses her view of the mayor's actions as: "C'est un homme qui a trop vécu, un vieux débauché. Il a peur de la mort, de l'enfer" (OE,I 1538). Perhaps indeed Arsène fears God's justice on account of his sins. The insensitive, non-believing doctor however views the mayor's obsession as a scientist. He tells Arsène: "Vous êtes un enfant, mon cher" (OE,I 1399) and then explains how he resembles a number of men in their sixties who suddeny become scrupulous over their past sins. For the most part, the doctor interprets Arsène's longing for childhood purity as sheer nonsense: "Alors, on rêve d'innocence, de pureté, de rachat - que sais-je? des bêtises" (OE,I 1400).

Receiving no understanding from the doctor, the mayor turns to his wife, Malvina, who also is unable to restore his innocence. She has listened to his disgusting "confessions" time after time and is willing enough to forgive all his indiscretions, but that is not sufficient for Arsène. He is vaguely aware of being called to something better than his present state: "Mais j'étais fait pour être autre chose que je suis, comprends-tu? - je ne sais quoi... tiens! une truite dans l'eau du moulin, quelque chose de frais, de pur..." (OE,I 1437). Arsène feels that no one but a child, a little child, can really understand his longing (OE,I 1438).

At the funeral of the little cowherd, the mayor makes a third attempt to free himself of his burden of guilt. When he begins his speech, he falsely interprets the looks on the faces of the villagers as fraternal sympathy. He wrongly concludes that everyone else is also looking for a deliverance from guilt: "Vont-ils connaître eux et lui, tous ensemble, l'oubli, le bienheureux oubli des fautes passées, le bienheureux pardon?" (OE,I 1496). But the jeering crowd sees only the ridiculous side of their mayor babbling incoherently at the graveside.

The fog-like pall of evil hanging over Fenouille and giving Bernanos' last novel its atmosphere of ambiguity is symbolical of Arsène's interior suffering as were Thérèse's images, "les plus épaisses ténèbres" (HA 241) and "un pays environné d'un épais brouillard" (HA 241), describing her own interior struggles. In her trial of faith the saint was to know the suffering of those who have never possessed, or who have ceased to possess, the gift of faith.

Interiorly Arsène's faith is dead. He suffers in solitude, for, as Yves Bridel notes with regard to the inhabitants in general of Fenouille: "Plus rien ne les retient ensemble, plus rien ne les relie à Dieu. Sa grâce ne peut pas circuler, il n'y a plus de communion, plus de barrière pour le péché" (EE 126). Arsène's suffering is virtually sterile because it does not bring spiritual good to others. So also would Thérèse's suffering have been sterile had she not, in a spirit of faith, accepted God's will for her. The Carmelite lovingly accepted her suffering in order to give spiritual life to others; thus, we read in her autobiography: "Je vois que la souffrance seule peut enfanter les âmes . . ." (HA 198) and "je sais que Jésus ne peut désirer pour nous de souffrances inutiles . . ." (HA 206). By willingly offering herself as a victim to merciful love for the salvation of others, Thérèse's trial of faith is transformed into productive suffering for the church.

In contrast to Thérèse, Arsène lacks faith, but the curé of Fenouille's attempt to help him spiritually is of no avail. Longing for some kind of salvation, the mayor declares: "Un homme ne peut-il une fois, une seule fois - une fois dans toute la vie - espérer le salut!" (OE,I 1517). Nor does the mayor seem to understand when the priest tells him that he is not supposed to hate himself.

When the priest continues trying to reason with Arsène he tells him that he could hardly expect the villagers to save him when only a few minutes after his speech their hands were to be steeped in Jambe-de-Laine's blood. Suddenly the word "blood" triggers in Arsène's mind his memory of tales of ancient purification rites. The priest insists that it is neither blood nor water that will restore purity of heart "Mais la grâce de Dieu fait du plus endurci un petit enfant" (OE,I 1520). He then offers the mayor the path to the restoration of childhood innocence through sacramental confession, but the latter cannot accept it.

Like Thérèse, Arsène suffers from a sense of impotence. Unlike her, he cannot accept himself in his human condition. Accepting her suffering in the spirit of Saint Paul, Thérèse of Lisieux joyfully proclaimed: "je ne me fais pas de peine en voyant que je suis la <u>faiblesse</u> même, au contraire c'est en elle que je me glorifie . . ." (<u>HA</u> 257).

The Carmelite's confidence in God's merciful love is also completely absent in Arsène. Thérèse stated that even if the burden of all the sins of the world were on her conscience she would still abandon herself to God because of His merciful love for sinners (<u>HA</u> 298). Arsène, however, acknowledges his wrongdoings, but refuses to love himself in spite of them, saying to the curé: "Je ne veux pas me pardonner . . ." (<u>OE</u>,I 1521). Neither does he believe that God will forgive him. Unable to recognize that through the simple admission of his need of God's mercy he could recover his childhood innocence, the mayor remains trapped in a vicious circle of guilt and despair.

v) *Monsieur Ouine*

Like Arsène, Monsieur Ouine has suffered much in his lifetime and now, near the hour of death, he longs to be reunited with his childhood. Ambiguous images of Thérèse appearing in the description of the former professor of languages bring to light the eponymous hero's rather complex role in the novel. As Claude-Edmonde Magny explains in her article, "La part du diable dans la littérature contemporaine," Monsieur Ouine "est vraiment l'incarnation du Mal; mais c'est en même temps un être concret, vivant, un personnage comme les autres, - comme nous."[11] While basically a reverse image of the saint, there is the occasional suggestion of a parallel image.

In Monsieur Ouine's description of himself to Steeny, we detect certain childlike qualities that could have been directed to a good purpose, but that have, on the contrary, become perverted. For example, the eponymous hero speaks to Steeny about what he considers to be his simplicity: "Je suis devenu un homme simple, très simple, je ne calcule plus" (OE,I 1368). These words recall similar ones spoken by Chantal de Clergerie who reflected so well the saint of Lisieux. When Monsieur Ouine describes himself as being: "Comme ces gelées vivantes, au fond de la mer, je flotte et j'absorbe" (OE,I 1368), what started out as a parallel image of Thérèse becomes a reverse image. Unlike the saint who in her simplicity freely and lovingly chose to abandon herself to God's will and to offer her life for the salvation of others, Monsieur Ouine chooses not to choose, but rather to draw into himself all that comes his way with no thought for anyone or anything other than satisfying his inordinate curiosity.

This perversion of childlike simplicity and generosity is the fruit of the suffering he experienced in childhood. Bernanos reveals how his eponymous hero was a lonely little boy seduced at the age of twelve by one of his teachers at the very moment when he was about to confide in him (OE,I 1472-1473).

As a result of the sacrifice of his own childhood, Monsieur Ouine's thoughts on childhood in general tend to be enigmatic. At one point he declares to the curé of Fenouille: "L'innocence, monsieur, est une maladie propre à l'âge mûr" (OE,I 1463), thus viewing childhood as something to be ridiculed and avoided. But, when he tells the school teacher that he has always honoured childhood, the former professor of languages seems to be advocating Thérèse's teaching of spiritual childhood: "L'enfance est le sel de la terre. Qu'elle s'affadisse, et le monde ne sera bientôt que pourriture et gangrène" (OE,I 1492). His apparent seduction of the young Steeny, however, would encourage us to believe that he does not practise what he preaches. Indeed, since his own childhood was violated, Monsieur Ouine tends to reject the spirit of childhood by projecting suffering on those who are still in possession of their innocence.

His own sad experience as a child has also led the eponymous hero to turn in on himself. The positive qualities of love and confidence which he had as a boy have changed into indifference and the desire to possess others, to know their innermost secrets and thereby control their actions. And just as Steeny desires to possess Monsieur Ouine's knowledge, so does the old professor desire to possess the adolescent's youth. As he has used Anthelme and Jambe-de-Laine, so now Monsieur Ouine makes use of the young boy who, when he observed him going along the road, reminded him so much of himself as a youth (OE,I 1369).

The eponymous hero is the opposite of Thérèse who in her frequent encounters with the novices under her care never gave in to curiosity or to the desire to possess them. Instead of looking for self-fulfilment in her position as assistant mistress of novices, she allowed the novices to use her, to exhaust her limited strength. "Le bon Dieu m'a permis que les novices m'épuisent" (DE 98), the saint confessed to her sister, Pauline. Monsieur Ouine's hunger for souls: "La curiosité me dévore . . . Telle est ma faim. Que n'ai-je été curieux des choses! Mais je n'ai eu faim que des âmes" (OE,I 1557-1558) also parallels in a negative manner the thirst Thérèse felt for souls after her conversion: "Je voulais donner à boire à mon Bien-Aimé et je me sentais moi-même dévorée de la soif des âmes..." (HA 115).

As a further reverse image of the saint's desire to offer souls to God, Monsieur Ouine plays God with the souls of those with whom he comes in contact: "La sécurité de ces âmes était entre mes mains, et elles ne le savaient pas, je la leur cachais ou découvrais tour à tour . . . je me donnais ce passe-temps de Dieu . . ." (OE,I 1558). A reaction to the fact that love was denied to him as a child, the eponymous hero's refusal to love is a reverse image of the saint who, through the experience of self-sacrificing love within her family, learned how to reach out to others in love. Genuine love of God and humanity enabled her to break the symbolic circle of self-centeredness, whereas the refusal to love continues to imprison Monsieur Ouine within the "cercle enchanté, rétréci chaque jour . . ." (OE,I 1470).

Although disillusioned as a child, Monsieur Ouine recognizes the importance of childhood and, like Arsène, deeply regrets the loss of his own innocence. Jambe-de-Laine tells Steeny how the old professor recognized himself in Steeny the first time he saw him: "Je viens de me revoir moi-même, dit-il, comme un mort regarde dans le passé... Le petit garçon que j'étais, je l'ai vu, j'aurais pu le toucher, l'entendre..." (OE,I 1422-1423). This longing for the restoration of his childhood innocence increases as Monsieur Ouine approaches his end. His words to Steeny: "Je m'épuise en efforts, non pour me retrouver: pour me rejoindre. Oui, pour me rejoindre, ainsi que les deux parts d'un serpent tranché par la bêche" (OE,I 1548) reveal his struggle to enter into death accompanied by his childhood.

Monsieur Ouine's death scene forms a negative counterpart to the death of the saint of Lisieux; yet it is not surprising that at Monsieur Ouine's deathbed one or two parallel images of Thérèse emerge. As William Bush points out, Monsieur Ouine's suffering is real and as such begs our compassion: "Monsieur Ouine, si grand pécheur qu'il soit, devient néanmoins humain et digne de notre compassion par l'effet de sa souffrance" (SE 89). Suffering was the eponymous hero's constant companion from childhood days just as it was the saint's.

Since both the saint and the eponymous hero suffer and die from tuberculosis (OE,I 1359), there are certain resemblances in the physical details of their suffering such as their spells of coughing and difficulty in breathing. Thérèse's rather surprising words on the day of her death: ". . . j'ai de force aujourd'hui! Non, je ne vais pas mourir! J'en ai encore pour des mois, peut-être des années!" (DE 183) are reflected in Madame Marchal's words about Monsieur Ouine the day of his death: "Et il peut vivre longtemps encore" (OE,I 1534). Similarly, Monsieur Ouine's feeling of hunger, "Je suis enragé de faim, je crève de faim" (OE,I 1551), when examined from a purely literal interpretation, parallels the saint's craving for food when she was no longer able to enjoy it: "C'est inouï, maintenant que je ne puis plus manger, il me prend des envies de toutes sortes de bonnes choses . . ." (DE 127-128).

The presence of Steeny at the deathbed scene is significant in that it emphasizes the old professor's longing for childhood to help him enter death:

"Que ne puis-je voir cette chose par vos yeux! Je dis vos yeux, vos vrais yeux, . . . vos yeux si neufs, si frais" (OE,I 1547).

But, as with Arsène, the desire for childhood is not enough in itself. Monsieur Ouine needs to recognize his impotence and abandon himself to God's merciful love. Contrary to the eponymous hero, Thérèse approached death with a childlike attitude of confidence and thus she was able to console her sisters: "Si vous me trouviez morte un matin, n'ayez pas de peine: c'est que Papa le bon Dieu serait venu tout simplement me chercher" (DE 41).

Thérèse's childlike relationship with God as heavenly Father strengthened her spiritually and made her aware of what was taking place in her soul. She was able, therefore, to describe how various trials and feelings affected her: "Si mon âme n'était pas toute remplie d'avance par l'abandon à la volonté du bon Dieu, . . . ce serait un flot de douleur bien amer et je ne pourrais le supporter" (DE 69). As a reverse image of the Carmelite saint, Monsieur Ouine's interior emptiness is so vast that in place of his soul he experiences "un vide, une attente, une aspiration intérieure" (OE,I 1560). And so the eponymous hero believes that his soul has become a spiritual void into which he has fallen. Although his words, "Je suis tombé en elle, jeune homme, de la manière dont les élus tombent en Dieu" (OE,I 1560), echo to some extent the saint's words, "c'est dans les bras du bon Dieu que je tombe!" (DE 169), the contrast between the state of Thérèse's soul and that of Monsieur Ouine's is striking.

The dying professor's spiritual emptiness is further portrayed in Steeny's story of the empty bottle. If, as William Bush suggests, the sailors represent Steeny and Monsieur Ouine and the captain of the ship is God whom "les marins ont renié pour s'embarquer à la recherche du secret de la vie, de cette bouteille vide . . ." (AM 180), the bottle is empty because true fulfilment cannot be found in material creation. Since Monsieur Ouine has never bothered to develop a relationship with the Creator, his soul is empty of spiritual values. For this reason, he has no secrets, no message of any importance to hand on to Steeny who represents the next generation. Nevertheless, at the hour of death, the elderly professor of languages is able to speak the truth of his inner being: "Je suis vide, moi aussi . . ." (OE,I 1550), "Je n'ai pas de secrets . . ." (OE,I 1554), and what is even more revealing, "J'ai besoin d'un secret . . ." (OE,I 1555) and "Cela me sauverait . . ." (OE,I 1555). Can these surprising statements possibly be the result of a special grace at the hour of death?

Examined in the light of Thérèse of Lisieux, salvation would be possible for Monsieur Ouine. William Bush's theory of the professor's rehabilitation illustrates how during his last moments Monsieur Ouine admits his wrongdoing and calls upon the spirit of childhood in the person of Steeny to help him. This act represents a supreme effort at his final hour "pour rassembler ses années en désordre et entrer dans la maison du Père, son enfance en tête, comme une avant-garde protectrice" (AM 29).

That Steeny may have dreamed the whole scene is not all that important in the sense that Bernanos allows his heroes to have their private moments with God in which their fate is known by Him alone. We certainly cannot deny the fact that Thérèse's words, "tout est grâce" (DE 41), are just as much present in this particular death scene as in the other death scenes in Bernanos' fictional world. And what is the secret Monsieur Ouine craves if not a longing for someone to reveal to him the way to discover the spiritual values that are absent in his soul? Through the simple admission of his weakness and his need for a new childhood, Monsieur Ouine can find Redemption, for God, in His merciful love, waits for the world to admit its guilt and its need of Him.

vi) The Parish of Fenouille

As for the congregation of the despiritualized parish of Fenouille, the words of their curé, "Dieu va se faire, dans cette paroisse, je le présume, plus petit que jamais!" (OE,I 1508), serve as a warning that if the spirit of childhood is not respected, if the true meaning of love is not fostered, and if suffering is not accepted with confidence in God's mercy, then God will no longer be present among His people. In contrast to Thérèse's suffering, that of the characters we have examined in <u>Monsieur Ouine</u> tends to be devoid of either temporal or spiritual value. The Carmelite's suffering would also have been sterile had she not lovingly united it with Christ's suffering in order to give spiritual birth to others.

Bernanos' fictional world of Fenouille stands as a symbol of modern civilization in which spiritual values are no longer present. When viewed from the front of the tapestry, we realize that the rich threads which are so invisible from the reverse side are those of a spirituality which is undisputedly Theresian in nature.

NOTES

CHAPTER 7

[1] William Bush, Genèse et structures d'"Un Mauvais rêve" (Paris: Minard Archives des Lettres Modernes, 1982) 30.

[2] Henri Debluë, Les romans de Georges Bernanos ou le défi du rêve (Neuchâtel: Editions de la Baconnière, 1965) 73-74.

[3] Charles Moeller, Man and Salvation in Literature, trans. Charles Underhill Quinn (Notre Dame, Indiana: University of Notre Dame Press, 1970) 116.

[4] William Bush, "Ordre de composition de 'M. Ouine,'" Bulletin de la société des amis de Georges Bernanos 48 (1962): 11-12.

[5] Alfred Cobban, A History of Modern France, vol. 2, From the First Empire to the Fourth Republic 1799-1945 (Harmondsworth, Middlesex, England: Penguin Books Ltd., 1961) 291-293.
  Leslie Derfler, The Third French Republic 1870-1940 (Malabar, Florida: Robert E. Krieger Publishing Company, 1982) 87-89.

[6] Hans Aaraas, "Les deux paroisses," La Revue des Lettres Modernes 108-110 (1964) "Etudes bernanosiennes" 5: 89.

[7] William Bush, "Vision créatrice et tentation littéraire," Courrier Georges Bernanos 2-3-4 (1971): 83.

[8] Claude-Edmonde Magny, "'Monsieur Ouine,' le dernier roman de Bernanos," La Revue des Lettres Modernes 108-110 (1964) "Etudes bernanosiennes" 5: 12. Cited hereafter as "MO."

[9] Soeur Raymond-Marie, "L'enfant, présence de choc," La Revue des Lettres Modernes 108-110 (1964) "Etudes bernanosiennes" 5: 108. Cited hereafter as "Enf."

[10] William Bush, L'angoisse du mystère (Paris: Minard Lettres Modernes, 1966) 57. Cited hereafter as AM.

[11] Claude-Edmonde Magny, "La part du diable dans la littérature contemporaine," Satan, ed. Père Bruno de Jésus-Marie (Paris: Desclée de Brouwer, 1948) 592.

CHAPTER 8

THERESIAN SPIRITUALITY ON THE SUPERNATURAL LEVEL IN JOURNAL D'UN CURÉ DE CAMPAGNE (1934-1936)

Bernanos abandoned Monsieur Ouine in the summer of 1934 to write Un crime which had been interrupted by the move to Majorca in October. The first version of Un crime completed by Christmas, the author began Journal d'un curé de campagne, the novel generally recognized as his masterpiece. It was completed towards the end of January, 1936. In his article, "Genèse du 'Journal d'un curé de campagne,'" Michel Estève emphasizes the relation between Monsieur Ouine and Journal d'un curé de campagne: "En novembre ou décembre 1934, le Journal d'un Curé de Campagne est ainsi né au premier tiers du chapitre XVI de Monsieur Ouine, abandonné environ quatre mois auparavant."[1] In complete contrast to the despair felt in writing Monsieur Ouine, Bernanos speaks with pleasure of his new novel in a letter written in January, 1935 to Robert Vallery-Radot: "J'ai commencé un beau vieux livre, que vous aimerez, je crois" (Corr. II 46). Journal d'un curé de campagne is the diary of a young priest posted to his first parish. Somewhat naïve, the curé of Ambricourt is easily taken in by others, and all his wonderful plans are doomed to failure right from the start. But in spite of this, Bernanos declares about his priest-hero: "alors qu'il croira tout perdu, il aura servi le bon Dieu dans la mesure même où il croira l'avoir desservi" (Corr.II 47).

Bernanos' apparent love for Journal d'un curé de campagne is due perhaps to the fact that the novel is in some ways a reply to Monsieur Ouine. In both novels the parish priest comes face to face with a parish entrenched in spiritual decay, but each priest handles the presence of evil differently. As Yves Bridel observes: "Nous voyons Fenouille à travers l'angoisse et peut-être le désespoir de l'auteur; nous voyons Ambricourt à travers la charité, l'espérance et la foi du curé et de Bernanos" (EE 143).

We have seen that although the curé of Fenouille portrays certain characteristics of the Carmelite saint, he seems powerless in his anguish over the presence of evil around him. In contrast, the curé of Ambricourt gradually learns to accept the presence of evil and to abandon himself to God's merciful love. He actually lives out in full the spirituality of Thérèse of Lisieux.

Almost every Bernanosian scholar has commented on the sole explicit reference to Thérèse in Journal d'un curé de campagne: her words, "tout est grâce" (DE 41), uttered by the curé of Ambricourt at the moment of his death (OE,I 1259). And though the saint's name never appears in the novel, her presence is implicit in the thoughts and actions of the novel's priest-hero, just as it is in his dying words.

Indeed several critics have already noted implicit images of the little Carmelite in Journal d'un curé de campagne. The first of these is Hans Urs von Balthasar who claims that the saint's presence in this great novel has been raised from the temporal to the spiritual plane (von B 289). Von Balthasar draws our attention to the fact that both Thérèse and the curé of Ambricourt refer constantly to their insignificance and that they possess a similar attitude of "all or nothing." This critic also detects how both saint and priest-hero express the desire to have an ordinary death (von B 289) and that, as the hour of death approaches, they experience the fear of not knowing how to die (von B 426). In the curé's words: "J'entends bien qu'un homme sûr de lui-même, de son courage, puisse désirer faire de son agonie une chose parfaite, accomplie. Faute de mieux, la mienne sera, ce qu'elle pourra, rien de plus" (OE,I 1256), Von Balthasar detects a parallel image of Thérèse's words: "Ma Mère, est-ce l'agonie?... Comment vais-je faire pour mourir? Jamais je ne vais savoir mourir!..." (DE 180).

In her article on Bernanos and the spirit of childhood, Soeur Raymond-Marie has also noticed certain elements of Thérèse's spirituality in the young curé. She believes that a comparative reading of the Derniers entretiens and the last fifty or so pages of Journal d'un curé de campagne is the best guide to discovering Theresian elements in the young priest's spirituality and his simplicity when facing death ("R-M" 309). Soeur Raymond-Marie maintains further that for both the saint and the priest-hero the words "tout est grâce" are far more than a simple acceptance of dying without the last sacraments of the Church. They testify rather to "une même adhésion pleine et amoureuse à la volonté divine" ("R-M" 306).

This same critic then draws up a list of parallel spiritual traits found in the Carmelite saint and the curé of Ambricourt such as their supernatural joy, simplicity, spiritual poverty, childlike abandonment, joy in the knowledge of their nothingness, humility, and loving confidence in God ("R-M" 309-310). For Soeur Raymond-Marie the nature and number of the parallels between the priest and the saint highlight the author's own spirituality: "Bernanos n'a pas imité sainte Thérèse, il a pénétré fort avant dans la voie d'enfance, la voie de son christianisme" ("R-M" 310).

Another interesting parallel established by this scholar concerns the similarity between Thérèse's and Bernanos' idea of the Virgin Mary. Thérèse felt that a sermon on the Mother of God should reveal her life as having been a very ordinary one, but one that was filled with hidden virtues that everyone can imitate (DE 141). As Soeur Raymond-Marie correctly states, the curé of Torcy's sermons on the Virgin Mary reveal the reality of her life, a life that consisted not in human glory and miracles, but rather in the practice of poverty, solitude, and simplicity ("R-M" 313-314).

In his 1960 article on Bernanos and Thérèse, Guy Gaucher also speaks of the little Carmelite's influence on the spirituality of Bernanos' country priest declaring that: "Lui est vraiment le fils spirituel de la carmélite, il vit de la petite voie d'enfance et meurt en prononçant les mots qui résument son message de paix et de joie" ("BT" 265).

Gaucher notes, in particular, how the saint and the priest-hero use the same imagery of a wall to describe the feeling that each has of being abandoned by God ("BT" 260). The young priest's words: "Derrière moi il n'y avait rien. Et devant moi un mur, un mur noir" (OE,I 1111) form a parallel image of Thérèse's description of her trial of faith: "c'est un mur qui s'élève jusqu'aux cieux et couvre le firmament étoilé..." (HA 244).

Similarly both the Carmelite and the curé of Ambricourt find the fulfilment of God's will in the practice of the simple virtues of ordinary daily life. Thérèse's statement: "Je m'appliquais surtout à pratiquer les petites vertus, n'ayant pas la facilité d'en pratiquer de grandes . . ." (HA 183) parallels the curé's comment about himself: "Car je n'ai de réussite qu'aux petites choses, et si souvent éprouvé par l'inquiétude, je dois reconnaître que je triomphe dans les petites joies" (OE,I 1255).

In addition, Gaucher notes that like Thérèse, Bernanos' saints die young ("BT" 254). Thus the young country priest believes that his journey here on earth will be of short duration. His thoughts: "Je me demandais: 'Que ferai-je à cinquante, à soixante ans?' Et, naturellement, je ne trouvais pas de réponse. Je ne pouvais pas même en imaginer une. Il n'y avait pas de vieillard en moi" (OE,I 1254) echo the Carmelite's words to her sister, Pauline: "...Depuis mon enfance, le bon Dieu m'a donné le sentiment profond que je mourrais jeune" (DE 75).

Gaucher reveals further evidence of Thérèse's presence in Journal d'un curé de campagne in the remarkable similarity between the saint and the priest-hero's mentor, the curé of Torcy, in their attitude towards life ("BT" 251). The critic compares the Carmelite's discovery of the way to become a saint "par la fidélité aux plus petites choses" (HA 87) to the curé of Torcy's advice to the younger priest about applying himself to the little tasks of daily life: "fais des petites choses, en attendant, au jour le jour. . . . Les petites choses n'ont l'air de rien, mais elles donnent la paix. . . . La prière des petites choses est innocente" (OE,I 1191-1192).

This same scholar shows a further correlation between the words of the older priest and those of Thérèse. His comment, "Mais c'est du sentiment de sa propre impuissance que l'enfant tire humblement le principe même de sa joie" (OE,I 1045) reflects the joy that the saint discovered in her feeling of impotence: "Je ne suis qu'une enfant, impuissante et faible, cependant c'est ma faiblesse même qui me donne l'audace de m'offrir en Victime à ton Amour, ô Jésus!" (HA 223). Such parallels in word and thought lead Gaucher to conclude that the analogy with Thérèse of Lisieux' teaching on the spirit of childhood is most striking in Journal d'un curé de campagne ("BT" 251-252).

In 1965 Henri Debluë reaffirmed in his critical study, Les romans de Georges Bernanos ou le défi du rêve, that "la spiritualité du curé d'Ambricourt est proche de celle de la sainte de Lisieux. Il a l'esprit d'enfance, d'humilité, de pauvreté, d'abandon, il est sous le signe de la divine Agonie."[2] Debluë adds to our knowledge of Thérèse's présence in the novel by établissant a rapport between the young priest's vision of the Virgin Mary and the saint's miraculous cure at the age of ten. Thus, the critic is able to proclaim that a parallel event from Thérèse's life gives credence to the curé's vision and imparts a supernatural sanction to his life (Défi 249).

The following year, Yves Bridel also commented on this vision. What interests him in particular is the similarity between Bernanos' description of the Virgin Mary's hands in Journal d'un curé de campagne and Thérèse's hands in Les Grands Cimetières sous la lune (EE 167). Bernanos writes of the former:

"C'était une main d'enfant, d'enfant pauvre, déjà usée par le travail, les lessives" (OE,I 1197), while of the latter he states that "de ses petites mains innocentes, de ses terribles petites mains expertes au découpage des fleurs de papier, mais aussi rongées par le chlore des lessives et les engelures" (OE,II 504) Thérèse has sown the seed of a spiritual message.

Bridel then discloses how the curé of Ambricourt's description of himself as "un malheureux mendiant qui va, la main tendue, de porte en porte, sans oser seulement frapper" (OE,I 1141) corresponds to what we have already seen to be one of Thérèse's favourite images of Christ: "Il se fait pauvre afin que nous puissions Lui faire la charité, Il nous tend la main comme un mendiant . . ." (LT 251). In his humble attitude of begging love or compassion from those with whom he comes in contact, the young priest thus imitates the saint's interpretation of the love that Christ practises towards humanity (EE 179). In his spiritual poverty the curé "fut, comme sainte Thérèse voyait Jésus, non celui qui console, mais celui qui doit être consolé et qui réclame l'amour" (EE 165). But the priest-hero's self-description also recalls the saint's own way of approaching God: "on agit comme les pauvres qui tendent la main afin de recevoir ce qui leur est nécessaire . . ." (HA 259). Thérèse advised Céline to approach God in a similar fashion by using words such as: "je vous tends la main comme une petite mendiante et je suis sûre que vous m'exaucerez pleinement . . ." (DE 198). Bridel further indicates (EE 179) how images used by Thérèse to describe her littleness, such as "Je suis une petite graine . . ." (DE 86), are echoed in the priest-hero's self-description, "Je n'ai d'abord été que cette étincelle, ce grain de poussière rougeoyant de la divine charité" (OE,I 1113).

In his various critical works on Bernanos, Michel Estève compares the spiritual as well as the physical suffering of the curé of Ambricourt to the Carmelite saint's suffering. He believes that the young priest's "nuit affreuse" is comparable to the saint's "nuit profonde" as described in the Histoire d'une âme.[3] In another of his critical works on Bernanos, Estève points out that for the curé of Ambricourt, as well as for the little Carmelite, the trial of faith "passe par un 'sombre tunnel': celui du silence et du doute, de l'angoisse et du sentiment d'abandon."[4]

Although he states incorrectly that both Thérèse and the curé of Ambricourt die at dawn,[5] Estève notes several important parallels between the death of the saint and that of the priest-hero. He focuses on the desire of both for an ordinary death, on the fear of death experienced by both, and on the curé's belief, similar to the saint's, that his hemorrhage was a sign of tuberculosis ("NG" 103-104). The curé's words shortly before his death: "Que le premier regard du Seigneur, lorsque m'apparaîtra sa Sainte Face, soit donc un regard qui rassure!" (OE,I 1256) recall the last part of Thérèse's name "de la Sainte-Face." Estève also claims that the curé of Ambricourt's statement that "l'agonie humaine est d'abord un acte d'amour" (OE,I 1256) reflects the saint's comment to Pauline: "Notre-Seigneur est mort sur la Croix, dans les angoisses, et voilà pourtant la plus belle mort d'amour" (DE 56).

As Estève has also observed, Manuscript C, the final part of the Histoire d'une âme which the saint composed in June, 1897, has the character of an intimate journal and Thérèse's temptation to suicide described here finds a parallel in the curé's account of his temptation ("NG" 104).

Certainly Bernanos' choice of a fictional diary corresponds well with the saint's autobiography since both literary forms tend to present an authentique first person account of the spiritual adventure of their respective "authors." The saint's aim in writing the story of her soul was to testify to God's presence in her life through the special graces He had bestowed upon her: "Voilà bien le mystère de ma vocation, de ma vie tout entière et surtout le mystère des privilèges de Jésus sur mon âme..." (HA 20). And as the saint reflects on the spiritual gifts she has received, her autobiography becomes an extension of her prayer. The curé of Ambricourt's goal in writing his diary is his desire to achieve a greater awareness of God's presence in his life, and so he says about his diary: "Dans mon idée, il devait être une conversation entre le bon Dieu et moi, un prolongement de la prière, une façon de tourner les difficultés de l'oraison, qui me paraissent encore trop souvent insurmontables . . ." (OE,I 1048).

Thérèse realized that the account of the events she intended to narrate in Manuscript C would come as no surprise to Mère Marie de Gonzague, at whose request she was writing this portion of her autobiography. Her statement: "vous connaissez depuis longtemps ce que je pense et tous les événements un peu mémorables de ma vie; je ne saurais donc vous apprendre rien de nouveau" (HA 289) finds a parallel image in the curé of Ambricourt's thoughts that if the curé of Torcy were to read his diary he would not learn anything new: "Ce que je vais fixer sur le papier n'apprendrait pas grand-chose au seul ami avec lequel il m'arrive encore de parler à coeur ouvert . . ." (OE,I 1036).

Both the saint and the priest-hero are aware of the value that their writing may have for others some day. Thus Thérèse's words, "ces pages feront beaucoup de bien" (DE 107), are paralleled in the curé d'Ambricourt's thoughts regarding the usefulness of his diary: "- qui sait? utile à moi, ou à d'autres" (OE,I 1117).

Journal d'un curé de campagne reflects the Histoire d'une âme in the sense that each work bears witness to evolution in the spirituality of its "author." Thérèse's autobiographical manuscripts reveal that she had to learn how to accept her impotence and that she did not always experience joy in suffering. Only gradually did the saint come to an awareness of the depths of her call to merciful love. Bernanos' novel shows the sincere efforts the young priest makes to understand and live out his vocation to the priesthood. Although much implicit general evidence of the Carmelite's presence in Journal d'un curé de campagne has already been detected, more specific observations can be made regarding the influence of the saint's spirituality on both the curé of Torcy and the curé of Ambricourt.

The Curé of Torcy

The role played by the curé of Torcy in helping the younger priest discern his vocation parallels certain events in the life of Thérèse of Lisieux. At times the older priest resembles Père Alexis Prou, the retreat master who reassured Thérèse about her special call, for although the curé of Torcy gently rebukes the curé of Ambricourt by telling him not to behave like a child, he nonetheless recognizes the potential spiritual strength the latter possesses in his natural childlike manner and innate sense of poverty. Just as Père Prou recognized Thérèse's superior spirituality and launched her on the way of confidence and abandonment to merciful love, so too does the curé of Torcy in his conversations with the curé of Ambricourt launch him on the path of spiritual childhood and poverty. The older priest's words to his young friend on the spirit of childhood are in essence the doctrine of Thérèse of Lisieux. The curé of Ambricourt proves to be fertile soil for his mentor's teaching, for he readily admits his impotence, his sense of failure and frustration in his undertakings. What the curé of Torcy succeeds in doing, therefore, is to offer his pupil the saint's way of dealing with her impotence: "Mais c'est du sentiment de sa propre impuissance que l'enfant tire humblement le principe même de sa joie. Il s'en rapporte à sa mère, comprends-tu?" (OE,I 1045). The curé of Torcy's description of the childlike joy in accepting one's impotence is at the heart of the saint's spirituality as is seen in a letter Thérèse wrote in July, 1890 to her cousin, Marie Guérin. Aware daily of her human weakness, she speaks of the grace of joyful acceptance of one's impotence, "car là seulement se trouve la paix et le repos du coeur, quand on se voit si misérable on ne veut plus se considérer et on ne regarde que l'unique Bien-Aimé!..." (LT 179).

The curé of Torcy's belief that each Christian has his particular role to play in the Gospel echoes Thérèse's discovery in the First Letter to the Corinthians that the Church is a body composed of many members, each having a special function (HA 221). This discovery is reflected in the curé of Torcy's thoughts: "Nous sommes tous appelés, soit, seulement pas de la même manière. Et, pour simplifier les choses, je commence par essayer de replacer chacun de nous à sa vraie place, dans l'Evangile" (OE,I 1186). The older priest's reflection leads the younger one to recognize that his place is that of a "prisonnier de la Sainte Agonie" (OE,I 1187) in the Garden of Gethsemani. The curé of Ambricourt's understanding of his call to be a prisoner of Christ's Agony reminds the reader of how the words of Saint Paul led Thérèse to discover her own calling and offer herself as a victim of holocaust to merciful love: "Oui j'ai trouvé ma place dans l'Eglise . . . dans le Coeur de l'Eglise, ma Mère, je serai l'Amour... . . ." (HA 222).

Like Thérèse, the curé of Torcy stresses the teaching that Christians are responsible for the salvation of others. During the course of their conversations, the older priest continually reminds the curé of Ambricourt that the Church looks sin in the face and that even "à l'exemple de Notre-Seigneur, elle le prend à son compte, elle l'assume" (OE,I 1044). Later on, he declares that because they have received special graces, the saints are obliged to pay for the redemption of others (OE,I 1122).

In a similar fashion, Thérèse wrote to Céline in March, 1889: "Offrons bien nos souffrances à Jésus pour sauver les âmes, pauvres âmes!... elles ont moins de grâces que nous, et pourtant tout le sang d'un Dieu a été versé pour les sauver... pourtant Jésus veut bien faire dépendre leur salut d'un soupir de notre coeur..." (LT 139). Other words written by the saint to her sister a few months later, "notre mission c'est de nous oublier, de nous anéantir... . . . et pourtant Jésus veut que le salut des âmes dépende de nos sacrifices, de notre amour, il nous mendie des âmes... . . ." (LT 157), are also reflected in the words of the curé of Torcy. His advice thus leads the younger priest to understand his vocation and accept his suffering in a way that closely resembles that of the saint of Lisieux.

The Curé of Ambricourt as a "Little" Saint and Servant of All

Both Thérèse and the curé of Ambricourt regard themselves as children. At one point in Manuscript C, for example, the saint declares: "Mais je m'amuse à parler comme un enfant . . ." (HA 290), while in the midst of a discussion with his fellow priests on the subject of savings banks, the curé of Ambricourt has "l'impression d'être un enfant fourvoyé dans une conversation de grandes personnes" (OE,I 1055).

Humility and simplicity are comparable traits in the saint and the priest. Always simple and humble in their interpersonal relations, they never judge themselves as superior to others. Although she recognized that God had given her extraordinary graces, Thérèse never considered herself a saint as we see from her words to Pauline: "Non, je ne suis pas une sainte; je n'ai jamais fait les actions des saints. Je suis une toute petite âme que le bon Dieu a comblée de grâces, voilà ce que je suis" (DE 123).

Similarly, as his reply to Dr. Laville indicates, the country priest considers himself as no better than his colleagues: "Je regrette seulement de vous donner une si mauvaise opinion de nous tous, ai-je répondu. Je suis un prêtre très ordinaire" (OE,I 1235). And also like his model, he is aware of having received special graces: "Dieu me comble de tant de grâces, et si inattendues, si étranges!" (OE,I 1223).

In both the saint and the priest-hero humility is connected with the spirit of poverty. Thérèse believed that it was simply because of her littleness that God gave her special gifts: "parce que j'étais petite et faible il s'abaissait vers moi, il m'instruisait en secret des choses de son amour" (HA 122). The saint further states that in order to learn the secrets of perfection, "il faut être pauvre d'esprit!..." (HA 122).

Her growth in spirituality is mirrored in the curé of Ambricourt's lucidity regarding his own spiritual development. It is because he is humble that he is able to admit the truth about himself: "Si sévèrement que je me juge parfois, je n'ai jamais douté d'avoir l'esprit de pauvreté. Celui d'enfance lui ressemble. Les deux sans doute ne font qu'un" (OE,I 1246). Thus, for both Bernanos and Thérèse of Lisieux, spiritual childhood and spiritual poverty go hand in hand.

In their simplicity, both the Carmelite saint and Bernanos' priest-hero are anxious to serve God well. Thérèse eagerly asked Mère Anne de Jésus in the dream she had of her: "dites-moi encore si le Bon Dieu ne me demande pas quelque chose de plus que mes pauvres petites actions et mes désirs. Est-Il content de moi?" (HA 218). The curé of Ambricourt shows a similar anxiety to follow God's will when he asks himself twenty times a day: "Suis-je là où Notre-Seigneur me veut?" (OE,I 1097).

Images of littleness used by the curé to describe himself are borrowed from Thérèse. The saint's belief that in God's eyes she was "un pauvre petit néant, rien de plus..." (HA 235) is reproduced in the priest-hero's humble admission to the countess: "Moi, je suis le serviteur de tous. Et encore, serviteur est-il un mot trop noble pour un malheureux petit prêtre tel que moi, je devrais dire la chose de tous, ou moins même, s'il plaît à Dieu" (OE,I 1146). In both saint and priest images of littleness gradually evolve into the desire to be forgotten. Thérèse wrote to Pauline in May, 1890: "je désire d'être oubliée, et non seulement des créatures mais aussi de moi-même, je voudrais être tellement réduite au néant que je n'aie aucun désir..." (LT 168). In the young priest's words to the curé of Torcy, the saint's statement becomes: "Je suis un malheureux petit prêtre qui ne demande qu'à passer inaperçu" (OE,I 1185).

Many parallels are observed in Thérèse of Lisieux and the curé of Ambricourt in the understanding of their respective vocations. Long before entering their teens, both felt called to religious life, but this call did not seem to suffice for either of them. So great was her desire to bring Christ to others that Thérèse felt within her the need to accomplish other vocations: "je me sens la vocation de GUERRIER, de PRETRE, d'APOTRE, de DOCTEUR, de MARTYRE . . ." (HA 219). The young priest's vocational aspirations are certainly along the same lines. The sentence that keeps running through his head, "'Mon coeur est avec ceux de l'avant, mon coeur est avec ceux qui se font tuer'. Ceux qui se font tuer... Soldats, missionnaires..." (OE,I 1222), suggests how he would like to have been a soldier or a missionary. He reflects in his diary on how whenever he would lose his courage during some trial, he would console himself "par l'espoir de quelque événement merveilleux, imprévisible - le martyre peut-être?" (OE,I 1244-1245).

The little Carmelite's call to offer herself as a victim to merciful love is implicit in the young priest-hero as he faithfully and lovingly pursues his duties as a parish priest. His attitude, "Moi, je suis le serviteur de tous" (OE,I 1146), corresponds with the saint's understanding of the Gospel passage on giving one's cloak as well as one's tunic to whoever should demand it: "Abandonner son manteau c'est, il me semble, renoncer à ses derniers droits, c'est se considérer comme la servante, l'esclave des autres" (HA 260).

For both Thérèse and the curé of Ambricourt prayer and the sharing of the sufferings of others are integral to their compassionate love for others. The saint's vocation as a Carmelite was to pray for the conversion of sinners and in particular to pray for priests. Thérèse soon had no doubt that this could be achieved only through prayer and sacrifice. In a letter written to Céline in August, 1892, she explained: "L'apostolat de la prière n'est-il pas pour ainsi dire plus élevé que celui de la parole? Notre mission comme Carmélites est de former des ouvriers évangéliques qui sauveront des milliers d'âmes..." (LT 222).

The curé of Ambricourt has similar thoughts on the power of contemplative prayer. He digresses in his diary about how, after years of prayer, old monks have become more compassionate and able to enter into the miseries of others: "Etrange rêve, singulier opium qui, loin de replier l'individu sur lui-même, de l'isoler de ses semblables, le fait solidaire de tous, dans l'esprit de l'universelle charité!" (OE,I 1112).

The young priest also tries to share Doctor Delbende's trial of faith: "J'essaie de la recevoir humblement dans mon coeur, telle quelle, je m'efforce de l'y faire mienne, de l'aimer" (OE,I 1096). And like the saint, he desires to give to others what he himself does not possess. Thérèse begged God to help her with the novices: "si vous voulez leur donner par moi ce qui convient à chacune, remplissez ma petite main . . ." (HA 271). As we recall, she wished to work for God alone, believing that she would one day appear before Him, "les mains vides . . ." (HA 317-318). Reflecting on how he was able to give the countess a peace he himself did not feel, the curé of Ambricourt uses Thérèse's image of empty hands: "O merveille, qu'on puisse ainsi faire présent de ce qu'on ne possède pas soi-même, ô doux miracle de nos mains vides!" (OE,I 1170).

Like the Carmelite saint, the country priest is convinced of the importance of prayer for the spiritual welfare of others. He enters wholeheartedly into the suffering of his parishioners by bringing them into his prayer. And so, when he finds Mademoiselle Louise in tears, he feels compassion for her solitude. The hatred and despair on the face of Chantal recall the suffering the priest-hero endured in his own childhood and, while he is praying for Chantal, it seems to him that his prayer takes on her sadness (OE,I 1135). His words to the teenager bear witness to his longing to suffer on her behalf: "Je réponds de vous, lui dis-je sans réfléchir, âme pour âme" (OE,I 1226).

The Countess Episode

Although young in years, both the Carmelite saint and the priest-hero reveal a psychological depth in their encounters with others often only achieved after many years. Prudence combined with a genuine compassion for the suffering of others plays a key role in their relations with those whose spiritual welfare is their concern. A brief glance at an event from Thérèse's life helps us understand how the curé of Ambricourt's treatment of the countess resembles the saint's way of giving spiritual guidance to the novices in her care.

Céline relates in <u>Conseils et souvenirs</u> how on one occasion she complained to Thérèse about another sister who had forgotten to help her with some work they were supposed to do together. What interests us is not so much the event itself, but rather the psychology used by the saint to reconcile Céline to the situation and help her use it for spiritual profit. Listening carefully to her sister's complaint about having to do all the work, Thérèse entered into her suffering even to the point of giving Céline the impression that she was justified in feeling annoyed. By accepting her sister as she was at that particular moment, Thérèse was offering her the psychological space needed to judge the situation objectively. Instead of trying to downplay or destroy the cause of Céline's annoyance, Thérèse tried to get her to view the unpleasant event in terms of an invitation to love. Céline declares how at this point she felt able to express her feelings and accept her own truth. Thérèse's way of dealing with Céline's struggle eventually made the latter discover the obstacle within herself that was blocking the way to union with her companion (<u>CSG</u> 10-11).

The psychology employed by Bernanos' priest-hero in the countess episode in <u>Journal d'un curé de campagne</u> is similar to that used by Thérèse in dealing with her novices. Disturbed over Chantal's unhappiness, the curé of Ambricourt decides to visit the mother. At the beginning of his visit he faces the countess with the truth: "Vous n'aimez pas votre fille . . ." (<u>OE</u>,I 1147). At the same time he assures her that he is not there to judge her, but that he, too, knows what suffering is: "Mais j'ai l'expérience de la souffrance, je sais ce que c'est." (<u>OE</u>,I 1148). The curé tries to get the mother to accept the reality of what is happening to her daughter and to deal with it in a way that allows her to keep her dignity. Because of the sincerity and sollicitude of the priest-hero, the countess begins to confide in him.

The curé learns that since the death of her infant son several years earlier, the countess has remained bitter over her loss and has also resigned herself to her husband's infidelities. In her present state of despair she refuses to love either her daughter or her husband. She has, in reality, ceased to love.

But now the countess receives new life through the curé's compassionate concern for her spiritual welfare. His understanding and acceptance of her feelings give her the freedom to speak openly of her bitter resignation. It is only then that she can accept the real truth of her situation. The curé can therefore point out to the countess her wrong in ceasing to love: "L'enfer, madame, c'est de ne plus aimer" (OE,I 1157). The countess comes to realize that her bitter resentment is opposed to God and His kingdom, where resides her infant son. The curé shows her that this is the very obstacle blocking her hope of ever being reunited with her lost child.

That the countess passes from sad resignation to hope and love is evident in her note to the curé written but a few short hours before her death. Her words, "Je ne suis pas résignée, je suis heureuse. Je ne désire rien" (OE,I 1165), recall not only Chantal de Clergerie's refusal to be resigned to God's will (OE,I 598), but also Thérèse's borrowing of Madame Swetchine's statement regarding resignation and the will of God (DE 90).

When her words are examined in the light of Thérèse's, the countess seems to have undergone a sudden change of heart whereby she now lovingly accepts God's will. But is it realistic for such a change to occur in so short a time? Once again the Carmelite saint provides the answer in her account of her Christmas conversion: "En un instant l'ouvrage que je n'avais pu faire en 10 ans, Jésus le fit se contentant de ma bonne volonté . . ." (HA 114). It was at this very moment that Thérèse experienced the birth of love within her and the feeling of happiness which accompanied it (HA 114-115). The countess episode thus shows not only that the curé's manner of reconciling the countess to God resembles the saint's psychology in dealing with the spiritual struggles of those in her charge, but also that the countess' conversion testifies to a genuine abandonment of herself to God's merciful love.

Suffering and the Trial of Faith

Closely linked with their desire to bring God to others are the various forms of suffering that both Thérèse of Lisieux and the curé of Ambricourt undergo during the brief span of their lives. Like the saint, the priest-hero suffers from a sense of his human impotence and from the attitudes of those with whom he comes in contact. Both speak of their excessive timidity, youth, and inexperience. The priest-hero laments his lack of knowledge regarding the daily concerns of his parishioners. The mistakes he believes he has made in certain encounters with them resemble the saint's difficulties in trying to accomplish the manual tasks assigned to her in the monastery. Just as her family background had not prepared her for household chores neither had the curé's background prepared him sufficiently for the shrewdness needed in handling financial matters. But both saint and priest accept the suffering occasioned by their weakness in a spirit of humility.

In addition, they also listen humbly to the judgments of others in their regard. Telling of how she preferred food seasoned with vinegar to sweets, Thérèse compares the novices' criticism of her to her delight in being served a delicious salad well-seasoned with vinegar (HA 279).

Little by little the priest-hero gradually learns to accept the judgments of his parishioners in a similar spirit. They talk behind his back, accusing him of being a secret drinker when all the while his unhealthy appearance and poor appetite are caused by cancer of the stomach. Arsène, his sacristan, tells him that people don't approve of how he teaches catechism to young girls. Even the children of the parish are cruel to their pastor by resisting in various ways his efforts to speak to them of God. When he tries to help Sulpice Mitonnet, a youth with suspect morals, the curé is subjected to more criticism. Séraphita, whom he mistakenly thinks is longing to make her first communion, disappoints the curé by telling him that she is more interested in his eyes than in his catechism lessons. The count's family brings him additional suffering. Instead of supporting the priest in his efforts to help the young people of the parish, the count disapproves of his plans and tries to block them by placing certain restrictions on the property he permits him to use for his youth organization. The count's daughter, Chantal, is openly rude to the priest-hero. Her governess, Mademoiselle Louise, sends him an anonymous letter in which she advises him to leave Ambricourt.

As if this is not enough, Bernanos' young curé must try to accept the fact that he is misunderstood by his superiors who, as the priest-hero discovers, are only too willing to listen to the malicious gossip of his parishioners. But, like Thérèse, his model, the curé of Ambricourt learns to accept the suffering occasioned by others, for he desires to take upon himself the suffering of his village whose victim he is. Does he not write with regard to his village: "et c'est vrai que parfois j'imagine qu'il m'a cloué là-haut sur une croix, qu'il me regarde au moins mourir . . ." (OE,I 1061)?

We have already observed how the curé of Ambricourt parallels Thérèse in his offering of himself as a victim of holocaust for others. But after each one of the above-mentioned encounters with his parishioners his own personal suffering increases and it seems as if their burdens have now become his. After the death of the countess, for example, the priest-hero believes that God is allowing him to take over the spiritual trial she has left behind: "Peut-être Dieu a-t-il voulu mettre sur mes épaules le fardeau dont il venait de délivrer sa créature épuisée" (OE,I 1184). Similar experiences can be found in the life of the Carmelite saint who claimed she could find no reasonable explanation for her extreme physical and spiritual sufferings other than her desire to suffer for the salvation of sinners. A few hours before her death she proclaimed: "Jamais je n'aurais cru qu'il était possible de tant souffrir! jamais! jamais! Je ne puis m'expliquer cela que par les désirs ardents que j'ai eus de sauver des âmes" (DE 185). Thérèse believed that God allowed a spiritual darkness to penetrate her soul so that she might better understand the interior suffering of those who did not believe in the existence of God or eternal life. She willingly accepted this trial of faith in order that God would offer salvation to those who did not believe: "Je Lui dis que je suis heureuse de ne pas jouir de ce beau Ciel sur la terre afin qu'Il l'ouvre pour l'éternité aux pauvres incrédules" (HA 243).

But the saint gradually discovered the joy that exists in suffering for others out of love: "Car est-il une joie plus grande que celle de souffrir pour votre amour?..." (HA 244). Further on, Thérèse adds that "la souffrance elle-même devient la plus grande des joies lorsqu'on la recherche comme le plus précieux des trésors" (HA 249). Is this not the joy that the curé of Ambricourt experiences upon giving the countess his blessing: "Dans le moment que je l'ai bénie, d'où me venait cette joie mêlée de crainte, cette menaçante douceur?" (OE,I 1184).

The curé of Ambricourt's trial of faith, symbolized by his sleepless nights filled with intense physical and spiritual suffering, the fury of the wind and rain, and the banging of the garden gate, suggestive of some unseen, diabolical presence, recalls Thérèse's attempt to describe her spiritual sufferings to Céline: "Le démon est autour de moi, je ne le vois pas, mais je le sens... il me tourmente, il me tient comme avec une main de fer pour m'empêcher de prendre le plus petit soulagement, il augmente mes maux afin que je me désespère" (DE 201) and, what is for the saint the greatest trial of all, "je ne puis pas prier!" (DE 201). And, indeed, is this not an explanation of what the curé of Ambricourt labels "une véritable hémorragie de l'âme" (OE,I 1099)? Like the saint of Lisieux, he, too, during his trial of faith, experiences difficulty in prayer: "Jamais je ne me suis tant efforcé de prier . . ." (OE,I 1111). The silence of God, of which Thérèse speaks as "Le Silence, voilà le langage qui peut vous dire seul ce qui se passe dans mon âme!..." (LT 173), becomes in the curé's words "ce hargneux silence de l'âme, presque haineux..." (OE,I 1113). Solitude and lack of spiritual consolation become his lot: "Même solitude, même silence . . . la nuit entre en moi . . . Je suis moi-même nuit" (OE,I 1113) as they became part of the Carmelite's trial of faith: "j'ai ressenti comme les angoisses de la mort... et avec cela aucune consolation!" (DE 41).

As they both struggle desperately to hold onto their faith, the temptation to despair appears on the threshold. The curé of Ambricourt's words: "Derrière moi il n'y avait rien. Et devant moi un mur, un mur noir" (OE,I 1111) correspond perfectly to Thérèse's statement: "c'est un mur qui s'élève jusqu'aux cieux et couvre le firmament étoilé..." (HA 244). Similarly, Thérèse's fear of speaking about her trial of faith: "cependant je ne veux pas en écrire plus long, je craindrais de blasphémer... j'ai peur même d'en avoir trop dit..." (HA 243) seems to be the very reason why the curé erases words and tears out pages here and there in his diary. And in what he does write: "la tentation m'est venue de..." (OE,I 1185) we believe that he was subjected to the temptation that Thérèse did not hesitate to name: "Si je n'avais pas eu la foi, je me serais donné la mort sans hésiter un seul instant..." (DE 174). As to how she faced such temptations, the saint stated: "tout en les subissant, je ne cesse de faire des actes de foi" (DE 224). And what saves the curé throughout his trial of faith is exactly what saved Thérèse: the knowledge that in spite of his trial, his faith is still intact: "Je n'ai perdu ni la Foi, ni l'Espérance, ni la Charité. . . . C'est le désir des biens éternels qui compte" (OE,I 1117).

Bernanos' young priest-hero parallels Thérèse of Lisieux in yet another attitude towards his trial of faith. In his effort to accept his suffering: "Je voulais seulement faire réellement le geste de l'acceptation totale, de l'abandon. J'étais couché au bord du vide, du néant . . ." (OE,I 1113) he imitates Thérèse's spirit of abandonment: "...Je suis abandonnée, j'attendrai tant qu'Il voudra" (DE 108).

For the curé of Ambricourt, death becomes a new opportunity for him to show his love for God. His first duty is to accept joyfully his own human impotence of which he has always been ashamed. Aware, as Thérèse also was, of the need for God's mercy at the hour of death, the priest humbly abandons himself to God: "Mon Dieu, je vous donne tout, de bon coeur" (<u>OE</u>,I 1245). His offering of himself reflects the saint's acceptance of her suffering: "J'accepte tout pour l'amour du bon Dieu . . ." (<u>DE</u> 41) and, on the day of her death, her words: "... Oui, mon Dieu, tout ce que vous voudrez . . ." (<u>DE</u> 184). The loving acceptance of himself and his death in a miserable apartment shared by an ex-priest and his char-woman mistress fills Bernanos' priest-hero with a fresh, new feeling: "Silence et paix" (<u>OE</u>,I 1255). And at this moment, Thérèse's words to Céline in April of 1889 could easily have been the curé's: "j'ai trouvé le secret de souffrir en paix... Qui dit <u>paix</u> ne dit pas joie, ou du moins joie <u>sentie</u>... Pour souffrir en paix, il suffit de bien vouloir tout ce que Jésus veut..." (<u>LT</u> 141). Realizing that he is to be deprived of the consolation of receiving the last rites of the Church, Bernanos' priest-hero slowly and distinctly utters the words Thérèse used when she became aware of the possibility that she might die without the sacraments: "Qu'est-ce que cela fait? Tout est grâce" (<u>OE</u>,I 1259). The curé of Ambricourt is indeed the Carmelite's spiritual son as Guy Gaucher has indicated ("BT" 265), for he dies in full possession of her spirit of childhood, her call to merciful love, and her acceptance of the trial of faith.

NOTES

CHAPTER 8

[1] Michel Estève, "Genèse du 'Journal d'un Curé de Campagne,'" <u>La Revue des Lettres Modernes</u> 67-68 (1961) "Etudes bernanosiennes" 2: 11.

[2] Henri Debluë, <u>Les romans de Georges Bernanos ou le défi du rêve</u> (Neuchâtel: Editions de la Baconnière, 1965) 240. Cited hereafter as <u>Défi</u>.

[3] Michel Estève, "La Nuit de Gethsémani," <u>La Revue des Lettres Modernes</u> 67-68 (1961) "Etudes bernanosiennes" 2: 97. Cited hereafter as "NG."

[4] Michel Estève, <u>Georges Bernanos: un triple itinéraire</u> (Paris: Hachette, 1981) 169.

[5] According to her sister, Pauline, Thérèse died on September 30, 1897 at shortly after 7:00 PM (<u>DE</u> 186). In addition, the Epilogue to the <u>Histoire d'une âme</u> states: "Puis elle ferme les yeux et expire. Il est 19 heures environ" (<u>HA</u> 312).

CHAPTER 9

**THERESIAN SPIRITUALITY ON THE NATURAL LEVEL IN
NOUVELLE HISTOIRE DE MOUCHETTE (1936-1937)**

In an interview with André Rousseaux in 1937, Bernanos spoke of how the sight of truckloads of wretched Majorcan peasants on their way to the firing squad during the Spanish Civil War prompted him to write his last novel, Nouvelle histoire de Mouchette. While admiring the courage exhibited by these men in the face of death, the author reacted vehemently to the terrible injustice of their dying from the imposture of a political situation totally incomprehensible to them.[1] Had he not witnessed events such as these, he said, he would not have written Nouvelle histoire de Mouchette. Rather than being the simple transposition of one such scene, however, the novel describes a young rape victim's suffering disillusionment from the indifference of those around her.

Nouvelle histoire de Mouchette is unlike Bernanos' other novels. No priest figure, no parish, no celebration of mass or reception of the sacraments is found in it. Mouchette's world, a world in which God seems no longer present, is a world similar to that also found in Monsieur Ouine.

Critics such as Marcel Arland and Père Brückberger both argue that Thérèse's words, "tout est grâce" (DE 41), can be applied to Nouvelle histoire de Mouchette. Proclaiming the role of grace to be the fundamental issue in all

Bernanos' work, Arland states: "Reconnaissons ce débat au coeur de l'<u>Histoire de Mouchette</u>; c'est par là qu'un tel livre, si particulier qu'il soit d'ailleurs, s'incorpore à l'oeuvre entier."² Arland maintains that grace can be found anywhere even though nowhere does Bernanos indicate which of his characters have received grace and been saved ("MA" 137).

In a similar vein, Brückberger contends that <u>Nouvelle histoire de Mouchette</u> develops in narrative form "à travers l'aventure d'un personnage inventé, les derniers mots du curé de campagne, qui sont aussi de Thérèse de l'Enfant-Jésus: 'Tout est grâce!'"³ This same critic draws an even further comparison between Bernanos' novel and the saint by stating that Mouchette is to Thérèse of Lisieux as a wild rose is to a cultivated one. Yet both belong to the same family (<u>BV</u> 62-63).

Yves Bridel has demonstrated how Mouchette's natural virtues and her extreme poverty do parallel the saint's doctrine of spiritual childhood as it would appear in a world where God was no longer present (<u>EE</u> 197). These parallels have also led Soeur Raymond-Marie in her study, "La simplicité des humbles et des petits," to assert that "Mouchette, une enfant pauvre, se présente comme le héraut de l'enfance naturelle . . ."⁴ and that the natural childhood displayed by Bernanos' characters is the basis for the spirit of childhood ("Sim" 317).

Mouchette, however, is far more than a natural reflection of Thérèse's spirit of childhood. Stripped totally in both a physical and spiritual sense, the young teenager can be seen as a parallel image on the natural level not only of Thérèse's spirit of childhood, but also of her call to merciful love, and her experience of the trial of faith.

Mouchette and the Spirit of Childhood

Thérèse of Lisieux transformed the positive qualities of natural childhood into supernatural qualities. Her teaching has a solid foundation rooted in the religious atmosphere of her home and in the loving parent-child relationship she experienced with her father which she transformed into a relationship of childlike confidence in God as heavenly Father.

Mouchette, on the other hand, has an alcoholic father whose only form of communication with his daughter consists in beatings and abusive language and about whom the wife of the game-warden remarks: "Un père? T'appelles ça un père, grand innocent? Il la vendrait pour une tournée de vieux rhum, sa fille!" (OE,I 1325). Her mother is too overburdened with drudgery, poverty, and ill health to give any concern to her teenage daughter's emotional needs. Her brothers show a complete lack of concern for their young sister. Indeed "Mouchette eût volontiers convenu avec elle-même n'avoir jamais connu la douceur d'une caresse, d'une vraie caresse" (OE,I 1341). At fourteen, the heroine is still at an age where she is vulnerable and dependent on others. All those with whom she comes in contact fail her. In addition to a lack of emotional support, the young heroine also suffers physical misery. She is forced to go to bed hungry if she does not arrive home from school on time. She has to share ill-fitting and worn-out clothing with family members. Her brother's galoshes on her tiny feet are "si larges qu'entre la tige elle peut passer les cinq doigts de sa petite main" (OE,I 1265). The family dwelling, situated on the edge of a swamp, is in such a state of disrepair that at the first frost the father is obliged to plug up the holes in the walls with sticks.

Spiritual deprivation completes this picture of misery. Mouchette finds herself belonging to a family where religion seems to have no place. In her village the Sunday celebration of high mass is no longer the focal point of parish life. As in time past, the church bells continue to ring out every Sunday morning but the streets remain deserted. Everyone is at home "getting ready," but, as Bernanos asks: "Se préparer à quoi? Car personne ne va plus à la grand-messe" (OE,I 1327). The heroine is thus deprived of any knowledge of God in her life.

Yet certain parallels between Mouchette's natural childhood and the life of Thérèse of Lisieux exist. First of all, it is significant that Bernanos' young heroine is only fourteen years of age, approximately the same age as the saint was at the moment of her Christmas conversion. Thérèse describes the period prior to this age as being a most painful one: "Cette période s'étend depuis l'âge de quatre ans et demi jusqu'à celui de ma quatorzième année, époque où je retrouvai mon caractère d'enfant tout en entrant dans le sérieux de la vie" (HA 43). Mouchette's childhood years, as we have just observed, have also been ones of suffering and now, she too, at age fourteen, comes face to face with the seriousness of life.

One of the common sources of suffering experienced by both Thérèse and Mouchette during childhood was their unhappiness at school. Instead of being a welcome opportunity for them to make new friends and expand their horizons, school tended, on the contrary, to highlight the differences between the two young girls and their peers. Thérèse even admitted that the five years she spent at school were the saddest of her life (HA 63). Unable to participate in games with her classmates whom she found to be so different from herself, Thérèse describes how she used to spend her recreation periods: "souvent pendant les récréations, je m'appuyais contre un arbre et là je contemplais le coup d'oeil, me livrant à de sérieuses réflexions!" (HA 96). Thérèse's words remind us to some extent of Bernanos' description of his heroine's experience of solitude at school. Forced to undergo humiliations doled out to her by her teacher and classmates, Mouchette rebels by refusing to participate in the singing lesson. She thus refuses, on the day the action takes place, to re-enter the school building after recreation, taking pleasure instead in hiding behind a hedge and contemplating at a distance her companions as they are dismissed from class (OE,I 1267). Mouchette thus feels as detached from her surroundings as did Thérèse during her schooldays at the abbey. The only one who recognizes the heroine's worth is the poacher, Arsène, who tells her: "Tu n'es pas une fille comme les autres, tu es une bonne fille . . . ." (OE,I 1278).

An even more significant parallel between the lives of Thérèse and Mouchette appears in the death of their mothers. In each case this event took place at a critical point in the development of the daughters. For the saint, the loss of her mother at the age of four and a half was a traumatic experience which led to a complete transformation of her natural happy and outgoing disposition. She confesses her feelings at the time: "je devins timide et douce, sensible à l'excès" (HA 43). Since she could not bear to be in the company of anyone but her immediate family, Thérèse experienced solitude right from her childhood days. As for Mouchette, her mother dies at the very moment when, for perhaps the first time in her life, she feels able to confide in her. Arriving home late after being raped by Arsène, Mouchette finds her mother in bed with severe chest pains. The young girl recognizes that "il y a dans la voix de la mère une tendresse incompréhensible, insolite" (OE,I 1307), but unaccustomed as she is to any signs of affection, she hesitates, unable at first to trust her with her terrible secret. Moments later when Mouchette finally summons up the courage to reveal her problems to her mother, the latter has already drawn her last breath. Scarcely conscious of the sense of despair welling up inside of her, Mouchette becomes gradually aware that "elle est seule, vraiment seule aujourd'hui, contre tous" (OE,I 1317).

The saint and the heroine also both experience deprivation. Mouchette's physical misery is not too far removed from the lack of physical comforts that Thérèse endured during her nine years in the Lisieux monastery. As the only fireplace was in the recreation room, the saint suffered greatly from the cold, damp climate of Normandy. Other sources of her suffering included fatigue from too few hours of sleep on an uncomfortable mattress, physical work to which she was unaccustomed, ill-fitting, coarse, homespun clothing handed out to her from a common supply cupboard, and, finally, an inadequate diet for a still growing teenager.

Thérèse, of course, contrary to Mouchette, was able to raise her deprivations to a higher level. In order to receive all from God, she actually desired to suffer physical poverty and lack of affection. Only then was she able to say: "On éprouve une si grande paix d'être absolument pauvre, de ne compter que sur le bon Dieu" (<u>DE</u> 117). For the saint, spiritual poverty and spiritual childhood are profoundly connected. In a letter to her sister, Marie, a year before her death, Thérèse commented on the psalmist's words that the person truly poor in spirit is found among the lowly. Inspired by this thought, the saint encouraged her sister to practise poverty of spirit: "Ah! restons donc <u>bien loin</u> de tout ce qui brille, aimons notre petitesse, aimons à ne rien sentir, alors nous serons pauvres d'esprit et Jésus viendra nous chercher, <u>si loin</u> que nous soyons il nous transformera en flammes d'amour..." (<u>LT</u> 360). Although poverty of spirit is impossible on the purely natural level, Bernanos has certainly succeeded in uniting natural childhood with natural poverty in the youngest of his heroines.

In addition to parallels between the circumstances of their lives, Mouchette displays certain natural qualities reminiscent of Thérèse's spirit of childhood. Among these are her attitude towards humiliations and her childlike expression of confidence in Arsène. Based on purely supernatural motives, Thérèse longed for humiliations and found joy in them. To this effect, she once said: "Tout le monde peut bien me mépriser, c'est toujours ce que j'ai désiré . . ." (<u>DE</u> 105). Mouchette's reaction to the scorn of others causes her to seek out further humiliations. She tries to get her clothing dirty and make herself as unattractive as possible.

Although their motives are different, both saint and heroine tend to treat humiliations in a similar fashion. Neither one shows concern for what others may think of her. With one sister telling her how well she looked and another how ill she looked, Thérèse soon decided that rather than allow herself to get upset over such conflicting opinions she would not attach any importance to them. The result was that both compliments and criticisms passed over her "sans laisser la plus légère empreinte" (DE 94). For her part, Mouchette, on a natural level, has also learned to ignore the unkind remarks and jeers of others. No longer ashamed of her clothing with all its holes, she takes pride in defying "par une souciance sauvage le jugement dédaigneux de ses compagnes et les moqueries des garçons" (OE,I 1281).

Courageous in accepting humiliations, Thérèse and Mouchette also show courage in the confidence they place in the one they have chosen to love. In spite of the extreme physical suffering she endured before her death, the saint was still able to proclaim: "la souffrance pourra atteindre des limites extrêmes, mais je suis sûre que le bon Dieu ne m'abandonnera jamais" (DE 56). Mouchette, unaccustomed to placing confidence in anyone, places her hand in Arsène's as a sign of the newly awakened feeling of confidence she discovers within herself for this man who has shown her some kindness: "Voilà tant d'années qu'elle n'a tendu à personne cette petite main! Elle a mis dans ce geste naïf toute la ferveur dont son coeur est plein" (OE,I 1293). As the Carmelite was ready to abandon herself freely to God's will, so too is Mouchette ready to go wherever Arsène leads her.

More important still, Mouchette parallels the saint's spirit of childhood on a natural level. Thérèse regards God as a loving Father who longs to provide for the needs of all His children. In answer to her sister Pauline's request to explain her "little way," the saint replied: "c'est la voie de l'enfance spirituelle, c'est le chemin de la confiance et du total abandon" (DE 223). On yet another occasion she described to this same sister just what she meant by remaining a little child before God: "C'est reconnaître son néant, attendre tout du bon Dieu, comme un petit enfant attend tout de son père; c'est ne s'inquiéter de rien, ne point gagner de fortune" (DE 119). Thérèse's way is destined, therefore, for those who humbly regard themselves as "little." Bernanos' youngest heroine exhibits this childlike simplicity quite naturally.

As Mouchette has barely entered her teens, there is still an air of childlike simplicity about the manner in which she acts and expresses her innermost thoughts and feelings. We notice how she quite innocently takes Arsène's hand, how she asks him where they are going, how she holds his head during his seizure, and how on that occasion she quite naturally begins to sing. Her negative reactions to the cruel words and actions of others are but a child's natural revolt to what it understands as unkindness and injustice. The heroine's reasoning powers have not yet matured to allow her to understand clearly why she feels such anguish after Arsène has forced himself on her. Although scarcely able to distinguish this violent act from her father's drunken brutality, Mouchette feels deeply wounded by the outrage: "la honte qui lui en reste est d'une espèce inconnue . . ." (OE,I 1304).

This same childlike simplicity will again appear in the heroine's free abandonment of herself to whatever death will have to offer her. Aware of her solitude and nothingness, she drowns herself in the belief that death will offer her what love has refused her (OE,I 1339). Thus the young girl reflects on the natural level Thérèse's attitude of simplicity in the acceptance of her impotence and her abandonment to the will of the Father.

Mouchette and the Call to Love

Just as the heroine's natural childhood reflects the saint's spirit of childhood, so also do certain aspects of Mouchette's search for true love on the natural level mirror Thérèse's search for her vocation of love. The concept of dream serves as a key instrument in the search of both young women, each of whom longs to translate her dream into reality.

In a letter to the abbé Bellière, Thérèse describes how her childhood dream of heroic adventures was fulfilled in her life. The exploits of Jeanne d'Arc had moved the young saint to the extent that she felt God calling her to perform similar deeds, but her vocation led her to a cloistered monastery. Mouchette, too, dreams of the great adventure that life offers. She seems to possess an unconscious desire for true love in which she places all her hope for earthly happiness. On account of her youth, however, she is unable to comprehend her interior yearnings fully. Her companions wonder about her belligerent attitude towards boys, but Mouchette has no desire to enter into the precocious sexual activities of her peers. On the contrary, she seems to take pride in an instinctive sense of purity and innocence whereby she unconsciously realizes the superior value of physical integrity. For Mouchette, love signifies more than a physical act. She has set up for herself a dream of love in which Arsène figures as her hero. The heroine dreams of her relationship with Arsène as one built on truth and admiration, the free gift of self to another. Her dream starts to disintegrate when her hero takes advantage of her in the isolated hut. In addition, Mouchette later discovers that Arsène has lied to her about the storm and the murder of the game-warden. Mouchette's ideal of love, like Thérèse's, is therefore a high one. Unlike the saint's, however, it cannot be realized, being centered on an unworthy lover.

Although the Carmelite and Bernanos' heroine view love on different levels, there are, nevertheless, certain similarities in their concepts of love. For both, love implies the total gift of self which leads to the overcoming of fear. Thérèse first began to understand the true meaning of love as a gift of self on that special Christmas night, a few days short of her fourteenth birthday, when, as she declares: "Je sentis en un mot la charité entrer dans mon coeur, le besoin de m'oublier pour faire plaisir et depuis lors je fus heureuse!..." (HA 114-115). As the young saint began to give herself in love, she became less fearful and more confident in God's mercy. And so, she was able to proclaim: ". . . la crainte me fait reculer; avec l'amour non seulement j'avance mais je vole..." (HA 198). On June 9, 1895 Thérèse made the total offering of herself in love in her "Acte d'offrande à l'Amour miséricordieux."

Mouchette's gift of self in love is symbolized in her singing to Arsène as she tenderly holds his head during his seizure: "Cela se fit si naturellement qu'elle ne s'en aperçut pas d'abord" (OE,I 1291). As her voice breaks forth in all its fragile beauty, Mouchette feels as if her unhappy childhood has suddenly vanished. Her voice symbolizes her sole treasure, the gift of herself in faith and trust to another. She is no longer afraid of letting her voice be heard. In his study, <u>Essai sur le langage de l'adhésion dans l'oeuvre de Bernanos</u>, Leopold Peeters comments: "Elle finira d'ailleurs par se donner totalement par le truchement du chant, sa voix étant la manifestation de sa personne la plus intime. Ce don est total car elle n'exige rien en retour."[5] And as Thérèse in her "Acte d'offrande à l'Amour miséricordieux" proclaimed: "Au soir de cette vie, je paraîtrai devant vous les mains vides . . ." (HA 317-318), Mouchette, having finished her song, "s'aperçut que ses mains étaient vides" (OE,I 1292).

As the saint's love for Christ grew through the contemplation of His Passion so too does Mouchette's love for Arsène develop through seeing him suffer an epileptic seizure. Shortly after her entrance into the monastery, the saint discovered the Carmelite devotion to the Holy Face. Her own devotion to this particular aspect of Christ's Passion was based on the Suffering Servant passage from Isaiah: "Without beauty, without majesty (we saw him), no looks to attract our eyes; a thing despised and rejected by men, a man of sorrows and familiar with suffering . . ." (Isaiah 53: 2-3).

In a letter to her sister, Céline, Thérèse reflects on the hidden beauties of the Holy Face: "il y a <u>si longtemps</u> ... et déjà l'âme du prophète Isaïe se <u>plongeait</u> comme la nôtre dans les BEAUTÉS CACHÉES de Jésus..." (LT 175). In yet another letter to Céline a certain tenderness is revealed in the saint's devotion to the Holy Face: "Regarde sa Face adorable!... Regarde ces yeux éteints et baissés!... regarde ces plaies... Regarde Jésus dans sa Face... Là tu verras comme il nous aime" (LT 142). Contemplating the Holy Face, Thérèse desired to share Christ's suffering: "Moi aussi, je désirais être sans beauté, seule à fouler le vin dans le pressoir, inconnue de toute créature..." (DE 115).

As Mouchette studies Arsène's face with its features distorted with suffering, feelings of love and compassion begin to rise up in her. Her hero's traits "gardent une telle expression de souffrance et d'étonnement qu'il ressemble à un enfant mort" (OE,I 1290). Bernanos' union of childhood and suffering in this passage reminds us of how Thérèse of Lisieux occasionally brought together images of the Christ Child with those of the Passion.[6] Arsène's face is not a handsome one, but in its expression of suffering and childlikeness Mouchette recognizes it as "seulement fait pour elle . . ." (OE,I 1288). It is also "un visage fraternel, un visage complice" (OE,I 1288) for Mouchette who, like Thérèse, longs to share in the suffering of her hero. And so, from the depths of her being there rises up a feeling of pleasure somewhat reminiscent of the saint's joy in suffering and her words: "Oh! que cette Sainte Face là m'a fait de bien dans ma vie!" (DE 115).

This awareness of love led both saint and heroine to an expansion of self and a concern for the well-being of others. It was only after Thérèse felt love enter her heart that she came to understand her vocation as a Carmelite: "Je suis venue pour sauver les âmes et surtout afin de prier pour les prêtres" (HA 172). While contemplating Arsène's suffering, Mouchette feels a tender compassion and a maternal instinct being born in her (OE,I 1289). Within this aspect of love both young women are to know intense suffering in their lives.

Mouchette and the Anguish of Deception

Bernanos portrays Thérèse of Lisieux' experience of the dark night of the soul in the anguish that Mouchette undergoes after Arsène has ruthlessly forced himself upon her. For the saint on the supernatural level and the young heroine on the natural level, the period of intense suffering which follows the offering of self in compassionate love is seen as a trial of faith. It was on Easter night, 1896, one year after her "Acte d'offrande à l'Amour miséricordieux," that the little Carmelite's trial of faith began. Part of her suffering consisted in temptations against faith that were so great that she had to struggle to keep on hoping and believing in God's promise of eternal life.

The saint's words reveal the extent of her suffering: "Mon âme est exilée, le Ciel est fermé pour moi et du côté de la terre, c'est l'épreuve aussi" (DE 52) and "quelles affreuses pensées m'obsèdent! . . . C'est le raisonnement des pires matérialistes qui s'impose à mon esprit . . ." (DE 223). Thérèse tells in her autobiography of how, during this entire period of suffering, she never felt the joy of having faith: "Lorsque je chante le bonheur du Ciel, l'éternelle possession de Dieu, je n'en ressens aucune joie, car je chante simplement ce que JE VEUX CROIRE" (HA 244). Stripped of virtually all spiritual consolation, the saint's only joy on earth was found in suffering out of love.

Thérèse s spiritual trial of faith is mirrored to some extent on the natural level in the suffering and solitude Mouchette feels from the moment Arsène takes advantage of her. The young teenager's dream of the ultimate gift of herself in love has turned into emptiness, "tout ce grand espoir n'était donc que le pressentiment d'une humiliation pire que les autres, bien que de la même espèce" (OE,I 1304). Instead of experiencing joy in love, all Mouchette knows is pure humiliation. Joy can find no place in her suffering. She tries to salvage what remains of her dream by trying to prove to herself that she has at least given her innocence to a hero who has bravely rescued her from a violent storm and killed M. Mathieu, the game-warden. Upon learning from her mother that there was no such storm, but simply a strong wind coming from the sea, Mouchette has to face the cruel reality that "Elle n'a même pas été dupe d'un homme, mais d'un rêve" (OE,I 1311).

The next morning, the truth is driven home further when the heroine discovers that M. Mathieu is alive and well. Mouchette now knows for certain that the precious gift of herself has been taken from her by a lover labeled by William Bush "a lying hero."[7] With this last element of her dream shattered, Mouchette loses all hope. She is alone "vraiment seule aujourd'hui, contre tous" (OE,I 1317).

Because she lacks the spiritual gifts we witness in Thérèse during her trial of faith, it is almost impossible for Mouchette, on the natural level, to arrive at the saint's acceptance of self and abandonment to hope. Despised by others, deceived by her own illusions, how can the young girl not be tempted to hate herself? "Une fois de plus, sa crainte et sa fureur se retournent déjà contre elle-même, c'est elle-même qu'elle hait" (OE,I 1320). She is conscious of the atmosphere of calm and quiet in the village, but "Elle n'y voit aucun motif d'espérance . . ." (OE,I 1321).

The church bells ring out, but the people whom Mouchette meets remain as indifferent to their sound as they do to the young girl's suffering. Nevertheless, the heroine possesses some interior force that spurs her on to hope. The expectancy detected in her final glance at Ménétrier and his mare shows that she would prefer to abandon herself to hope rather than despair. "Elle eût voulu crier, appeler, courir au-devant de ce grotesque sauveur. Mais il s'éloigna de son pas pesant . . ." (OE,I 1344). Thus it is that in her temptation to despair, Mouchette's desire to abandon herself to a natural saviour parallels Thérèse's spiritual abandonment to God during her trial of faith.

From time to time Bernanos uses certain images recalling those of the Carmelite saint to express in concrete terms the interior suffering of his young heroine. The trial of faith which Thérèse depicts as a wall, "un mur qui s'élève jusqu'aux cieux et couvre le firmament étoilé..." (HA 244), is thus paralleled in Mouchette's suffering: "la nuit est si épaisse qu'elle s'y sent comme derrière un mur" (OE,I 1306). And like Thérèse who portrays her trial of faith in terms of darkness, preferring to remain "dans la nuit de la foi" (DE 126) so that others may come to know God, Mouchette, on the natural level, thinks of the night of her trial as "la nuit plus noire, plus traîtresse" (OE,I 1273). The saint compares her night of the soul to having been born "dans un pays environné d'un épais brouillard" (HA 241), while Bernanos describes Mouchette's anguish as resembling "une espèce de brouillard . . ." (OE,I 1315).

To describe the darkness of her soul during her retreat for profession, Thérèse wrote to Pauline that it was as if Christ had led her into a subterranean passage: "où je ne vois rien qu'une clarté à demi voilée, la clarté que répandent autour d'eux les yeux baissés de la face de mon Fiancé!..." (LT 181). Thérèse's difficulty in distinguishing the face of her loved one in the darkness is reflected in Mouchette's attempt to discern Arsène's face: "Mouchette lève la tête, essaie de distinguer le visage penché vers elle dans les ténèbres" (OE,I 1273).

Bernanos parallels in his young heroine not only Thérèse's trial of faith and her description of it, but also her temptation to suicide. We can readily understand why Mouchette, for whom God has no real meaning, is so tempted to give into despair when Thérèse, a canonized saint, underwent a similar temptation as witnessed in her revelation to Pauline: "Oh! comme je sens que je me découragerais si je n'avais pas la foi! ou plutôt si je n'aimais pas le bon Dieu" (DE 112). And, only eight days before her death, she again referred to her temptation to suicide: "quelle grâce d'avoir la foi! Si je n'avais pas eu la foi, je me serais donnée la mort sans hésiter un seul instant..." (DE 174).

It was, therefore, the saint's faith alone that kept her from despair. Since Mouchette's parents failed in their responsibility to pass on to their daughter the Christian faith of her ancestors, the young girl knows nothing beyond a natural faith and hope that death will offer her what life has refused her. Michel Estève has fittingly noted in his work, Le sens de l'amour dans les romans de Bernanos, that through her despair, Mouchette continues none the less to wait for something or some one to save her. "Si elle cherche à quitter la vie, ne serait-ce pas précisément pour découvrir une autre Vie, plus belle, plus mystérieuse, plus digne d'être vécue?"[8]

But what exactly are the heroine's thoughts on death? Do they in any way resemble the saint's? When Thérèse suffered her first hemorrhages she felt happy over the prospect of soon meeting God face to face. She declared: "la pensée du Ciel faisait tout mon bonheur . . ." (HA 240). Death was for the saint, then, something to which she looked forward. Until her experience of the previous night, Mouchette had never seriously thought about death. It is Philomène, the old woman who keeps watch with the dead of the village, who gives Mouchette the impression that death is a positive experience. She assures the young girl that the day of one's death is a most special one. She then gives her some white sheets for her mother's burial and, for the funeral itself, a beautiful white dress to wear which had belonged to a young victim of tuberculosis.

In Mouchette's mind the idea of death thus begins to attach itself to the idea of regaining her original innocence, symbolized by the whiteness of the sheets and the dress (OE,I 1331). Does she long to possess the childlike innocence of the young girl to whom the dress belonged and who, in her youth and manner of death, recalls the saint of Lisieux? In any case, Mouchette's longing for the restoration of the purity and innocence of her childhood is not too far removed from the desires of Thérèse to have her childhood joys restored in eternity as seen in a letter to Céline: ". . . bientôt nous serons dans notre terre natale, bientôt les joies de notre enfance, les soirées du Dimanche, les causeries intimes... tout cela nous sera rendu pour toujours et avec usure . . ." (LT 212). Observed in this light, death can be regarded as something for which Mouchette longs.

Thérèse's thoughts on death hold yet another positive feature: the transformation of her humanity into something divine. The saint once explained to Céline in a letter that some day they would know a divine existence: "nous sommes plus grandes que l'univers entier, un jour nous aurons nous-mêmes une existence Divine..." (LT 135). Philomène suggests something similar to Mouchette when she tells her of how in former times the dead were honoured:

"les morts étaient des dieux, quoi! ça devrait être la vraie religion . . ." (OE,I 1332).

Following in the footsteps of her model, the heroine is now able to look at death no longer with fear but with the excitement of a marvelous discovery, "l'imminente révélation d'un secret, ce même secret que lui avait refusé l'amour" (OE,I 1339). Michel Estève determines that Mouchette is longing for the happiness that life has denied her. He sees this as an unconscious quest for love on the part of the unhappy teenager who is ignorant of the fact that God alone can fulfill this desire: "Le 'désir' de Mouchette n'est-il pas une aspiration vers un Infini de beauté et d'Amour?" (SA 80). As this critic indicates, the heroine's suffering in love comes from her longing for the kind of love which can only be achieved in eternity. In words borrowed from John of the Cross, Thérèse described to Céline the suffering of love: "L'amour ne se paie que par l'amour et les plaies de l'amour ne se guérissent que par l'amour" (LT 138). Is this not the secret that death will reveal to Mouchette?

Mouchette and Salvation

We have already seen how Marcel Arland and Père Brückberger believe that Thérèse's words "tout est grâce" (DE 41) pervade the entire novel. The saint also often stated that God could in an instant transform us to come into His presence. It is interesting to note, too, that Bernanos did not see his heroine as despairing. In the above-mentioned interview with André Rousseaux, the author declares that Mouchette's death was not really a suicide: "Mouchette ne se tue pas vraiment. Elle tombe et s'endort après avoir attendu jusqu'au bout un secours qui ne lui venait pas" ("AR" 245).

If we attempt to interpret the author's thinking here, it would seem that he believes his heroine unconsciously acts out Thérèse's statement: "c'est dans les bras du bon Dieu que je tombe!" (DE 169). For although she was a saint, Thérèse was ever aware of her constant need of God's mercy, especially at the hour of death. As she told her sister, Pauline: "Oh! que je suis heureuse de me voir imparfaite et d'avoir tant besoin de la miséricorde du bon Dieu au moment de la mort" (DE 98).

In the "dédicace" to his novel, Bernanos points out that the Mouchette of Nouvelle histoire de Mouchette shares the same tragic solitude as the Mouchette of Sous le soleil de Satan. He concludes by recommending both of his beloved young heroines to the mercy of God: "A l'une et à l'autre que Dieu fasse miséricorde!" (OE,I 1263).

Thérèse of Lisieux' implicit presence in Nouvelle histoire de Mouchette shows the extent to which the saint has penetrated the author's thought. Until now certain characters of Bernanos' fictional world have tended to be either parallel or reverse images of the saint on the supernatural level. In the little Mouchette, however, we detect for the first time an image of the threefold nature of the Carmelite's spiritual doctrine as it might be lived on the purely natural level: the spirit of childhood, the call to love, and the experience of the trial of faith.

NOTES

CHAPTER 9

[1] André Rousseaux, "Misère et grandeur de Mouchette, visite à M. Georges Bernanos," Bernanos, by Michel Estève (Paris: Gallimard, 1965) 244. Cited hereafter as "AR."

[2] Marcel Arland, "Mouchette et la grâce," Georges Bernanos. Essais et témoignages, ed. Albert Béguin (Paris: Editions du Seuil; Neuchâtel: Editions de la Baconnière, 1949) 137. Cited hereafter as "MA."

[3] R.-L. Brückberger, o.p., Bernanos vivant (Paris: Editions Albin Michel, 1988) 64. Cited hereafter as BV.

[4] Soeur Raymond-Marie, "La simplicité des humbles et des petits," Culture XX (1959): 317. Cited hereafter as "Sim."

[5] Leopold Peeters, Une prose du monde: essai sur le langage de l'adhésion dans l'oeuvre de Bernanos (Paris: Lettres Modernes Minard, 1984) 164.

[6] Thérèse's recreational play, "Les anges à la crèche," presents the Infant Saviour as already dreaming of Calvary (RP 91-109), while in a letter written in 1894 to Pauline Thérèse describes a similar dream of the Christ Child: "son visage enfantin et si beau, Il le voit défiguré, sanglant!... méconnaissable!..." (LT 270).

[7] William Bush, Georges Bernanos (New York: Twayne Publishers, Inc., 1969) 103.

[8] Michel Estève, Le sens de l'amour dans les romans de Bernanos (Paris: Minard Lettres Modernes, 1959) 79. Cited hereafter as SA.

CHAPTER 10

REFORMERS AND SAINTS: "FRÈRE MARTIN" (1943) AND "NOS AMIS LES SAINTS" (1947)

Two brief but remarkable texts, "Frère Martin" and "Nos amis les saints," allow us a rare glimpse of Bernanos' penetrating insight into the mystery of the Church as he neared his end. The author originally intended that "Frère Martin," written in Brazil in 1943, be enlarged to form a whole work devoted to the reformer, Martin Luther. The few pages of the text he did write were subsequently mislaid however and later discovered by Pedro Octavio Carneiro da Cunha and published posthumously by Albert Béguin in 1951 ("FM" 433).[1] The second text, referred to earlier, is that of a conference given by Bernanos in Tunisia on April 4, 1947 to a group of women religious of the order of Charles de Foucauld and published in 1953 by Albert Béguin in a volume of Bernanos' post-war lectures, La liberté pour quoi faire?.[2]

Why have well-intentioned reformers so often ended up outside the Church? Why have obscure religious just as often found themselves raised to the altars of the Church? In his attempt to answer these thought-provoking questions in these two texts, Bernanos seems to have created the contrasting sides of a tapestry. As in Monsieur Ouine where Thérèse's spirit of childhood appeared as it would on the reverse side of a tapestry, so, too, in "Frère Martin" do we find the reverse image of the saint in the reformer. In "Nos amis les saints" however the parallel image of the saint appears on the right side of the tapestry in Bernanos' own vision of how a person becomes a saint.

Although the only explicit reference to Thérèse of Lisieux in these two texts appears in "Nos amis les saints," the saint's presence seems implicitly felt in the author's attempt to explain the difference between a reformer and a saint and to present a definition of sanctity within the grasp of the ordinary person.

"Frère Martin"

Thérèse of Lisieux' presence is felt in "Frère Martin" in Bernanos' compassion for Martin Luther and in his portrayal of the reformer as the reverse image of a saint. Certain passages in the text are reminiscent of Thérèse's letter to her sister, Céline, in July, 1891 in which she speaks of Père Hyacinthe Loyson, the Carmelite priest who had left the Church and for whom she would offer her last communion. That Bernanos entitles his text "Frère Martin" rather than simply "Martin Luther" parallels the Carmelite's sisterly concern for Père Loyson to whom she referred as "notre frère" (LT 210).

A similar compassion is revealed in the sympathetic way in which the author and the saint speak of the one who has wandered away from the fold. For the author, the German reformer is "ce malheureux, égaré par la haine et pris au piège du mal dont il subit visiblement la fascination" ("FM" 438), while for the saint, the ex-Carmelite priest is "Le malheureux prodigue" and "cette pauvre brebis égarée" (LT 209) for whom she has offered her suffering.

But an even more significant parallel between Bernanos' attitude and Thérèse's lies in their obvious refusal to condemn the "sinner" and in their confidence that God in His merciful love will take pity on him. Bernanos believes that what is most important about the above image of the unfortunate

Luther caught in the snare of evil is "qu'il y a plutôt là de quoi nous faire rêver aux mystérieux desseins de la toute-puissante miséricorde sur cet homme étrange" ("FM" 438).

Bernanos shows sympathy for Luther in his suffering by stating that we cannot underestimate the power of God's merciful love with regard to Luther's salvation: "qui peut savoir, en effet, où la douce pitié de Dieu cachera ceux qu'elle a volés à l'enfer, par quelque stratagème irrésistible, pour l'éternelle confusion des justes et des sages?" ("FM" 439). Confident in God's merciful love, Thérèse similarly believed God to be capable of "quelque stratagème irrésistible" to lead Père Loyson back to the fold: "il est bien coupable, plus coupable peut-être que ne l'a jamais été un pécheur qui se soit converti, mais Jésus ne peut-il pas faire une fois ce qu'Il n'a encore jamais fait?" (LT 209).

Just as Bernanos seems to have portrayed his fictional "sinners" as reverse images of the Carmelite saint, so, too, do we find him portraying Martin Luther as a reverse image of Thérèse.[3] But in order for us to understand how it is possible for a reformer such as Luther to become the reverse image of a saint, Bernanos discusses, first of all, three important features about the Church. Declaring that "Il y a un mystère dans l'Eglise" ("FM" 436), he affirms that if a person looks for anything in the Church other than Christ, he will end up by becoming a part of the mediocrity he is certain to find there. It is also essential to understand the difference between the visible Church and the invisible Church. The former, belonging to the temporal order, is the institutional Church with all its many problems and injustices. The latter, belonging to the eternal order, is the realm of the saints. Finally, proclaiming that "L'Eglise n'a pas besoin de réformateurs, mais de saints" ("FM" 440), Bernanos establishes a contrast between reformers and saints. A reformer, he contends, could just as easily have been a saint. Specially chosen for an extraordinary destiny, "les grands hérésiarques qui ont ravagé l'Eglise auraient pu aussi bien en devenir la gloire . . ." ("FM" 442).

Bernanos claims that reformers have often received great graces and have cast them away. The author's thoughts in this regard remind us of Père Pichon's words of caution to Thérèse in which he urges her to thank God for the many graces He had given her: "car s'il vous abandonnait, au lieu d'être un petit ange, vous deviendriez un petit démon" (HA 173). We also recall how as a child Thérèse was so inspired by the deeds of Jeanne d'Arc that she felt that she too had a marvelous destiny marked out for her and that she would become a great saint (HA 84-85).

Throughout much of his essay Bernanos elaborates on the contrast between a reformer, witnessed explicitly as Martin Luther, and a saint, felt implicitly as Thérèse of Lisieux. It is not surprising then to find Bernanos reflecting on what could have been Luther's childhood "conversion" had he co-operated with the graces God might have offered him. The author imagines God speaking to the young Martin as a father to a son, begging him not to lose his childlike relationship with Him and "de rester humble et docile dans l'accomplissement de sa tâche . . ." ("FM" 443). And, according to the author, Martin Luther seems to have had certain natural qualities that could have encouraged this childlike attitude and loving acceptance of his daily task for: "il était plutôt fait pour la joie, la rude joie du travail ouvrier, du travail quotidien, du fardeau mis sur l'épaule, ou déchargé d'un coup de reins" ("FM" 441). What we are really witnessing in this passage is God inviting Luther to follow Thérèse's attitude of joyfully and confidently expecting everything from God day by day as a little child expects everything from his father: "C'est reconnaître son néant, attendre tout du bon Dieu, comme un petit enfant attend tout de son père; c'est ne s'inquiéter de rien, ne point gagner de fortune" (DE 119).

Bernanos then borrows Theresian imagery of littleness to describe what Luther's relationship with God could have been. As the saint desired to be the Christ Child's "petite balle de nulle valeur qu'il pouvait jeter à terre" (HA 159) or "presser sur son coeur" (HA 159), so Bernanos envisages Luther as being offered the choice to be "une petite pierre dans la main du Très-Haut, ramassée hier, rejetée demain" ("FM" 443).

In addition, he sees God as having offered Luther special graces to perform his task as reformer, but the latter must not take false pride in these gifts. God reminds him that health, physical strength, and a gift for eloquence and debate are not "les armes préférées" ("FM" 443) of His saints, but only the means to "déblayer, arracher, déraciner les souches pourries" ("FM" 443).

God then warns Luther that unless a person has humility he will experience great difficulty in trying to find Him in His Church: "plus difficile encore à découvrir que dans la petite étable de Bethléhem, pour ceux qui ne vont pas humblement vers moi, derrière les Mages et les Bergers" ("FM" 444). All that is necessary to find Him are "une étoile et un coeur pur" ("FM" 444). The Wise Men and the Shepherds discovered the Redeemer of the world in the guise of a helpless Infant lying in a manger. They were the first to meditate on the mystery of Christ's greatness in His weakness just as centuries later Thérèse of Lisieux would relate how the Christ Child, only one hour old, rendered her strong and courageous (<u>HA</u> 113).

Bernanos gives us to understand that because Luther did not search for God with a similar spirit of humility, he failed to find Him in the visible Church. Instead, the reformer became so overwhelmed by the scandals of the Renaissance Church that he entirely misunderstood what the term "reform" really means. Declaring that "Le malheur de Martin Luther fut de prétendre réformer" ("FM" 439), the author proclaims that the Church cannot be reformed by means similar to those used to reform a temporal society: "on ne réforme l'Eglise visible qu'en souffrant pour l'Eglise invisible. On ne réforme les vices de l'Eglise qu'en prodiguant l'exemple de ses vertus les plus héroïques" ("FM" 439).

Bernanos portrays Luther as not realizing the spiritual value contained in the acceptance of suffering. At the age of fourteen, Thérèse already understood this sublime concept when she believed that God was destining her to become "l'apôtre des apôtres par la prière et le sacrifice" (<u>HA</u> 125). A few months before her death, the saint remarked to Pauline: "C'est par la prière et le sacrifice que nous pouvons seulement être utiles à l'Eglise" (<u>DE</u> 64).

The writer depicts Luther as failing to love, "égaré par la haine" ("FM" 438), consumed by anger against the injustices and mediocrity of the Renaissance Church. Thus he appears as a reverse image of the Carmelite saint who offered herself as a victim of holocaust to God's merciful love and who, in the above mentioned letter where she speaks of Père Loyson, realized that "il n'y a que la souffrance qui puisse enfanter des âmes à Jésus..." (<u>LT</u> 209).

In his refusal to use prayer and sacrifice, "les armes préferées" ("FM" 443) of the saints, Luther can be interpreted as a negative image of the saint who lovingly offered her intense suffering for the conversion of sinners. Although Thérèse certainly did not set out to reform the Church, her example of heroic virtue, her message of God's merciful love, and the acceptance of her impotence helped break down the narrow confines of late nineteenth century spirituality. Bernanos leaves his reader with the impression that, in his attempt to reform the Church, Luther's rejection of God's invitation to remain childlike in his spirituality and his refusal to use the weapons of the invisible Church are what really led him outside the walls of the visible Church.

"Nos amis les saints"

Forming a contrasting parallel with "Frère Martin" is "Nos amis les saints," Bernanos' lecture to a group of women religious in which he presents his own thoughts on how the average person can attain sanctity in his daily life. Thérèse of Lisieux' presence seems implicit in the author's various statements pointing out the qualities and attitudes necessary to become a saint.

The Church, Bernanos declares, is not some type of refuge or spiritual inn. It is, on the contrary, "une force en marche" (<u>Lib</u> 214), kept from straying away from the right path by the constant vigilance of the saints.

The author imagines that one can learn to be a saint in much the same way that children learn grownup ways of behaving by playing "monsieur" and "madame." Perhaps, he suggests, this is how Thérèse of Lisieux learned sanctity: "En tout cas, il semble bien que la petite soeur Thérèse ne s'y soit pas prise autrement, on pourrait dire qu'elle est devenue sainte en jouant aux saints avec l'Enfant Jésus . . ." (<u>Lib</u> 213). If, as Bernanos argues, children's games can give a boy the longing to be a mechanic or a railroad engineer, cannot the desire to become a saint be experienced in a similar fashion? Certainly the <u>Histoire d'une âme</u> reveals how the little Thérèse practised virtue and mortification from her earliest years.

Bernanos' reflection on the Carmelite's desire to be a saint shows how childhood and sanctity are closely linked in his thought. During his Brazilian exile, he wrote in the autograph book of a young girl a message in which he gives her this advice: "restez fidèle à l'enfance! Ne devenez jamais une grande personne! Il y a un complot des grandes personnes contre l'enfance, et il suffit de lire l'Evangile pour s'en rendre compte."[4] Even in the author's personal life this union of childhood and sanctity were important as is seen in his letter to Dom Paul Gordan in March, 1943: "je retourne à ma vie très ordinaire, qui n'est plus l'enfance, hélas! car j'ai perdu l'enfance, je ne pourrais la reconquérir que par la sainteté - . . ." (<u>Corr</u>.II 503).

Bernanos' fusion of childhood and sanctity forms a close parallel with Thérèse's thoughts such as witnessed in her letter to Père Roulland in May, 1897: "je vois qu'il suffit de reconnaître son néant et de s'abandonner comme un enfant dans les bras du Bon Dieu. . . . je me réjouis d'être petite puisque les enfants seuls et ceux qui leur ressemblent seront admis au banquet céleste" (<u>LT</u> 409).

Reflecting on what type of person it takes to be a saint, Bernanos declares that saints are very ordinary people who in no way resemble the modern idea of supermen or the heroes of ancient history: "Les saints ne sont pas des héros, à la manière des héros de Plutarque. Un héros nous donne l'illusion de dépasser l'humanité, le saint ne la dépasse pas, il l'assume . . ." (Lib 228). Accepting his human weakness, the saint tries to imitate as closely as possible his Divine Model. He rests confident in the knowledge that "le Christ n'est pas mort seulement pour les héros, il est mort aussi pour les lâches" (Lib 228).

Although no explicit reference is made to Thérèse of Lisieux, her presence seems implicit in Bernanos' reflection on sanctity as it reminds us of a similar passage in Lettre aux Anglais in which the saint is named (Ang 28). And indeed what saint can seem more appealing to Christians than one who recognizes her own impotence and complete dependence on God's merciful love? Thérèse certainly never thought of herself as being superhuman. Shortly before her death she confessed to Pauline: "...Non, je ne me crois pas une grande sainte! Je me crois une toute petite sainte; mais je pense que le bon Dieu s'est plu à mettre en moi des choses qui font du bien à moi et aux autres" (DE 112). It was simply the grace of God that raised Thérèse to the heights of sanctity, for she saw herself as but a weak child: "Je ne suis qu'une enfant, impuissante et faible" (HA 223), "je suis trop petite pour faire de grandes choses..." (HA 229), and these words of encouragement for others: "Jésus ne demande pas de grandes actions, mais seulement l'abandon et la reconnaissance . . ." (HA 215). Thérèse also longed to imitate Christ, her model, in His suffering: "il nous faut ressembler à Jésus, à Jésus dont le visage était caché..." (LT 252). Her simplicity and love for Christ were so perfect that she no longer feared death: "Si j'ai peur du Voleur! Comment voulez-vous que j'aie peur de quelqu'un que j'aime tant?!" (DE 60).

In this lecture on the saints, love plays an important role in Bernanos' concept of what sanctity is, just as it does also in Thérèse of Lisieux.' The author reminds us that God is Love and that creation is above all an act of love. Moreover, man was given a free will so that he could freely choose to love: "l'amour est un choix libre, ou il n'est rien" (Lib 219). The world of God's love is the dwelling place of the saints; indeed, Bernanos declares, "Les saints ont le génie de l'amour" (Lib 229). Because of their awareness of God's love for them, they are not at all scandalized by the faults of the visible Church. Perhaps this is why they are so willing to offer their suffering for others. Moved by God's love for her, Thérèse freely chose to offer herself as a victim of holocaust to merciful love (HA 318).

Like Thérèse, Bernanos believes that the saint makes a total gift of himself in love. He does not work just for his own salvation: "Un saint ne vit pas du revenu de ses revenus, ni même seulement de ses revenus, il vit sur son capital, il engage totalement son âme" (Lib 225). A fourteen page manuscript of an article of the author's, dated August, 1943, contains a similar statement: "Car il n'y a qu'une manière de se donner, c'est de se donner tout entier . . ." (VS 97) which corresponds with the saint's statement: "Je ne veux pas être une sainte à moitié . . ." (HA 36). Without worrying about her own personal salvation, Thérèse also desired to work solely for the conversion of others: "je veux travailler pour votre seul Amour, dans l'unique but de vous faire plaisir, de consoler votre Coeur Sacré et de sauver des âmes qui vous aimeront éternellement" (HA 317).

This concept of working for the salvation of others stands out in statements made by both the author and the saint regarding the Communion of saints. Bernanos asks: "Quels sont les riches et les pauvres de cette étonnante communauté? Ceux qui donnent et ceux qui reçoivent? Que de surprises!" (Lib 226), thus repeating an earlier statement he made in Les enfants humiliés: "Nous apprendrons de Dieu, le jour venu, quels liens mystérieux lient les grands pécheurs aux grands saints . . ." (OE,II 814). Thérèse had similar thoughts: "Combien de fois ai-je pensé que je pouvais devoir toutes les grâces que j'ai reçues aux prières d'une âme qui m'aurait demandée au bon Dieu et que je ne connaîtrai qu'au Ciel" (DE 80).

Bernanos also parallels the Carmelite saint in his idea that sanctity consists in the loving acceptance of the sufferings and trials of daily life. He claims that when suffering is considered by the intellect alone, it is refused as an evil, but that saints tend to look on suffering as the manifestation of God's will and so they lovingly accept it. A person's "yes" to God's will is all that is needed to make him a saint as seen in the author's examples of the poor man's prayer of gratitude for the gift of freedom and the mother's acceptance of the death of her child: "Oui, au moment où cet homme, cette femme acceptaient leur destin, s'acceptaient eux-mêmes, humblement, - le mystère de la Création s'accomplissait en eux . . . Bref, ils étaient des saints" (Lib 225). As William Bush has aptly pointed out, it is not the suffering itself but rather the acceptance of suffering that makes one a saint (SE 15). This concept is witnessed in the influence that Bernanos' fictional "saints" have on the lives of those with whom they come in contact.

This acceptance of suffering and abandonment to God's will is exemplified by the Carmelite saint in such statements as: "Mon seul but serait donc d'accomplir la volonté du bon Dieu, de me sacrifier pour Lui de la manière qu'il lui plairait" (HA 249); "Je ne m'inquiète pas du tout de l'avenir, je suis sûre que le bon Dieu fera sa volonté, c'est la seule grâce que je désire . . ." (LT 396); "Mais, au fond, je suis bien abandonnée pour vivre, pour mourir, pour guérir, et pour aller en Cochinchine, si le bon Dieu le veut" (DE 31).

Finally, if we were to summarize the various qualities and attitudes of a saint which Bernanos has mentioned in "Nos amis les saints," we would arrive at what we might consider to be the author's own statement on sanctity. The saint is a very ordinary person who desires simply and humbly to imitate Christ's life and suffering. There are no half-measures for the saint, for his life consists in a total gift of himself to God and the loving "yes" to the will of the Father in his sufferings.

If we compare this "statement" with two of Thérèse of Lisieux' statements on sanctity, we can see how closely the elements of Bernanos' concept of what it means to be a saint parallel the saint's thoughts on sanctity. "La Sainteté ne consiste pas à dire de belles choses, elle ne consiste pas même à les penser, à les sentir!... elle consiste à <u>souffrir</u> et à souffrir <u>de tout</u>" (<u>LT</u> 145). "La sainteté n'est pas dans telle ou telle pratique, elle consiste en une <u>disposition du coeur</u> qui nous rend humbles et petits entre les bras de Dieu, conscients de notre faiblesse, et confiants jusqu'à l'audace en sa bonté de Père" (<u>DE</u> 110). As Guy Gaucher has observed: "Cette disposition de l'âme est celle des saints de Bernanos" ("BT" 165).

Implicit evidence of Thérèse of Lisieux' presence in "Nos amis les saints" thus reveals how the spirituality that Bernanos admired so greatly in the Carmelite saint is not only the type of spirituality that informs his fictional "saints," but that it is also the same spirituality that has become so much a part of his own thought on how the average person can become a saint through ordinary means. We have already seen how the author believed that the nineteen twenties' canonizations of Jeanne d'Arc and Thérèse of Lisieux signified the relevance of their message of heroic childhood for modern times. So perhaps is it with such a thought in mind that Bernanos concludes his text on the saints in this fashion: "Oh! sans doute, on pourrait croire que ce n'est plus l'heure des saints, que l'heure des saints est passée. Mais comme je l'écrivais jadis, l'heure des saints vient toujours" (<u>Lib</u> 230).

NOTES

CHAPTER 10

[1] "Frère Martin" is also published in Georges Bernanos, <u>Les prédestinés</u>, textes rassemblés et présentés par Jean-Loup Bernanos, préface de Mgr Daniel Pézeril (Paris: Editions du Seuil, 1983) 105-123, and in Georges Bernanos, <u>La vocation spirituelle de la France</u>, inédits rassemblés et présentés par Jean-Loup Bernanos (Paris: Plon, 1975) 223-238.

[2] "Nos amis les saints" is also published in <u>Les prédestinés</u> (81-104).

[3] We might note in passing that Bernanos' implicit comparison of Thérèse of Lisieux and Martin Luther is not without a certain justification. René Laurentin devotes nine pages of his volume on the Carmelite saint to showing how modern scholars and post Vatican II theologians have drawn points of comparison between the saint and the reformer [René Laurentin, <u>Thérèse de Lisieux: mythes et réalité</u> (Paris: Beauchesne, 1972: 23-32)].

[4] Georges Bernanos, "Sur un album," <u>Bulletin de la société des amis de Georges Bernanos</u> 12-13 (1952): 4.

CHAPTER 11

BERNANOS' SPIRITUAL TESTAMENT:
DIALOGUES DES CARMÉLITES (1947-1948)

Based on the martyrdom of sixteen Carmelites of Compiègne on July 17, 1794, ten days before the fall of Robespierre on July 27, Dialogues des Carmélites is not only Bernanos' last fictional work, but it is also his spiritual testament. Although no explicit reference can be found to either Thérèse of Lisieux' name or quotes, her influence seems more pervasive in this work than in any other. This is all the more remarquable in that the author was supposedly under contract to provide merely the dialogues for a film scenario based on Gertrud von le Fort's Die Letzte am Schafott and written by the Dominican, Père Brückberger, and Philippe Agostini.

Critics such as Joseph Boly have pointed out that with the exception of a few modifications, Dialogues des Carmélites remains faithful to the basic themes of the short German novel. Boly further states that Bernanos based his dialogues on the scenario which Brückberger had sent him and which was true to von le Fort's work. Although he had read Die Letzte am Schafott several years earlier, Bernanos did not re-read it while writing Dialogues des Carmélites.[1]

Bernanos' fidelity to the original work can be partially explained by the fact that the essential themes of Die Letzte am Schafott are ones that by their very nature would strike a resounding chord in Bernanos' own heart. In his spiritual biography of the author, Guy Gaucher explains that in writing <u>Dialogues des Carmélites</u>, Bernanos was preparing for his own death and that "Les thèmes de la peur, de l'angoisse, de l'agonie, de l'espérance, de l'abandon à Dieu, de la victoire définitive sont la substance même de sa vie spirituelle" (<u>IE</u> 138).

Yet <u>Dialogues des Carmélites</u> differs from <u>Die Letzte am Schafott</u> in the type of spirituality portrayed by the Carmelite heroines. Critics such as Michel Estève are quick to note that in comparison with the German story, Bernanos' play possesses a greater spiritual depth. Estève declares that while Bernanos retains much of the original work, "il s'avance beaucoup plus loin que Gertrude von Le Fort sur le chemin de l'exploration du surnaturel."[2]

In his above-mentioned work, Gaucher also remarks on how Bernanos' spirituality has flavoured <u>Dialogues des Carmélites</u> to the extent that it is a "véritable testament spirituel où Bernanos a tout mis de lui-même et qui ne peut laisser aucun doute sur la profondeur de sa vie spirituelle" (<u>IE</u> 138). Then, in his article on Bernanos and Thérèse, this same critic indicates that the spirituality found in the author's last work is definitely that of Thérèse of Lisieux. Gaucher feels confident in stating that "A un niveau très profond, l'esprit thérésien est présent dans ce scénario" ("BT" 238). But how can it be possible for Thérèse of Lisieux' spirituality to be so strongly felt in a work which, after all, has respected the themes of the work on which it was based?

If we re-examine the explicit references to the little Carmelite found in Bernanos' polemical works of the nineteen forties, we are not at all surprised at her obvious influence on <u>Dialogues des Carmélites</u>. We are immediately struck by the similarity between the themes of the passages containing these references and the themes of <u>Dialogues des Carmélites</u>. In <u>Lettre aux Anglais</u>, for example, we recall that Beranos used Thérèse as an example of how the French are able to put their misfortunes to best use. At her weakest moment, the saint showed heroism by her childlike acceptance of God's will. Her weakest moment became, therefore, her finest moment. For Bernanos, this is honour raised to the supernatural level (Ang 28-30).

We have also seen how at the ceremony for the christening of the Brazilian airplane, "Jeanne d'Arc," Bernanos pointed to the fact that the twentieth century canonizations of Jeanne d'Arc and Thérèse of Lisieux were a sign of France's historic mission to the world (Che 651). Both young women saints symbolize the innocence of childhood and supernatural heroism in the face of fear and anguish.

Themes appearing in Bernanos' late polemical works are thus echoed in Dialogues des Carmélites: fear, honour, the Communion of saints, agony, spiritual childhood, and spiritual poverty are all inter-connected in the play. Not only Blanche de la Force, the young heroine, but all the members of the Carmelite community, embark on a spiritual adventure that will lead them to a deeper awareness of the nature of their vocation of offering themselves as innocent victims for the salvation of Carmel and of France. It is a journey in which parallel images of the diverse aspects of Thérèse of Lisieux' spirituality will be found, not just in one or two characters, but in several, in much the same way as a beam of light refracted and dispersed by a prism forms a brilliant display of colours. Bernanos' Dialogues des Carmélites shows the gradual evolution in the spirituality of the future martyrs who set forth on the road travelled by Thérèse of Lisieux leading to Divine Love. As the saint stated: "ce chemin c'est l'abandon du petit enfant qui s'endort sans crainte dans les bras de son Père..." (HA 214).

After Bernanos' death his manuscript for these dialogues describing the road leading to Divine Love was edited by Albert Béguin for publication as a volume divided into a prologue and five sequences (Boly 20). In the prologue we come to understand why Blanche de la Force suffers from an innate sense of fear. Indeed we are told that on the night of Blanche's birth, her mother, the Marquise de la Force, was so terrified by a frenzied mob surrounding her carriage that she went into premature labour and died giving birth to her daughter.

First Sequence

In the first sequence, Blanche, now a young woman of fifteen, is ashamed of her weakness, judging it to run counter to the code of honour expected of a member of the nobility. Her brother supports this belief by telling their father that Blanche's fear is an inherent weakness: "Le mal est entré en elle comme le ver dans le fruit..." (OE,I 1571).

Blanche, however, makes a noble effort to combat her weakness in a way that parallels Thérèse of Lisieux' acceptance of her impotence. But at this stage in her spiritual journey, the young heroine is far from ready to accept herself and let God act in her through her weakness. The joy the Carmelite saint felt in suffering and accepting her weakness out of love will be experienced by Blanche only at the very end of the play. But already in the first sequence, the young woman recognizes God's presence in her weakness, and so she declares to her father: "Loin d'en ressentir de la honte; je devrais plutôt être tentée de tirer gloire d'une telle prédestination" (OE,I 1578).

Although Bernanos' young heroine gives the outward appearance of accepting her weakness, there is no real joy in her acceptance. It will be through suffering alone that she will discover the joy of participating in the Holy Agony. Yet even at this stage on the road to perfect love that banishes fear, taught by Saint John (I John, iii,18), Blanche resembles the saint of Lisieux. For neither did Thérèse, in the beginning of her spiritual life, experience any joy in suffering, but as time passed she was able to claim: "j'ai reconnu bien vite que plus on avance dans ce chemin, plus on se croit éloigné du terme, aussi maintenant je me résigne à me voir toujours imparfaite et j'y trouve ma joie..." (HA 182). Also, in her growing awareness that it is possible for her to find glory in her inordinate fear, Blanche parallels Thérèse's thoughts as a young girl that God was destining her to become a great saint in spite of her impotence (HA 85).

Certain elements pertaining to Blanche's call to enter the monastery of Compiègne are also present in the saint's vocation. Thérèse's sole purpose in entering the Carmel of Lisieux was for God alone. Blanche similarly desires to sacrifice all to God: "Je lui sacrifie tout, j'abandonne tout, je renonce à tout pour qu'il me rende l'honneur" (OE,I 1579). Although her motive for entering religious life is, like the saint's, a noble one, there is a basic difference in the aspirations of the two young women.

Blanche hopes that by sacrificing everything to God, He will restore her honour. Thérèse had no such expectation upon entering the monastery, for God had already on that special Christmas night of 1886 restored her strength of character: "la petite Thérèse avait retrouvé la force d'âme qu'elle avait perdue à 4 ans et demi et c'était pour toujours qu'elle devait la conserver!..." (HA 114). With regard to life in the monastery, Blanche displays beforehand a certain lucidity regarding the courage she will need to live at close quarters with companions inferior to herself in birth and education. This, as we know, was one of the sufferings Thérèse had to face in the Lisieux Carmel. Finally, both young women enter the monastery at age fifteen.

Second Sequence

Through the words and actions of Madame de Croissy, the first prioress, and through the events that take place in the days following Blanche's entrance into the monastery, the second sequence gives us our first impression of what the Carmelite vocation to love entails. In her interview with Blanche, Madame de Croissy's words reveal a spirituality that combines Thérèse of Lisieux' spirit of poverty with her spirit of childhood. The saint's thoughts on spiritual poverty,

"On éprouve une si grande paix d'être absolument pauvre, de ne compter que sur le bon Dieu" (DE 117), indicate a poverty that consists in a total détachment from self. The prioress' concept of the poverty demanded of a religious is very similar to this: "Mais à quoi bon, pour une religieuse, être détachée de tout, si elle n'est pas détachée de soi-même, c'est-à-dire de son propre détachement?" (OE,I 1581).

At the same time, Madame de Croissy also informs Blanche about what she can expect to find in the daily life of a Carmelite. She explains how tasks that give the outward appearance of being the lightest are often the most difficult to perform: "On franchit une montagne et on bute sur un caillou" (OE,I 1582). Sanctity can thus be found in the faithful performance of little daily tasks, a lesson which Thérèse's sister, Marie, had taught her early in life (HA 87).

When Blanche confesses to the prioress her desire to be unnoticed by others, "Je ne demande qu'à passer inaperçue..." (OE,I 1583), her words seem to echo the saint's request to her sister, Marie, in May, 1888: "Demandez que votre petite fille reste toujours un petit grain de sable bien obscur, bien caché à tous les yeux, que Jésus seul puisse le voir . . ." (LT 86).

Madame de Croissy feels obliged to warn Blanche about some of the trials of monastic life, one of which is the extreme solitude "où une véritable religieuse est exposée à vivre et à mourir" (OE,I 1584). This is the type of solitude about which Thérèse of Lisieux during her final illness could only state: "le bon Dieu seul peut me comprendre" (DE 69). The prioress then speaks of other trials that the young heroine can expect to encounter in the monastery. Blanche's reply: "Qu'importe, si Dieu me donne la force" (OE,I 1585) parallels Thérèse's remark: "le bon Dieu me donne ce qu'il me faut" (DE 215), and as such indicates that the heroine is in the right direction on the road to confidence and abandonment.

A brief instruction on the childlike virtues of simplicity and abandonment to God that are so characteristic of the Carmelite saint's spirit of childhood also forms part of Blanche's interview with Madame de Croissy. Thérèse's definition of spiritual childhood, "la voie de l'enfance spirituelle, c'est le chemin de la confiance et du total abandon" (DE 223), finds a corresponding explanation in the prioress' comparison of the Carmelites' prayer to the prayer of a little shepherd boy. The Carmelites spend their lives trying to acquire a similar childike spirit of simplicity and abandonment to God's will, "car c'est un don de l'enfance qui le plus souvent ne survit pas à l'enfance... Une fois sorti de l'enfance, il faut très longtemps souffrir pour y rentrer . . ." (OE,I 1586). Thus, for Madame de Croissy, and for Bernanos as well, the importance of maintaining or regaining a childlike attitude to God is as essential as it was for the Carmelite saint who stated: "L'âge n'est rien aux yeux du bon Dieu, et je m'arrangerai bien à rester petite enfant, même en vivant très longtemps" (DE 35).

From the outset of her religious life, Blanche seems placed under the two aspects of Thérèse's spirituality: her spirit of childhood and especially her call to suffering. The young heroine's choice of name, Soeur Blanche de l'Agonie du Christ, not only recalls the second part of the saint's name, but further reveals, through Madame de Croissy's startled reaction, that Blanche, like Thérèse, will be invited to enter more deeply into Christ's Passion wherein lies His true glory, and ultimately her own. But Blanche is also placed under the protection of the Christ Child. At her entrance to the monastery, the Carmelites bring her to pray before a statue of the Little King of Glory to whom they have a special devotion.

In the remaining scenes of the second sequence, Thérèse's participation in Christ's redemptive suffering and her spirit of childhood are echoed in the events that take place. Shortly after Blanche's arrival, we witness the final illness and deathbed scene of the prioress. Much to everyone's surprise, Madame de Croissy appears to be afraid of death. Nevertheless, in her abandonment to God: "Je m'en remets à Lui pour guérir ou mourir, selon Sa Volonté" (OE,I 1590), she faithfully imitates Thérèse's attitude: "Mais, au fond, je suis bien abandonée pour vivre, pour mourir, pour guérir, et pour aller en Cochinchine, si le bon Dieu le veut" (DE 31). Moreover, when Mère Marie, the sub-prioress, informs the doctor that Carmelites strive to merit peace for others and not for themselves, we begin to understand that Madame de Croissy is suffering in place of someone else. Thérèse's image of God filling her empty hands with spiritual goods for others seems implied in the prioress' suffering which also recalls the curé of Ambricourt's words: "O merveille, qu'on puisse ainsi faire présent de ce qu'on ne possède pas soi-même, ô doux miracle de nos mains vides!" (OE,I 1170).

Then, momentarily leaving aside this scene of anguish, Bernanos introduces us to Constance, the postulant destined to become Blanche's companion in life and death and who, according to Yves Bridel, "est l'une des plus pures incarnations de l'esprit d'enfance de toute l'oeuvre bernanosienne" (EE 221). Her steps never once falter along the road of Theresian abandonment to God's merciful love. It is Constance who, as Luc Estang was the first to point out,[3] represents Thérèse de l'Enfant-Jésus. The young postulant's childlike simplicity and joy in the simple pleasures of family life reflect the saint's happiness in the midst of her family circle. Constance also parallels Thérèse's fidelity in her daily tasks: "J'essaie de faire le mieux possible ce qu'on me commande, mais ce qu'on me commande m'amuse..." (OE,I 1593). For Blanche's companion, happiness consists in doing God's will. Endowed with a generous nature, she is also willing to substitute her life for Madame de Croissy. Like Thérèse of Lisieux, Constance is not afraid of death and would prefer to die young. And as the saint told her sister, Pauline: "Depuis mon enfance, le bon Dieu m'a donné le sentiment profond que je mourrais jeune" (DE 75), Constance similarly declares to Blanche: "J'ai compris que Dieu me ferait la grâce de ne pas me laisser vieillir . . ." (OE,I 1595).

If we look again at the deathbed scene, we find Madame de Croissy in the midst of extreme suffering and solitude resembling what Thérèse endured before her death. The saint's description of her spiritual suffering: "Mais c'est l'agonie toute pure, sans aucun mélange de consolation" (DE 183) is reflected in Madame de Croissy's words to Mère Marie as "Je suis seule, ma Mère, absolument seule, sans aucune consolation" (OE,I 1597). Like the saint, the prioress is a prisoner of Christ's Agony. She soon begins to realize that just as Christ came to fulfill the old law, so too, are the Carmelites, through the acceptance of their suffering, called to raise honour from its worldly level to the supernatural plane.

The influence of Theresian spirituality is further seen in the prioress' desire to offer herself as a victim of love to save Blanche, her youngest and most vulnerable daughter. Since she can no longer give her life for Bernanos' young heroine, Madame de Croissy willingly offers her death in all its poverty. In the humiliation of her extreme suffering at the hour of her death and her frightening vision of the Carmelites' chapel, desecrated and stripped of its ornaments, can indeed be found an echo of the saint's explanation of her dreadful suffering shortly before her death: "Jamais je n'aurais cru qu'il était possible de tant souffrir! jamais! jamais! Je ne puis m'expliquer cela que par les désirs ardents que j'ai eus de sauver des âmes" (DE 185).

But in spite of the fact that Madame de Croissy offers her death for Blanche, the end of sequence two finds the young heroine still in the grips of her weakness. Left alone to watch beside the body, Blanche takes fright and runs out of the chapel.

Third Sequence

The third sequence deepens our understanding of the Carmelite vocation and, through Constance's spirit of childhood and Blanche's role of expiatory victim, allows us to penetrate further the twofold nature of the saint's name: Thérèse de l'Enfant-Jésus et de la Sainte-Face. In the opening scene we find the two postulants busy making a cross of flowers for Madame de Croissy's grave and, at the same time, discussing who will be the new prioress. Constance shows a childlike attitude in her belief that God will answer her prayer that Mère Marie be elected: "Dieu est parfaitement capable de faire nommer Mère Marie, seulement pour faire plaisir à un pauvre petit ver de terre comme moi" (OE,I 1613). Indeed Constance's simplicity is not too far removed from Thérèse's belief that God would do her will: "Il faudra que le bon Dieu fasse toutes mes volontés au Ciel, parce que je n'ai jamais fait ma volonté sur la terre" (DE 73).

But Constance is also preoccupied with the idea that somehow the prioress' death was not suited to her, that it was as if God had given her the wrong death. She tries to explain these thoughts to Blanche: "Oui, ça devait être la mort d'une autre, une mort pas à la mesure de notre Prieure, une mort trop petite pour elle . . ." (OE,I 1613). According to Constance, when this other person comes to die, she is going to be surprised at how easy it will seem. Her thoughts certainly seem to have an effect on Blanche. Do not her silence, and then the shakiness in her voice, both suggest that it is already beginning to dawn on Bernanos' young heroine that it was really her death that Madame de Croissy suffered?

The prioress' gift of her death to Blanche, a death without fear, recalls how following the death of Mère Geneviève, Thérèse felt a sudden unexpected change take place in her interior disposition: "en un clin d'oeil je me suis sentie remplie d'une joie et d'une ferveur indicibles, c'était comme si Mère Geneviève m'avait donné une partie de la félicité dont elle jouissait . . ." (HA 193). Constance's thoughts on the Communion of saints also correspond with Thérèse's statement: "Combien de fois ai-je pensé que je pouvais devoir toutes les grâces que j'ai reçues aux prières d'une âme qui m'aurait demandée au bon Dieu et que je ne connaîtrai qu'au Ciel" (DE 80).

The next scene finds the Carmelites assembled in the Chapter Room ready to make their obedience to Madame Lidoine, the newly elected prioress. Invited by the new prioress to assist her in addressing the community, Mère Marie reminds the religious of the importance of obedience, an obedience which consists in the complete abandonment of oneself to God's will. Thérèse's words: "Ce qui me contente uniquement c'est de faire la volonté du bon Dieu" (DE 155) show this to be the degree of obedience achieved by the saint of Lisieux. This, as we see, is the obedience to which the Carmelites of Compiègne are being called.

At this point in the play, the revolution breaks in upon the scene. The community is now forced to face a new situation in which fidelity to their vocation will become even more demanding. Mère Marie becomes concerned that Blanche's intense fear will prove dangerous for the community's honour. When the young novice becomes distressed by the discussion of the revolution during the recreation hour, the prioress is forced to remind the sisters once again that the desire for physical martyrdom goes against their vocation of praying for the conversion of sinners. Their martyrdom could even imperil their executioners' eternal salvation (OE,I 1627). Madame Lidoine thus steers her daughters away from the desire for personal glory which is contrary to the Carmelite saint's offering of herself as a victim of holocaust for the salvation of sinners. In this way, the prioress indirectly urges her daughters to abandon themselves to God's will.

Shortly after this discussion on martyrdom, Blanche's brother arrives at the monastery to coax his sister to return home. Convinced that she is where God wants her to be, the young heroine retorts: "Je ne suis plus desormais ici que la pauvre petite victime de Sa Divine Majesté. Dieu fera de moi selon son bon plaisir" (OE,I 1630). Her reply proves that she is now struggling to accept her weakness and abandon herself to God. Blanche is thus once again setting out on a straight course following Thérèse who stated: "Les grands saints ont travaillé pour la gloire du bon Dieu, mais moi qui ne suis qu'une toute petite âme, je travaille pour son unique plaisir . . ." (DE 84-85). The young religious informs her brother, therefore, that her duty in the monastery is to suffer for him and thus it is as important as his is on the battlefield. Begging him to think of her as "un compagnon de lutte" (OE,I 1633), she explains the similarity in their struggle: "nous allons combattre chacun à notre manière, et la mienne a ses risques et ses périls comme la vôtre" (OE,I 1633).

Blanche's words to her brother echo those of Thérèse of Lisieux to her spiritual brothers, Père Roulland and Abbé Bellière, two missionary priests with whom the saint corresponded and for whom she offered prayers and sacrifices. A letter dated February 24, 1897 shows how Thérèse longed to continue sharing their battle for souls even after her death: "Nos rôles resteront les mêmes, à vous les armes apostoliques, à moi la prière et l'amour..." (LT 392). But when Blanche's brother takes his departure, the young woman's childlike nature reappears in her words to Mère Marie: "Oh! ne serai-je jamais pour eux qu'une enfant?" (OE,I 1633) paralleling how Thérèse felt treated like a child by her director, Père Pichon (DE 56).

In the next few scenes, Blanche's fear intensifies as delegates from the municipality enter the monastery to interrogate the religious, especially the younger ones. The entire community now enters into Christ's Passion as the chaplain says the last Mass the law will permit him to say. With the tabernacle empty, the priest reminds the sisters that now is the hour for consecrated souls to be sacrificed. The idea that God's grace is not limited to the simple reception of the sacraments is an echo of Thérèse's words, "tout est grâce" (DE 41).

Scene fifteen presents the various reactions of the Carmelites to the possibility of their martyrdom. On account of her great fear, Blanche feels herself to be a burden to Mère Marie: "Je suis pour vous une charge bien lourde" (OE,I 1646), in much the same way that Thérèse, during the extreme weakness of her last illness, felt herself to be a burden to her sisters. But if Blanche is like a child who gives the sub-prioress many worries, Constance also resembles a child in her way of accepting the possibility of death. Constance, like Thérèse, believes that the best preparation for death is being where God wants her to be at the particular moment. Why can she not prepare herself just as well in the chapel, at work, or, even at recreation (OE,I 1647)?

In the last scene of the third sequence, parallel images of the Carmelite saint can be detected in both Madame Lidoine and Mère Marie as they discuss the decree dispensing all religious of enclosed orders from their vows and depriving Blanche and Constance of the privilege of making their vows. Mère Marie reflects Thérèse in her belief that Carmelites must enter into the solitude and terror of Christ's Agony. Did not the saint of Lisieux ask: "...Pourquoi serais-je plus à l'abri qu'une autre d'avoir peur de la mort?" (DE 66). The sub-prioress judges it as a sign from heaven that the Carmelites' honour has been placed in the hands of the community's weakest member, Blanche de la Force. Her thoughts remind us of how, in his writings, Bernanos so often stressed the fact that Thérèse's message of acceptance of weakness is an urgent one for our times.

Madame Lidoine realizes that with her notion of honour based on worldly standards, Mère Marie can unexpectedly come upon a dangerous curve on the road to merciful love. She therefore warns her: "C'est vous, ma fille, qui serez sacrifiée à cette faiblesse et peut-être substituée à ce mépris" (OE,I 1649). By nature a generous soul, the sub-prioress gladly consents to the possible substitution of herself for Blanche. In this way she will gradually be set on the right path and come to a fuller understanding of the type of martyrdom suffered by Thérèse: "le martyre du coeur n'est pas moins fécond que l'effusion du sang . . ." (LT 383).

Fourth Sequence

The opening scene of the fourth sequence leads us deeper still into the mystery of the Carmelites' vocation of prayer and suffering. Madame Lidoine now invites Blanche and Constance to accept the generous sacrifice of the revolutionary law forbidding them to pronounce their vows in public. She then reminds the entire community of its duty of expiation for others: "car notre vocation n'est nullement de nous opposer à l'injustice, mais simplement de l'expier, d'en payer la rançon . . ." (OE,I 1651-1652). Those who are persecuting the Carmelites have a far greater poverty and are thus in need of their prayers. Although her words testify to her awareness of the possibility of martyrdom for her community, the prioress once again tells the sisters that seeking martyrdom for personal honour is wrong. The life and death of a Carmelite have to be placed at the loving service of God: "Une carmélite qui souhaite le martyre est aussi mauvaise carmélite que serait mauvais soldat le militaire qui chercherait la mort avant d'avoir exécuté les ordres de son chef" (OE,I 1652).

Thérèse's presence is detected in the differing attitudes toward martyrdom witnessed in Madame Lidoine and Mère Marie. The prioress' viewpoint seems to approach Thérèse of Lisieux' concept of martyrdom as being essentially an act of love. In Mère Marie, we discover the saint's longing for martyrdom.

Madame Lidoine's thoughts on martyrdom parallel Thérèse so well that she could certainly have borrowed the saint's words to Céline in October, 1889 to address her daughters: ". . . Jésus veut que le salut des âmes dépende de nos sacrifices, de notre amour, il nous mendie des âmes. . . . Faisons de notre vie un sacrifice continuel, un martyre d'amour . . ." (LT 157). In her simplicity, the prioress encourages her community to trust that God will give them the courage needed to face whatever the future holds in store for them: "Au surplus, quoi qu'il arrive, ne comptons jamais que sur cette espèce de courage que Dieu dispense au jour le jour, et comme sou par sou" (OE,I 1652). According to the prioress, this is the courage best suited to a Carmelite. Madame Lidoine's definition of courage resembles Thérèse's comment to her three Carmelite sisters on how she practised courage: "Je ne m'appuie pas sur mes propres forces mais sur la force de Celui qui sur la Croix a vaincu les puissances de l'enfer" (LT 428).

The prioress then shows her daughters how their anguish and fear are united to Christ's Agony. Since Christ divinized all human suffering in the Garden of Gethsemani, she believes that there is scarcely any difference between fear and courage (OE,I 1653). We are thus reminded here of the Carmelite saint's reflection on her own intense anguish: "Notre-Seigneur est mort sur la Croix, dans les angoisses, et voilà pourtant la plus belle mort d'amour" (DE 56).

In scene two, Blanche's anguish increases as she learns that Mère Marie intends to obey unquestioningly the prioress' decision against allowing the novices to pronounce their vows secretly. But what appears in Blanche as a question: "En sommes-nous venues à ce degré d'infortune que notre seul espoir soit de passer inaperçues, ainsi qu'un lièvre au gîte?" (OE,I 1654), is, for Thérèse, a desire: "Fais que je ne sois jamais à charge à la communauté mais que personne ne s'occupe de moi, que je sois regardée foulée aux pieds oubliée comme un petit grain de sable à toi, Jésus" (HA 315). In her spiritual journey, Blanche is, therefore, at the place along the road where she still longs for some consolation to still the anguish of her fear. She has yet to discover, as Thérèse discovered shortly after her entrance into the monastery, the real treasures hidden in Christ's suffering (HA 175).

The next few scenes depict the mob of revolutionaries desecrating and looting the chapel. The statue of the Little King of Glory is stripped of its cloak and crown. Madame Lidoine attempts to console her daughters by recalling that poverty is the first condition of a Carmelite and that no matter how poor they are they are still far removed from the poverty of Christ. The prioress' attitude on poverty corresponds once again with Thérèse's image of Christ coming to us as a beggar: "Il se fait pauvre afin que nous puissions Lui faire la charité, Il nous tend la main comme un mendiant . . ." (LT 251). This, too, as we recall, is the image of Christ which shows up in the entry for January 19, 1948 in Bernanos' "Dernier agenda": "Il n'est pas venu en vainqueur, mais en suppliant."[4]

Scene six then finds that the young heroine has advanced along the road to Theresian abandonment. Her changing of the wording of the prayer of Saint Teresa of Avila: "Donnez-moi refuge ou angoisse mortelle, Comment voulez-vous disposer de moi?" (OE,I 1657) mirrors in a positive manner Thérèse of Lisieux' attitude: "Ce que le bon Dieu aime mieux et choisit pour moi, voilà ce qui me plaît davantage" (DE 162). The parallel between these words uttered scarcely three weeks before the saint's death and Blanche's new attitude testifies to the evolution in the young woman's spirituality that has taken place since the first sequence. Now better prepared than ever to accept her weakness as God's will, Bernanos' heroine is able to declare: "Car enfin, ma Mère, Dieu m'a peut-être voulue lâche . . ." (OE,I 1658).

The ninth scene portrays the Good Friday Service being celebrated in secret. In his sermon recalling how Christ came among the poor, the chaplain urges the Carmelites to remain little and willing to offer themselves as victims: "Faisons-nous donc aussi maintenant tout petits, non pas, comme eux, pour échapper à la mort, mais pour la souffrir le cas échéant, comme Il l'a soufferte Lui-même . . ." (OE,I 1659). The priest's words thus parallel Thérèse's advice to her sister, Marie, on how to practise poverty of spirit: "Le seul désir d'être victime suffit, mais il faut consentir à rester pauvre et sans force et voilà le difficile . . ." (LT 360).

While awaiting the arrival of the chaplain on Easter Sunday, the Carmelites discuss their thoughts on fear. In her words: "Oui, il n'est d'autre remède à la peur que de se jeter à corps perdu dans la volonté de Dieu . . ." (OE,I 1662), Mère Marie imitates Thérèse's confidence in God's mercy and abandonment to His will. The saint's idea of "tout est grâce" (DE 41) is once again hidden in Dialogues des Carmélites in the prioress' reply to one of the sisters who is wondering what they will do when there are no longer any priests left to administer the sacraments. Grace, the prioress declares, will be restored by a surplus of martyrs (OE,I 1662).

In the following scenes, the Carmelites reflect together on Christ's Agony in the Garden of Gethsemani as did Thérèse during her agony. Aware that her sisters might easily become distressed over her intense suffering, Thérèse reminded them: "Notre-Seigneur est bien mort Victime d'Amour, et voyez quelle a été son agonie!..." (DE 40). The Carmelites' suffering becomes intensified as they contemplate how they will spend their last night. In much the same way as Thérèse tried to accept her suffering during the long months of her final illness, they try to relate their own passion to Christ's suffering, solitude, and fear of death.

Each Carmelite, in her own way, portrays an aspect of the Carmelite saint during her last few months. Thus Blanche's fear of death resembles the anguish Thérèse endured during her trial of faith, while Constance utters the words of Madame Jourdain that Thérèse loved to quote, "c'est dans les bras du bon Dieu que je tombe!" (DE 169), when she laughingly reassures one of her companions that God will take care of them: "Mais nous, ma Soeur, nous ne pouvons tomber qu'en Dieu!" (OE,I 1672).

It is during the absence of Madame Lidoine that the Carmelites finally make the vow of martyrdom for the salvation of Carmel and France. Afraid that Blanche will vote against the vow, Constance generously decides to support her companion by also opposing the vow. Then, discovering that she is the only one to have voted against the vow, Constance humbly asks the community to allow her to change her decision. When the prioress returns she is distressed to hear that the vow has been made, for such an action could jeopardize the salvation of its weakest member. She tells Mère Marie that it is the Christ Child in the person of Blanche that risks paying the price of their heroism. Realizing her fault, the sub-prioress humbly begs pardon and asks God to permit her to expiate her fault in such a way that she be the only one to suffer from it.

Mère Marie must learn that God alone has the right to decide whether or not the Carmelites will have the privilege of martyrdom. Although her proposal is inspired by a desire for glory based on honour according to worldly standards, it is also inspired, as von Balthasar points out, "par fidélité au principe de substitution, lié lui-même à la vocation du Carmel" (von B 468).

Fifth Sequence

Sequence five is the final step in the Carmelites' spiritual adventure leading them into the heart of the mystery of Christ's Incarnation and Redemption. The first few scenes show the little community disbanded, desolate, and destitute. Blanche has fled to Paris, but shortly after her return home her father is guillotined. Now more alone than ever, Bernanos' young heroine is forced to perform menial tasks and is humiliated and mistreated by those who were her former servants. Mère Marie departs for Paris to urge Blanche to go back to Compiègne with her. The young woman accepts her weakness at this point, but she has encountered a new stumbling block on the road to confidence and abandonment: hatred of self. Still judging her weakness according to the worldly code of honour, Blanche believes that since others despise fear, it is only right for her to hate herself. By means of calling Blanche by her religious name, Soeur Blanche de l'Agonie du Christ, Mère Marie attempts to set her back on the right path. The young woman is thus reminded of her call to share in Christ's redemptive suffering.

A short time later, the young heroine learns of the arrest of the Carmelites of Compiègne. Still fearful of death herself, she is anxious to save them from death too, and so hastens to Mère Marie for help, only to find the latter convinced of their duty to join the others in martyrdom. Uppermost in Mère Marie's thoughts is the glory to be obtained from the sacrifice of innocent victims. With Blanche a victim of her fear and Mère Marie a victim of her pride, both religious are stalled on the road to confidence and abandonment.

But <u>Dialogues des Carmélites</u> testifies to the Carmelite saint's idea that sanctity can be achieved through perfect obedience to God's will. Her presence is implicit in the scene where the Carmelites of Compiègne are in prison awaiting their death sentence. Soeur Claire's explanation of what is meant by active obedience is simply another way of describing one's abandonment to God: "Une vieille religieuse comme moi ne souhaite rien de plus que mourir dans l'obéissance, mais dans une obéissance active et consciente" (OE,I 1711). Religious possess nothing of their own in this world, she adds, yet: "Il n'en est pas moins vrai que notre mort est notre mort, personne ne peut mourir à ma place" (OE,I 1711). Active obedience signifies, therefore, the free offering of oneself in love as Thérèse of Lisieux freely offered herself as a victim of holocaust to God's merciful love. Completely stripped of everything, the Carmelites freely and lovingly choose to offer the gift of their lives for the salvation of others. As Thérèse bravely endured her trial of faith for those who had no faith, the Carmelites of Compiègne are to be martyred for those persecuting the faith.

Madame Lidoine's courage in accepting the vow of martyrdom which she herself did not personally make, and her words of encouragement to her spiritual daughters reveal new heights of her simplicity and generosity. Her words inject a childlike confidence into the others and, so, one of the young sisters kneels before her and kisses her hand. "On voit les larmes couler encore sur son visage, qui exprime maintenant une confiance naïve, enfantine" (OE,I 1713). And, in Bernanos's description of this young Carmelite whose name is not revealed, are not Thérèse's spirit of childhood, Thérèse de l'Enfant-Jésus, and her call to suffering, Thérèse de la Sainte-Face, united in a final act of abandonment to God?

And as for the two absent members of the Carmelite community, they also have a special destiny awaiting them. When Mère Marie learns that she is not to fulfill her vow of martyrdom, she is totally devastated. But fortunately, the chaplain arrives on the scene in time to remind her that what is more important than her vow of martyrdom is her vow of obedience: "vous avez prononcé ce voeu dans l'obéissance et c'est dans l'obéissance que vous devez l'accomplir" (OE,I 1709). Thus, in urging the sub-prioress to abandon herself to God's will, the chaplain shares the saint's belief that "Jésus ne demande pas de grandes actions, mais seulement l'abandon et la reconnaissance . . ." (HA 215).

The chaplain points out to Mère Marie that since she made her vow to God alone, it is, therefore, to God alone that she is responsible for it. Her cry: "Je suis déshonorée!" (OE,I 1718) betrays the true nature of her suffering. But, as the priest tells her, God wishes her to endure another kind of martyrdom, one which she will find far more difficult, requiring much love and sacrifice on her part: "Voilà ce sang, oui, voilà ce sang que Dieu vous demande, et qu'il vous faut verser!" (OE,I 1718).

Mère Marie could certainly have been consoled at this point by Thérèse of Lisieux who also longed for martyrdom, but who realized that instead of being a martyr for her faith, God destined her to be a martyr of love. One of the saint's letters to Céline dated July 14, 1889 describes the heroism required by this type of martyrdom: "le martrye ignoré, connu de Dieu seul, que l'oeil de la créature ne peut découvrir, martyre sans honneur, sans triomphe... Voilà l'amour poussé jusqu'à l'héroïsme..." (LT 154). This martyrdom to which Thérèse felt called is also to be the martyrdom reserved for Mère Marie, one in which she will take on the suffering of Blanche.

As for Bernanos' young heroine, God in His merciful love has come to her assistance. Thérèse's presence is so evident in Blanche as she bravely makes her way to the scaffold that she could well borrow the saint's words to tell us how her fear has vanished: "mais à la loi de crainte a sucédé la loi d'Amour, et l'Amour m'a choisie pour holocauste, moi, faible et imparfaite créature..." (HA 223). Through her joyful acceptance of God's will, Blanche has raised honour to the supernatural level. And in her face now free from all fear, we read other words of the Carmelite saint: "mais je ne meurs pas, j'entre dans la vie . . ." (LT 426).

Finally, as the radiant colours of the spectrum are all united into one beam of light, so do the various parallel images of Thérèse of Lisieux found in Blanche de la Force, Constance, Madame de Croissy, Madame Lidoine, Mère Marie, and indeed in the entire Carmelite community come together in one loving act of confident abandonment to God. And as the characters of the author's fictional world unite under one banner, so, too, do the various questions and fears posed by the diverse themes of Bernanos' work find their answer in the words of the little saint of Lisieux written to her sister, Marie, in September, 1896: "C'est la confiance et rien que la confiance qui doit nous conduire à l'Amour..." (LT 360).

NOTES

CHAPTER 11

[1] Joseph Boly, o.s.c., <u>Dialogues des Carmélites: étude et analyse</u> (Paris: Les Editions de l'Ecole, 1960) 21-22. Cited hereafter as <u>Boly</u>. See also: Meredith Murray, o.p., <u>La genèse des "Dialogues des Carmélites"</u> (Paris: Editions du Seuil, 1963) 20-26.

[2] Michel Estève, <u>Georges Bernanos: un triple itinéraire</u> (Paris: Hachette, 1981) 275-276.

[3] Luc Estang, "Les Dialogues des Carmélites," <u>Bulletin de la société des amis de Georges Bernanos</u> 1 (1949): 14.

[4] Albert Béguin, <u>Bernanos par lui-même</u> (Paris: Editions du Seuil, "Ecrivains de toujours," 1958) 146.

CONCLUSION

"DANS LA DOUCE PITIÉ DE DIEU"

CONCLUSION

"DANS LA DOUCE PITIÉ DE DIEU"

Was Bernanos aware of the extent to which he used the Carmelite saint as a model for his fictional world? In a letter written in 1935 to the Vicomtesse Villiers de la Noue, Bernanos explains how people he knew inspired the creation of his characters. Beings that he knew and loved appear in his works and it was only later on, when they had ceased to act and speak, that he recognized them or perhaps, as he states: "je ne les reconnais pas du tout, parce qu'ils se sont transformés peu à peu, font, mêlés à d'autres, une créature imaginaire plus réelle pour moi qu'un vivant . . ." (Corr.II 115). Thus, Bernanos' love for Thérèse may have led him not only to use her consciously, but also unconsciously as a model for his characters, incorporating her Christian emphases as part of his own thought.

Certainly there seems to be no doubt that in his evolution as a writer it was always in the direction of the saint's attitude of approaching God with "une disposition du coeur qui nous rend humbles et petits entre les bras de Dieu, conscients de notre faiblesse, et confiants jusqu'à l'audace en sa bonté de Père" (DE 110).

A letter written to Père Brückberger in May, 1948, barely two months before the author's death, shows moreover the extent to which Thérèse's message burned in him as a Christian. Faced with the prospect of his approaching death from cancer of the liver, Bernanos was able to declare: "J'ai plus que jamais confiance dans la douce pitié de Dieu" (<u>Corr</u>.III 466).

That this personal tie with the saint would be constantly found in Bernanos' writings is therefore perhaps not too surprising. From "La Malibran" in 1913 to <u>Dialogues des Carmélites</u> in 1948, Thérèse of Lisieux' presence testifies to the tremendous impact she had on the life and thought of the author. Yet it was an influence which evolved over the years. We have seen how the author's life itself often provides the key to understanding this evolution.

In his "Notice autobiographique" written in January, 1945, Bernanos highlighted the Spanish Civil War as a major event in his life: "Cette expérience d'Espagne a été, peut-être, l'événement capital de ma vie" (<u>Len</u> 13). The experience of Majorca was indeed to have a lasting influence on both his thought and work, for prior to the Spanish Civil War, Bernanos' fictional works show a balance of explicit and implicit evidence of the Carmelite saint appearing in words, images, character traits, and incidents. Thérèse's presence is observed both explicitly and implicitly in the abbé Chevance and in his spiritual daughter, Chantal de Clergerie. Though a character tends to be either a parallel or a reverse image of the saint, he often may exhibit elements of both as in the case of Donissan and the first Mouchette.

The works arising from the years spent in Majorca however indicate a change: the Carmelite saint's influence becomes more interiorized. In contrast to a relative dearth of explicit evidence of the saint, implicit evidence of her presence increases as we see her spirit of childhood lived out on the supernatural level in the young priest-hero of <u>Journal d'un curé de campagne</u> and on the natural level in the little Mouchette of <u>Nouvelle histoire de Mouchette</u>. Or it may be completely destroyed as in <u>Monsieur Ouine</u>.

In contrast, in <u>Les Grands Cimetières sous la lune</u>, the great conclusion to the author's Majorcan experience, the saint is not only explicitly present, but more so than anywhere else in Bernanos' writings. We have seen the author use the non-believer's sermon for the saint's feast day as the occasion to give an unequivocal statement on the relevance of her message of childhood for the twentieth century.

After <u>Les Grands Cimetières sous la lune</u> there are burning references to the urgency of her message in <u>Lettre aux Anglais</u> in 1942 and in Bernanos' "Discours pour le baptême de l'avion brésilien 'Jeanne d'Arc'" in 1943, as also by implication in "Frère Martin." As for her presence in "Nos amis les saints," it cannot be disputed. But it is in <u>Dialogues des Carmélites</u> that her presence will make itself felt on every page and in every character to the extent that we begin to wonder if certain lines are the saint's or the author's. In <u>Dialogues des Carmélites</u> Thérèse's message had become so internalized that it had become Bernanos' own.

BIBLIOGRAPHY

BIBLIOGRAPHY

PRIMARY SOURCES

i) Georges Bernanos

Bernanos, Georges. Le Chemin de la Croix-des-âmes. Nouvelle édition, complétée, corrigée et annotée par Brigitte et Jean-Loup Bernanos d'après les manuscrits. Augmentée de tous les articles et messages écrits au Brésil. Monaco: Editions du Rocher, 1987.

---. Correspondance inédite, recueillie par Albert Béguin, choisie et présentée par Jean Murray, o.p. Paris: Plon, 1971. Tome I. 1904-1934 Combat pour la vérité. Tome II. 1934-1948 Combat pour la liberté.

---. Correspondance inédite, recueillie, choisie, annotée et présentée par Jean-Loup Bernanos. Paris: Plon, 1983. Tome III. 1904-1948 Lettres retrouvées.

---. Le crépuscule des vieux. Paris: Gallimard, 1956.

---. "Dans l'amitié de Léon Bloy." Présence de Bernanos. By Luc Estang. Paris: Plon, 1947. vii-xxix.

---. "Discours pour le baptême de l'avion brésilien 'Jeanne d'Arc.'" Bulletin de la société des amis de Georges Bernanos 24-25 (1955): 1-8.

---. Essais et écrits de combat. Tome I. Textes présentés et annotés par Yves

Bridel, Jacques Chabot et Joseph Jurt sous la direction de Michel Estève. Paris: Gallimard, "Bibliothèque de la Pléiade," 1971.

---. Français, si vous saviez 1945-1948. Paris: Gallimard, 1961.

---. La France contre les robots. Suivi de textes inédits. Présentation et notes de Jean-Loup Bernanos. Paris: Plon, 1970.

---. "Frère Martin." Présenté par Albert Béguin. Esprit 183 (octobre 1951): 433-445.

---. Le lendemain, c'est vous!. Paris: Plon, 1969.

---. Lettre aux Anglais. Paris: Gallimard, 1946.

---. La liberté pour quoi faire?. Paris: Gallimard, 1953.

---. Oeuvres romanesques, suivies de Dialogues des Carmélites. Préface par Gaëtan Picon. Texte et variantes établis par Albert Béguin. Notes par Michel Estève. Paris: Gallimard. "Bibliothèque de la Pléiade," 1984.

---. Les prédestinés. Textes rassemblés et présentés par Jean-Loup Bernanos. Préface de Mgr Daniel Pézeril. Paris: Editions du Seuil, 1983.

---. "Quelques pages des brouillons inédits de Monsieur Ouine." Transcription de la lecture faite par Mgr Daniel Pézeril de quelques pages du onzième chapitre. Courrier Georges Bernanos 2-3-4 (février 1971): 86-92.

---. Sous le soleil de Satan. Première édition conforme au manuscrit original. Texte établi et annoté par William Bush. Paris: Plon, 1982.

---. "Sur un album." Bulletin de la société des amis de Georges Bernanos 12-13 (1952): 3-4.

---. La vocation spirituelle de la France. Inédits rassemblés et présentés par Jean-Loup Bernanos. Paris: Plon, 1975.

Sarrazin, Hubert. L'oeuvre de Bernanos à l'époque de la seconde guerre mondiale, suite chronologique de 1938 à 1945 / texte et commentaire établis sur documents originaux. Weldon Library University of Western Ontario Special Collections: London, Ontario, 1984.

ii) Thérèse of Lisieux

Thérèse de l'Enfant-Jésus et de la Sainte-Face. Conseils et souvenirs. Recueillis par Soeur Geneviève de la Sainte Face, soeur et novice de sainte Thérèse de l'Enfant-Jésus. Paris: Editions du Cerf, 1988.

---. Une course de géant: lettres. Edition intégrale. Paris: Editions du Cerf et Desclée de Brouwer, 1977.

---. Histoire d'une âme. Lisieux: Editions de l'Office Central de Lisieux (France), 1924.

---. Histoire d'une âme: manuscrits autobiographiques. Paris: Editions du Cerf et Desclée de Brouwer, 1972.

---. J'entre dans la vie: derniers entretiens. Paris: Editions du Cerf, 1973.

---. Poésies. Edition intégrale. Paris: Editions du Cerf et Desclée de Brouwer, 1979.

---. Prières: L'offrande à l'Amour Miséricordieux. Paris: Editions du Cerf et Desclée de Brouwer, 1988.

---. Théâtre au Carmel: "récréations pieuses." Paris: Editions du Cerf et Desclée de Brouwer, 1985.

---. Le triomphe de l'humilité (RP 7). Thérèse mystifiée (1896-1897). L'affaire Leo Taxil et le Manuscrit B. Paris: Editions du Cerf et Desclée de Brouwer, 1975.

SECONDARY SOURCES

i) Books

Aaraas, Hans. A propos de "Journal d'un curé de campagne": essai sur l'écrivain et le prêtre dans l'oeuvre romanesque de Bernanos. Paris: Archives des Lettres Modernes, 1966.

---. Littérature et sacerdoce: essai sur "Journal d'un curé de campagne" de Bernanos. Paris: Lettres Modernes Minard, 1984. "Situation" No 44.

Ballesteros Gaibrois, Manuel. Breve historia de España. Buenos Aires: Editorial "El Ateneo," 1967.

Balthasar, Hans Urs von. Bernanos. Cologne: Jakob Hegner, 1954. Trad.: Le chrétien Bernanos. Trad. Maurice de Gandillac. Paris: Editions du Seuil, 1956.

Béguin, Albert. Bernanos par lui-même. Paris: Editions du Seuil, "Ecrivains de toujours," 1958.

Bernanos, Jean-Loup. Bernanos. Iconographie recueillie, choisie et présentée par Jean-Loup Bernanos. Paris: Plon, 1988.

---. Georges Bernanos à la merci des passants. Paris: Plon, 1986.

--- and Luc Balbont. Bernanos aujourd'hui. Paris: Nouvelle Cité, 1987.

Blumenthal, Gerda. The Poetic Imagination of Georges Bernanos. Baltimore: The John Hopkins Press, 1965.

Boisdeffre, Pierre de. Métamorphose de la littérature. Tome 1. Barrès, Gide, Mauriac, Bernanos, Montherlant, Malraux. Verviers, Belgique: Gérard et Cie., 1974.

Boly, Joseph, o.s.c. "Dialogues des Carmélites": étude et analyse. Paris: Editions de l'Ecole, 1960.

Brémond, Henri. Histoire littéraire du sentiment religieux en France depuis la fin des guerres de religion jusqu'à nos jours. Tome II. L'invasion mystique. Paris: Librairie Bloud et Gay, 1930.

Bridel, Yves. L'esprit d'enfance dans l'oeuvre romanesque de Georges Bernanos. Paris: Minard Lettres Modernes, 1966. "Thèmes et Mythes No 10."

Bro, Bernard, o.p. The Little Way: The Spirituality of Thérèse of Lisieux. Trans. Alan Neame. Westminster, Maryland: Christian Classics, 1980.

Browne, Harry. Spain's Civil War. Harlow, Essex, England: Longman Group Limited, 1983.

Brückberger, R.-L., o.p. Bernanos vivant. Paris: Editions Albin Michel, 1988.

Bush, William. L'angoisse du mystère: essai sur Bernanos et "Monsieur Ouine." Paris: Minard Lettres Modernes, 1966. "Situation" No 11.

---. Genèse et structures de "Sous le soleil de Satan." Paris: Archives des Lettres Modernes, 1988.

---. Genèse et structures d'"Un mauvais rêve." Paris: Archives des Lettres Modernes, 1982.

---. Georges Bernanos. New York: Twayne Publishers Inc., 1969. "Twayne World Author Series No 71."

---. Souffrance et expiation dans la pensée de Bernanos. Paris: Minard Lettres Modernes, 1962. "Thèmes et Mythes No 8."

Cobban, Alfred. A History of Modern France. Volume II. From the First Empire to the Fourth Republic 1799-1945. Harmondsworth, Middlesex, England: Penguin Books Ltd., 1961.

Combes, Mgr. André. The Heart of Saint Thérèse. Trans. A Carmelite Nun. New York: P.J. Kennedy and Sons, 1951.

---. Saint Thérèse and Her Mission: The Basic Principles of Theresian Spirituality. Trans. Alastair Guinan. New York: P.J. Kennedy and Sons, 1955.

---. The Spirituality of Saint Thérèse. (An Introduction). Trans. Mgr. Philip E. Hallett. New York: P.J. Kennedy and Sons, 1950.

Cooke, John E. Georges Bernanos: A Study of Christian Commitment. Amersham, Buckinghamshire: Avebury Publishing Company, 1981.

Crisógono de Jesús, o.c.d. Vida y enseñanzas de Santa Teresita. Madrid: Editorial de Espiritualidad, 1982.

Daniel-Rops, Henri. L'Eglise des Révolutions: un combat pour Dieu. Paris: Librairie Arthème Fayard, 1963.

Dansette, Adrien. Histoire religieuse de la France contemporaine: l'église catholique dans la mêlée politique et sociale. Edition revue et corrigée. Paris: Flammarion, 1965.

Debluë, Henri. Les romans de Georges Bernanos ou le défi du rêve. Neuchâtel: Editions de la Baconnière, 1965.

Derfler, Leslie. The Third French Republic 1870-1940. Malabar, Florida: Robert E. Krieger Publishing Company, 1982.

Estang, Luc. Présence de Bernanos. Précédé de "Dans l'amitié de Léon Bloy" par Georges Bernanos. Paris: Plon, 1947.

Estève, Michel. Bernanos. Paris: Gallimard, 1965.

---. Le Christ, les symboles christiques et l'Incarnation dans l'oeuvre de Bernanos. Lille: Service de reproduction des thèses Université de Lille III, 1982.

---. Georges Bernanos: un triple itinéraire. Paris: Hachette, 1981.

---. Le sens de l'amour dans les romans de Bernanos. Paris: Minard Lettres Modernes, 1959, "Thèmes et Mythes No 7."

Fabrègues, Jean de. Bernanos tel qu'il était. Tours: Mame, 1963.

Fragnière, Marie-Agnès. Bernanos fidèle à l'enfant. Fribourg: Editions Universitaires, 1963.

Gaucher, Guy, o.c.d. Georges Bernanos ou l'invincible espérance. Paris: Plon, 1962.

---. Histoire d'une vie: Thérèse Martin (1873-1897). Paris: Editions du Cerf, 1982.

---. La passion de Thérèse de Lisieux. Paris: Editions du Cerf et Desclée de Brouwer, 1972.

---. Le thème de la mort dans les romans de Georges Bernanos. Paris: Minard Lettres Modernes, 1967, "Thèmes et Mythes No 2."

Gibson, Ralph. A Social History of French Catholicism 1789-1914. London: Routledge, 1989.

Gillespie, Jessie Lynn. Le tragique dans l'oeuvre de Georges Bernanos. Genève: Librairie E. Droz; Paris: Librairie Minard, 1960.

Gosselin, Monique. L'écriture du surnaturel dans l'oeuvre romanesque de Georges Bernanos. 2 tomes. Lille: Atelier Reproduction des thèses Université de Lille III; Paris: Librairie Honoré Champion, 1979.

Guillemin, Henri. Regards sur Bernanos. Paris: Editions Gallimard, 1976.

Halda, Bernard. Bernanos ou la foi militante et déchirée. Paris: Téqui, 1980.

Hebblethewaite, Peter, s.j. Bernanos: An Introduction. New York: Hilary House Publishers Ltd., 1965.

Huot, Cécile-J., c.n.d. "Dialogues des Carmélites, principaux thèmes et valeur dramatique." Diplôme d'études supérieures. U Laval, 1967.

Jamart, François, o.c.d. Complete Spiritual Doctrine of St. Therese of Lisieux. Trans. Walter Van de Putte, c.s.sp. New York: Alba House, 1961.

Jamet, Henry. Un autre Bernanos. Lyon: E. Vitte, 1959.

Johnson, Vernon. Spiritual Childhood: A Study of St. Teresa's Teaching. London: Sheed and Ward, 1953.

Kedward, H.R. Occupied France: Collaboration and Resistance 1940-1944. Oxford UK: Basil Blackwell Ltd., 1985.

Lafrance, Jean. Thérèse de Lisieux et sa mission pastorale: essai de pédagogie thérésienne. Paris: Desclée de Brouwer, 1968.

Laurentin, René. Thérèse de Lisieux: mythes et réalité. Paris: Beauchesne, 1972.

Lawrence of the Ressurection, o.c.d. The Practice of the Presence of God. Trans. Donald Attwater. Springfield, Illinois: Templegate Publishers, 1974.

Leclerq, Pierre Robert. Introduction à "Monsieur Ouine" de Bernanos. Paris: Lettres Modernes Minard, 1978. "Situation" No 38.

Le Touzé, Philippe. Le mystère du réel dans les romans de Bernanos. Paris: Librairie A.-G. Nizet, 1979.

Marie-Céleste, Soeur. Bernanos et son optique de la vie chrétienne. Paris: A.-G. Nizet, 1967.

Marín, Diego. La civilización española. Edición revisada. New York: Holt, Rinehart and Winston, 1969.

Meester, Conrad de. Les mains vides: le message de Thérèse de Lisieux. Trans. A. Patfoort, o.p. Paris: Editions du Cerf, 1972.

Milner, Max. Georges Bernanos. Paris: Desclée de Brouwer, 1967.

Moeller, Charles. Littérature du XXe siècle et christianisme. Tome 1. Silence de Dieu. Paris: Castermann, 1953.

---. Man and Salvation in Literature. Trans. Charles Underhill Quinn. Notre Dame: University of Notre Dame Press, 1970.

Morris, Daniel R. From Heaven to Hell: Imagery of Earth, Air, Water and Fire in the Novels of Georges Bernanos. New York: Peter Lang, 1989.

Murray, Meredith, o.p. La genèse de "Dialogues des Carmélites." Paris: Editions du Seuil, 1963.

O'Connor, Patricia. In Search of Thérèse. Wilmington, Delaware: Michael Glazier, 1987.

O'Mahoney, Christopher, o.c.d., ed. and trans. St. Thérèse of Lisieux by Those Who Knew Her: Testimonies from the Process of Beatification. Huntington, Indiana: Our Sunday Visitor, Inc., 1975.

O'Sharkey, Eithne M. The Role of the Priest in the Novels of Georges Bernanos. New York: Vantage Press, 1983.

Peers, E. Allison. Mother of Carmel: A Portrait of St. Teresa of Jesus. New York: Morehouse-Gorham Co., 1946.

Peeters, Leopold. Une prose du monde: essai sur le langage de l'adhésion dans l'oeuvre de Bernanos. Paris: Lettres Modernes Minard, 1984. "Situation" 45.

Pernoud, Régine. Jeanne d'Arc par elle-même et par ses témoins. Paris: Editions du Seuil, 1962.

---, Geneviève Baïlac, and Guy Gaucher. Jeanne et Thérèse. Paris: Editions du Seuil, 1984.

Picon, Gaëtan. <u>Georges Bernanos</u>. Paris: Robert Marin, 1948. Collection "Les hommes et les oeuvres."

Riaud, Alexis. <u>La "science d'amour" en sainte Thérèse de l'Enfant Jésus</u>. Paris: Editions du Seuil, 1984.

Rideau, Emile. <u>Thérèse de Lisieux: la nature et la grâce</u>. Paris: Fayard, 1973.

Rivard, Yvon. <u>L'imaginaire et le quotidien: essai sur les romans de Georges Bernanos</u>. Paris: Lettres Modernes Minard, 1978. "Bibliothèque des lettres modernes" No 21.

Rohrbach, Peter Thomas, o.c.d. <u>The Search for Saint Thérèse</u>. Garden City, New York: Hanover House, 1961.

Sackville-West, V. <u>The Eagle and the Dove: A Study in Contrasts St. Teresa of Avila, St. Thérèse of Lisieux</u>. Garden City, New York: Doubleday, Doran and Company, Inc., 1944.

Sion, Victor. <u>Réalisme spirituel de Thérèse de Lisieux</u>. Préface de Mgr Guy Gaucher. Paris: Editions du Cerf, 1986.

Six, Jean-François. <u>Thérèse de Lisieux au Carmel</u>. Paris: Editions du Seuil, 1973.

---. <u>La véritable enfance de Thérèse de Lisieux: névrose et sainteté</u>. Paris: Editions du Seuil, 1972.

Speaight, Robert. <u>Georges Bernanos: A Study of the Man and the Writer</u>. London: Collins and Harvill Press, 1973.

Teresa de Jesús. <u>Libro de su vida</u>. Garden City, New York: Doubleday and Company, Inc., 1961. "Colección Hispánica."

<u>The Jerusalem Bible</u>. Garden City, New York: Doubleday and Company, Inc., 1966.

Tobin, Michael Robinson. "Incarnation and Desincarnation in the Thought of Bernanos." Ph.D. Diss. U of Western Ontario, 1985.

Warner, Marina. <u>Joan of Arc: The Image of Female Heroism</u>. London: Weidenfeld and Nicolson, 1981.

ii) Articles in Books

Aaraas, Hans. "La conversion de Bernanos." <u>Bernanos: continuités et ruptures</u>. Actes du Colloque international organisé par le Groupe d'Informations et de Recherches sur Bernanos, Nancy - 1987. Etudes réunies par Pierre Gille et Max Milner. Nancy: Presses Universitaires de Nancy, 1988. 13-23.

Arland, Marcel. "Mouchette et la grâce." <u>Georges Bernanos: essais et témoignages</u>. Ed. Albert Béguin. Paris: Editions du Seuil; Neuchâtel: Editions de la Baconnière, 1949. 133-137.

Beaumont, Ernest. "Georges Bernanos, 1888-1948." <u>The Novelist as Philosopher</u>. Ed. John Cruickshank. London: Oxford University Press, 1962. 29-54.

Béguin, Albert. "Le témoin de la Sainte Agonie." <u>Georges Bernanos: essais et témoignages</u>. Ed. Albert Béguin. Paris: Editions du Seuil; Neuchâtel: Editions de la Baconnière, 1949. 138-145.

Bridel, Yves. "Jeanne d'Arc et Bernanos." <u>Bernanos. Centre culturel de Cerisy-la-Salle 10 au 19 juillet 1969</u>. Ed. Max Milner. Paris: Plon, 1972. 289-302.

Bush, William. "Cet autre aspect..." <u>Paradoxes et permanence de la pensée bernanosienne</u>. Études publiées sous la direction de Joël Pottier. Paris: Aux Animateurs de livres, 1989. 169-178.

Chabot, Jacques. Notice and Notes. <u>Essais et écrits de combat</u>. Tome 1. By Georges Bernanos. Textes présentés et annotés par Yves Bridel, Jacques Chabot et Joseph Jurt sous la direction de Michel Estève. Paris: Editions Gallimard, "Bibliothèque de la Pléiade." 1532-1581.

Congar, Yves, o.p. "Bernanos, romancier de la grâce et théologien de l'église." <u>Georges Bernanos: essais et témoignages</u>. Ed. Albert Béguin. Paris: Editions du Seuil; Neuchâtel: Editions de la Baconnière, 1949. 89-98.

Day, Dorothy. Introduction. <u>The Practice of the Presence of God</u>. By Brother Lawrence of the Resurrection, o.c.d. Springfield, Illinois: Templegate Publishers, 1974. 7-20.

Gaucher, Guy, o.c.d. "La prière dans l'oeuvre de Bernanos." <u>Bernanos. Centre</u>

culturel de Cerisy-la-Salle 10 au 19 juillet 1969. Ed. Max Milner. Paris: Plon, 1972. 323-340.

Gendre, Claude. "Rencontres spirituelles autour des Carmélites de Compiègne et de Blanche de la Force." Paradoxes et permanence de la pensée bernanosienne. Études publiées sous la direction de Joël Pottier. Paris: Aux Animateurs de livres, 1989. 131-154.

Glueckert, Leopold. "The World of Thérèse: France, Church and State in the Late Nineteenth Century." Carmelite Studies: Experiencing St Thérèse Today. Washington: Institute of Carmelite Studies, 1990. 10-27.

Le Touzé, Philippe. "Monsieur Ouine et le mythe du mal." Mythe-Symbole-Roman. Actes du Colloque d'Amiens, réunis par Jean Bessiere. Paris: Presses Universitaires de France, 1980. 56-64.

Magny, Claude-Edmonde. "La part du diable dans la littérature contemporaine." Satan. Ed. Bruno de Jésus-Marie. Paris: Desclée de Brouwer, 1948. 573-606.

Malraux, André. Préface. Journal d'un curé de campagne. By Georges Bernanos. Paris: Plon, 1974.

Michaud, Monique. "Les Grands Cimetières sous la lune revisités." Paradoxes et permanence de la pensée bernanosienne. Études publiées sous la direction de Joël Pottier. Paris: Aux Animateurs de livres, 1989. 81-93.

Mounier, Emmanuel. "Un surnaturalisme historique." Georges Bernanos: essais et témoignages. Ed. Albert Béguin. Paris: Editions du Seuil; Neuchâtel: Editions de la Baconnière, 1949. 99-132.

Pézeril, Daniel. "Bernanos et sa mort." Georges Bernanos: essais et témoignages. Ed. Albert Béguin. Paris: Editions du Seuil; Neuchâtel: Editions de la Baconnière, 1949. 341-358.

---. "Le saint de Lumbres." Bernanos. Centre culturel de Cerisy-la-Salle 10 au 19 juillet 1969. Ed. Max Milner. Paris: Plon, 1972. 303-322.

Pottier, Joël. "Un jugement de Gertrud von le Fort sur 'Jeanne, relapse et sainte' de Georges Bernanos." Paradoxes et permanence de la pensée bernanosienne. Études publiées sous la direction de Joël Pottier. Paris: Aux Animateurs de livres, 1989. 179-189.

Renard-Georges, Pierrette. "La femme dans l'oeuvre de Bernanos." Bernanos. Centre culturel de Cerisy-la-Salle 10 au 19 juillet, 1969. Ed. Max Milner. Paris: Plon, 1972. 267-280.

Rousseaux, André. "Bernanos et la démission de la France." Georges Bernanos: essais et témoignages. Ed. Albert Béguin. Paris: Editions du Seuil; Neuchâtel: Editions de la Baconnière, 1949. 318-337.

---. "La voix de Bernanos et le silence de Mouchette." Littérature du vingtième siècle. Vol. I. By Rousseaux. Paris: Editions Albin Michel, 1938. 163-173.

---. "Misère et grandeur de Mouchette. Visite à M. Georges Bernanos." Bernanos. By Michel Estève. Paris: Gallimard, 1965. 243-246.

Russell, John, o.carm. "The Religious Plays of St Thérèse of Lisieux." Carmelite Studies: Experiencing St Thérèse Today. Washington: Institute of Carmelite Studies, 1990. 41-58.

Sayre, Robert. "Journal d'un curé de campagne: The Saint's Gethsemane." Solitude in Society. A Sociological Study in French Literature. By Sayre. Cambridge, Massachusetts: Harvard University Press, 1978. 133-154.

"Swetchine," New Catholic Encyclopedia, 1967 ed.

iii) Articles in Journals

Aaraas, Hans. "Les deux paroisses." La Revue des Lettres Modernes 108-110 (1964) "Etudes bernanosiennes" 5: 69-92.

Ackerman, Colette, o.c.d. and Joseph Healey, m.m. "Reinterpreting Thérèse for Today's World." Spiritual Life 35.2 (1989): 83-98.

Astorg, Bertrand d'. "Enfance et littérature." Esprit 216 (juillet 1954): 12-33.

Balthasar, Hans Urs von. "The Timeliness of Lisieux." Trans. C. Latimer. Carmelite Studies 1 (1980): 103-121.

Beaumont, Ernest. "Le sens christique de l'oeuvre romanesque de Bernanos." La Revue des Lettres Modernes 81-84 (1963) "Etudes bernanosiennes" 3-

4: 85-106.

Bénier, Jean. "Bernanos at Pirapora: A Personal Memoir (1939-1940)." Renascence XLI.1-2 (Fall 1988/Winter 1989): 55-68.

Blanchard, P. "Georges Bernanos et l'Esprit d'enfance." Vie Thérésienne 14 (avril 1964): 60-74.

Bush, William. "Bernanos et la Malibran: commentaire et présentation d'un texte retrouvé." Courrier Georges Bernanos 15 (1974): 3-10.

---. "Les enfants humiliés: composition, thèmes et titre." La Revue des Lettres Modernes 340-345 (1973) "Etudes bernanosiennes" 14: 7-24.

---. "Honneur, enfance et désincarnation: composition et thèmes des Grands cimetières sous la lune." La Revue des Lettres Modernes 290-297 (1972) "Etudes bernanosiennes" 13: 7-17.

---. "In His Image: Georges Bernanos (1888-1948)." Canadian Catholic Review 4.9 (1986): 13-16.

---. "The Novelist's Critique of the Clergy." Renascence XL1. 1-2 (1988-1989): 107-119.

---. "Ordre de composition de M. Ouine." Bulletin de la société des amis de Georges Bernanos 48 (1962): 5-12; 51-52 (1963): 19-26.

---. "Scènes et chronologie." La Revue des Lettres Modernes 108-110 (1964) "Etudes bernanosiennes" 5: 25-46.

---. "Les ténèbres: structure souhaitée et structure réalisée." La Revue des Lettres Modernes 409-412 (1974) "Etudes bernanosiennes" 15: 5-22.

---. "Vision créatrice et tentation littéraire." Courrier Georges Bernanos 2-3-4 (1971): 78-86.

Conn, Joann Wolski. "Conversion in Thérèse of Lisieux." Spiritual Life 24.3 (1978): 154-163.

Copiz, Pietro. "The Drama of Christian Vocation." Renascence XL1. 1-2 (1988-1989): 81-90.

Delvaux, Pierre-Paul. "Chantal de Clergerie: la dialectique du don ou le combat de la lumière et des ténèbres." La Revue des Lettres Modernes 340-345 (1973) "Etudes bernanosiennes" 14: 145-181.

---. "Esquisse pour une lecture de Monsieur Ouine à la lumière de René Girard." La Revue des Lettres Modernes 857-864 (1988) "Etudes bernanosiennes" 19: 209-228.

Demorest, Jean-Jacques. "L'ambiguïté de Monsieur Ouine." Symposium 13 (1959): 32-41.

Emmanuel, Pierre. "Epic of Fear." Commonweal LI.26 (April 7, 1950): 680, 682.

Estang, Luc. "Les Dialogues des Carmélites." Bulletin de la société des amis de Georges Bernanos 1 (1949): 12-14.

Estève, Michel. "Genèse du Journal d'un curé de campagne." La Revue des Lettres Modernes 67-68 (1961) "Etudes bernanosiennes" 2: 3-15.

---. "La nuit de Gethsémani." La Revue des Lettres Modernes 771-776 (1986) "Etudes bernanosiennes" 18: 87-107.

Frison, François. "Le thème de la chevalerie et le mythe personnel de Bernanos." La Revue des Lettres Modernes 290-297 (1972) "Etudes bernanosiennes" 13: 197-219.

Gaucher, Guy, o.c.d. "Bernanos et Sainte Thérèse de l'Enfant-Jésus." La Revue des Lettres Modernes 56-57 (1960) "Etudes bernanosiennes" 1: 228-268.

---. "Comment est-on canonisé? ou la solitude des saints." La Vie spirituelle 126.590 (1972): 335-346.

---. "L'appel de Bernanos." Courrier Georges Bernanos 2-3-4 (1971): 93-108.

---. "La prière du curé de campagne." Carmel 10 (1972): 97-139.

---. "Quelques réflexions sur les poésies de Thérèse." Carmel 2 (1980): 139-151.

Gordan, Dom Paul. "Bernanos au Brésil." Bulletin de la société des amis de Georges Bernanos 5 (1950): 2-6; 6 (1951): 3-6.

Guers-Villate, Yvonne. "Les premiers écrits de Bernanos." La Revue des

Lettres Modernes 203-208 (1969) "Etudes bernanosiennes" 10: 125-145.

Jurt, Joseph. "Bernanos as a Resistance Writer." Renascence XLI.1-2 (Fall 1988/Winter 1989): 43-54.

---. "Georges Bernanos et la France libre." Lettres romanes XXVII.3 (1973): 225-247.

Kelly, Louis. "'Childhood' as a Spiritual Force in Le Journal d'un curé de campagne." Culture XXVI (1965): 84-96.

Ladd, George. "Le journal de bord du curé d'Ambricourt." La Revue des Lettres Modernes 290-297 (1972) "Etudes bernanosiennes" 13: 177-196.

Lafon, Guy. "Le romancier et le théologien." La Vie spirituelle XCVI.425 (février 1957): 179-185.

---. "L'homme libre selon l'honneur (aperçus sur le concept d'honneur dans l'oeuvre 'polémique' de Bernanos)." La Revue des Lettres Modernes 81-84 (1963) "Etudes bernanosiennes" 3-4: 61-84.

Leclerq, Pierre-Robert. "Cénabre et Ouine, même âme de ténèbres." La Revue des Lettres Modernes 409-412 (1974) "Etudes bernanosiennes" 15: 63-77.

Léthel, François-Marie. "La passion de Jeanne d'Arc et de Thérèse de Lisieux." Carmel 2 (1980): 152-164.

Lye, John. "The Diary of a Country Priest and the Christian Novel." Renascence XXX.I (Fall 1978): 19-32.

Magny, Claude-Edmonde. "Monsieur Ouine, le dernier roman de Bernanos." La Revue des Lettres Modernes 108-110 (1964) "Etudes bernanosiennes" 5: 7-23.

Milford, James E. "Saint for a Violent Society." Spiritual Life 31.3 (1985): 131-139.

Molinari, Marthe. "Donissan, le champion de Dieu." La Revue des Lettres Modernes 81-84 (1963) "Etudes bernanosiennes" 3-4: 107-137.

Morris, Thomas H. "Thérèse's Story of a Soul: Wisdom for Today." Spiritual Life 33.2 (Summer 1987): 89-96.

O'Connell, David. "Georges Bernanos: Country Priests and Christian Soldiers." Renascence XXXII.4 (Summer 1980): 248-255.

O'Donoghue, Noel Dermot, o.c.d. "The Greatness of the Little Way." The Furrow 28.10 (1977): 599-610.

O'Sharkey, Eithne M. "Portraits of the Clergy in Bernanos' Journal d'un curé de campagne." Dublin Review 504 (Summer 1965): 183-191.

Peeters, Leopold. "Narration et tendresse dans Nouvelle histoire de Mouchette." La Revue des Lettres Modernes 637-642 (1982) "Etudes bernanosiennes" 17: 145-159.

Pézeril, Daniel "'Si vous vouliez cesser de vous haïr....'" Par Georges Bernanos. Esprit 351 (juillet-août 1966): 1-10.

Pfeifer, Josef. "La passion du Christ et la structure de Dialogues des Carmélites." La Revue des Lettres Modernes 81-84 (1963) "Etudes bernanosiennes" 3-4: 139-169.

Raymond-Marie, Soeur, s.s.a. "Bernanos et l'esprit d'enfance." Carmel 4 (1959): 292-317.

---. "L'enfant, présence de choc." La Revue des Lettres Modernes 108-110 (1964) "Etudes bernanosiennes" 5: 93-112.

---. "La simplicité des humbles et des petits." Culture XX (1959): 315-336; 403-419.

Renard-Georges, Pierrette. "Au pays de la soif et de la peur." La Revue des Lettres Modernes 203-208 (1969) "Etudes bernanosiennes" 10: 31-55.

Rousseaux, André. "Bernanos nous a donné rendez-vous." Bulletin de la société des amis de Georges Bernanos 4 (1950): 2-4.

Sarrazin, Hubert. "On Being French and Catholic (1938-1945)." Renascence XLI.1-2 (Fall 1988/Winter 1989): 69-80.

Saward, John. "Faithful to the Child I Used To Be: Bernanos and the Spirit of Childhood." The Chesterton Review XV-XVI.4-1 (1988-1989): 465-485.

Sonet, Jean, s.j. "Georges Bernanos et les Dialogues des Carmélites." Les Etudes classiques XVIII.3 (juillet 1950): 304-311.

Storelv, Sven. "La vocation de la France chez Péguy et Bernanos." <u>La Revue des Lettres Modernes</u> 127-129 (1965) "Etudes bernanosiennes" 6: 101-128.

Tobin, Michael Robinson. "The Christian Core: 'Ejus divinitatis esse consortes.'" <u>Renascence</u> XLI.1-2 (Fall 1988/Winter 1989): 91-97.

---. "Thérèse de Lisieux and Bernanos' First Novel." <u>French Forum</u> 10.1 (1985): 84-96.

Vallery-Radot, Irénée. "Bernanos en face de la mort." <u>La Table ronde</u> 243 (avril 1968): 81-92.

Vilain, Max. "Bernanos et les <u>Novissima Verba</u>." <u>Vie Thérésienne</u> (janvier 1974): 57-65.

Winter, Nicole. "Conception bernanosienne du sacerdoce à partir du <u>Journal d'un curé de campagne</u>." <u>La Revue des Lettres Modernes</u> 67-68 (1961-1962) "Etudes bernanosiennes" 2: 55-83.

INDEX

Except for the names of Bernanos and Thérèse of Lisieux which appear on virtually every page, this index includes historic personnages, fictional characters, and titles of works by Bernanos and Thérèse.

Aaraas, Hans, 12*n*, 142, 161*n*
Action Française, 35-36, 55*n*, 84
Agostini, Philippe, 68, 215
André, 136-137, 139
Anne de Jésus, Mère, 21, 174
Arland, Marcel, 185-186, 200, 202*n*
Arsène (*Monsieur Ouine*), 147, **151-154**, 156, 158
Arsène (*Nouvelle histoire de Mouchette*), 189-198

Balthasar, Hans Urs von, xviii, 3-7, 9-10, 18, 49, 88-89, 164-165, 231
Beaumont, Ernest, 12*n*
Béguin, Albert, 68, 70-71*n*, 84, 202*n*, 203, 217, 236*n*
Bellière, Abbé, 77, 103, 128, 192, 226
Belperron, Pierre, 39
Benedict XV, 42
Bernanos, Jean-Loup, 10, 14*n*, 70-71*n*, 214*n*
Bernanos, Mme Georges (Jehanne Talbert d'Arc), 65, 79-80
Blanchard, P., 12*n*
Blanche de la Force/Blanche de l'Agonie du Christ, 3, 9, 68-69, 117, **217-227**, **229-232**, 234
Blum, Léon, 142
Blumenthal, Gerda, 12*n*
Boisdeffre, Pierre de, 12*n*
Boly, J., 12*n*, 215, 217, 236*n*
Bourdel, Maurice, 34, 36, 38-39
Brémond, Henri, 13*n*
Bridel, Yves, 8-10, 14*n*, 41-42, 55*n*, 69, 70*n*, 110, 130*n*, 153, 164, 167-168, 186, 222

Bro, Bernard, 12*n*
Brückberger, R.-L., 12*n*, 68, 185-186, 200, 202*n*, 215, 239
Brun, Louis, 37
Bush, William, 7, 9-10, 14*n*, 18-19, 21-22, 29, 31*n*, 52, 55*n*, 71*n*, 84, 91*n*, 93, 97, 102, 119, 122, 132, 142, 151, 157-159, 161*n*, 197, 202*n*, 212

Carneiro da Cunha, Pedro Octavio, 203
Cénabre, 18, **25-26**, 29, 113-114, 116, **126-129**
"*Ce qui ne meurt pas*", 83
Chabot, Jacques, 61, 70*n*
Chantal (*Journal d'un curé de campagne*), 176-177, 180
Chantal de Clergerie, 5-8, **23-29**, 34, 44, 103, 113, **115-126**, 129, 155, 178, 240
Chaplain (*Dialogues des Carmélites*), 9, 226, 230, 233-234
Le Chemin de la Croix-des-âmes, 57-61, 65, 68, 70-71*n*
Chevance, 7, 23-24, 27, 44, **113-116**, 118, 121, 123-124, 126-127, 129, 240
Christoflour, Raymond, 53-54
Cobban, Alfred, 161*n*
Coleville, Maxence de, 58
Combes, Mgr André, 17
Conseils et souvenirs, 42, 86, 177
Constance, 3, 9, 68, 222-224, 226-227, 231, 234
Cooke, John E., 12*n*
Correspondance inédite I, 30, 35-40,

42, 55n, 76-80, 112, 132, 142
Correspondance inédite II, 34, 41, 45, 141, 143, 163-164, 209, 239
Correspondance inédite III (Lettres retrouvées), 36, 39, 55n, 79, 81-82, 103, 240
Coty, François, 36
Countess (*Journal d'un curé de campagne*), 176-181
Une course de géant: lettres, 28, 42, 50, 66, 77-78, 82-83, 94-95, 103-104, 111, 114, 128, 135, 137-138, 140-141, 168, 171-172, 174-175, 182-183, 190, 194-195, 198-200, 202n, 204-205, 208-210, 212-213, 220, 226-230, 234-235
Le crépuscule des vieux, 84
Un crime, 33-34, 40, **131-133, 136-141**, 143, 163
curé d'Ars, xx
curé of Ambricourt, xix, 5-6, 8, 11, 40-41, 45, **163-183**, 222, 240
curé of Fenouille, 143, **145-146**, 153-155, 159, 164
curé of Torcy, 45, 165, 167, **170-172**, 174

Daudet, Léon, 37
Dawson, Christopher, 62
Day, Dorothy, 9n
Debluë, Henri, 12n, 138, 161n, 167, 184n
De Gaulle, Charles, 59, 65
Derfler, Leslie, 161n
"Dernier agenda", 67, 229
"Derniers appels", 67-68
Derniers entretiens, 4-5, 9, 11, 13n, 18, 20-21, 23-24, 26-27, 31n, 40, 42-43, 55n, 70, 77-80, 82-84, 86-89, 95-96, 98, 108-109, 113-115, 117, 119-122, 125-127, 129, 130n, 136, 139-141, 144, 156-159, 164-166, 168-170, 173, 178, 181-183, 184n, 185, 190-191, 195-196, 198, 200-201, 206, 208, 210-213, 220-227, 229-231, 239
"Les Deux Fils", 83-84
"Dialogue d'ombres", 88-90
Dialogues des Carmélites, xx, 3, 7, 9, 12-13n, 57, 68-69, 71n, 117, **215-235**, 236n, 240-241
"Discours pour le baptême de l'avion brésilen 'Jeanne d'Arc'", 65, 71n, 217, 241
Donissan, 7, 10, **18-22**, 43-44, 75, 91n, 93, **96-105**, 119, 240
Drumont, Edouard, 33, 111
Dumanoir, Cosmao, 81

Les Enfants humiliés, 211
Estang, Luc, 3, 9, 13n, 68, 71n, 222, 236n
Estève, Michel, 5-6, 11, 13-14n, 55n, 70n, 163, 168-169, 184n, 198-200, 202n, 216, 236n
Evangeline, 133, **136-141**, 143

Foucauld, Charles de, 67, 203
Fragnière, Marie-Agnès, 7, 13n
Français, si vous saviez 1945-1948, 65-66
La France contre les robots, 71n
Francis of Assisi, xx
Franco, 47
François-Xavier, St., 70n
"Frère Martin", xix, **203-208**, 214n, 241
Frison, François, 12n

García, María Felicia, see *"La Malibran"*
Gaucher, Guy, xviii, 3, 6-7, 9, 11, 14n, 17-18, 23, 25-30, 52, 56n, 66, 68, 75, 91n, 122, 130n, 166-

167, 183, 213, 216
Geneviève, Mère, 88, 117, 224
"Le Geste du roi", 83
Gille, Pierre, 12*n*
Gillespie, Jessie Lynn, 12*n*
Gordan, Dom Paul, 4, 13*n*, 60, 70*n*, 209
Gosselin, Monique, 13*n*
La Grande peur des bien-pensants, 33, 36, 39, 111-112
Les Grands cimetières sous la lune, xviii-xix, 4, 6, 10, 12*n*, 14*n*, 33, 43, **45-52**, 54, 55*n*, 64, 131, 167-168, 240-241
Guérin, Marie, 140-141, 171
Guers-Villate, Yvonne, 90, 91*n*
Guillaume, 143-145, 149
Guillemin, Henri, 12*n*
Gusman, Dominic, see also *"Saint Dominique"*, xx

Halda, Bernard, 12*n*
Hebblethewaite, Peter, 12*n*
Hello, Ernest, 78
Histoire d'une âme, xvii, 9, 13*n*, 18-23, 25, 27-28, 31*n*, 35, 38, 41, 54, 55*n*, 70-71*n*, 76-79, 81-82, 84, 86-88, 90, 94-104, 108, 110, 114-126, 128, 132, 135-136, 138, 140, 144-150, 152-154, 156, 166-170, 172-176, 178-179, 181-182, 184*n*, 188-189, 193-199, 206-212, 217-220, 224, 229, 233-234
Hitler, 58, 61

L'Imposture, 17-18, **23-28**, 44, 107, **112-116**, 121, **126-129**
Isaiah, 9, 194

Jamart, François, 43, 55*n*
Jamet, Annie, 40-41
Jeanne d'Arc, xvii, xx, 4, 6-7, 10, 14*n*, 30, 41-42, 44, 52-54, 55*n*, 60, 62-65, 71*n*, 107, 110-112, 130*n*, 135, 193, 206, 213, 217
"Jeanne, relapse et sainte", 7, 12*n*, 30, 41-42, 44, 53-54, 64, 107, **109-111**
J'entre dans la vie: derniers entretiens, see *Derniers entretiens*
John of the Cross, 138, 200
La Joie, 5, **23-30**, 33-35, 39, 44, 107, 112-113, **117-126**, 129, 178
Jourdain, Madame, 13*n*, 231
Journal d'un curé de campagne, xix, 5-6, 12-13*n*, 33, 40-41, 45, 131, **163-183**, 184*n*, 240
Jurt, Joseph, 70*n*

Kedward, H.R., 70*n*

Lagrange, Abbé, 76-78
Laurentin, René, 11, 14*n*, 121, 130*n*, 214*n*
Lawrence of the Resurrection, Brother, 91*n*
Lefèvre, Frédéric, 82, 103
Le Fort, Gertrud von, 68, 215-216
Leo XIII, 98
Le Touzé, Philippe, 12*n*
Lettre aux Anglais, 58, **62-64**, 210, 216-217, 241
La liberté pour quoi faire?, 58, 65, 203
Loyson, Père Hyacinthe, 25, 114, 126, 204-205, 208
Luther, Martin, xix-xx, 203-208, 214*n*

"Madame Dargent", xix, 4, 9, 18, 88-90
Madame de Croissy, 117, 219-224, 234
Madame Lidoine, 224-229, 231,

233-234
"Mademoiselle Triomphe", 83-84
Magny, Claude-Edmonde, 142-143, 154, 161*n*
Maid of Orleans, see Jeanne d'Arc
Maître, Jean-Marie, 79-80
"La Malibran", xviii, 84-88, 91*n*, 240
Malraux, André, xvii, 3, 12*n*
Manificat, Christiane, 39
Marchand, Jacques, 38-39
Marie-Celeste, Sister, 12*n*
Marie de Gonzague, Mère, 170
Martin, Céline, 42, 50, 82, 86, 114, 137, 168, 172, 175, 177, 181, 183, 194-195, 199-200, 204, 228, 234
Martin, Marie, 23, 42, 102, 190, 220, 230, 235
Martin, Pauline, 22-23, 42, 55*n*, 70*n*, 77-80, 87, 95, 98, 109, 120, 125, 127, 130*n*, 156, 166, 169, 173-174, 184*n*, 191, 198, 201, 202*n*, 210, 222
Massis, Henri, 35, 112
Maurras, Charles, 36, 61
Un mauvais rêve, 33, 36, **131-141**, 143, 161*n*
Menou-Segrais, 10, 19-21, 97-102
Mère Marie de l'Incarnation, 221-234
Michaud, Monique, 12*n*
Milner, Max, 8-10, 12-14*n*, 55*n*, 130*n*
Moeller, Charles, 4, 13*n*, 17, 31*n*, 141, 161*n*
Monsieur Ouine, 33, 36, 38, 57, 131-132, **141-160**, 161*n*, 163-164, 185, 203, 240
Monsieur Ouine, xix, 75, 144-145, 147, 149-151, **154-159**
"La Mort avantageuse du chevalier de Lorges", 83
Mouchette (in *Nouvelle histoire de Mouchette*), xix, 8, **186-201**, 202*n*, 240
Mouchette (in *Sous le soleil de Satan*), 10, 19, 21-22, **93-96**, 98-99, 101, 131, 201, 240
"La Muette", 83-84
Murray, Meredith, 12*n*, 236*n*
Mussolini, 61

"Nos amis les saints", xx, 67, 203-204, **208-213**, 214*n*, 241
"Notice autobiographique", 240
Nous autres Français, 57, 60-61
Nouvelle histoire de Mouchette, xix, 8, 33, 57, **185-201**, 202*n*, 240
Novissima Verba, see *Derniers entretiens*
"Une nuit", 89

"On passera!", 83
O'Sharkey, Eithne M., 12*n*

Paésie, 22, 31*n*
Paul, St., 102, 119, 145-146, 154, 172
Peeters, Leopold, 194, 202*n*
Péguy, Charles, 59
Pétain, 58-59
Pézeril, Daniel, 214*n*
Pichon, Père, 99, 120, 131-132, 206, 226
"La Pitié du chouan", 83
Pius X, xvii, xxi*n*
Pius XI, 35, 70*n*
Pius XII, 61, 70*n*
Pottier, Joël, 12*n*
Poulenc, Francis, 68
"Pour préserver les lys", 83
Pranzini, 24, 100
Les prédestinés, 214*n*

"Preface for Louis le Cardonnel, pèlerin de l'invisible", 52-54
Prou, Père Alexis, 21, 99, 120-121, 171
Pujo, Maurice, 37

Raymond-Marie, Soeur, 6, 23-25, 121, 148-149, 161n, 165-166, 186, 202n
Renard, Pierrette, 10, 14n
Rideau, Emile, 12n, 130n
Rivard, Yvon, 12n
Rohrbach, Peter-Thomas, 13-14n
Roulland, Père, 83, 104, 209, 226
Rousseaux, André, 58, 66, 70n, 185, 200, 202n
Russell, John, 91n

"Saint Dominique", 44, 107-109
Sarrazin, Hubert, 70-71n
Saward, John, 12n
Simenon, Georges, 39
Simone Alfieri, 75, **132-141**, 143
Six, Jean-François, 13n, 98, 106n
Sous le soleil de Satan, 7, 9-10, **18-22**, 31n, 35, 37-39, 43-44, 75, **93-105**, 107, 112-113, 119, 201
Speaight, Robert, 13n, 38, 62, 132-133
Steeny, 143-144, **147-151**, 154-159
Sudre, Abbé André, 35
"Sur un album", 209, 214n
Swetchine, Madame, 125, 130n, 178

Taxil, Léo, 111-112, 130n
Tenant, Jean, 36
Teresa of Avila, xviii, xx, 10, 40, 85, 87-88, 91n, 229
Théâtre au Carmel: récréations pieuses, 110-112, 202n
Tobin, Michael, 10, 19-22, 47, 50, 55n, 93-94, 98, 131

"La Tombe refermée", 83
Le triomphe de l'humilité (RP 7), 112, 130

Vallery-Radot, Marie, 45, 142
Vallery-Radot, Robert, 30, 35-36, 38, 41, 45, 132, 141, 163
Vaughan, Diana, 111-112
Vilain, Max, 13n
Villiers de la Noue, Vicomtesse, 239
"Virginie ou le Plaisir des champs", 83
La vocation spirituelle de la France, 70n, 211

Warner, Marina, 109-110, 130n
Winter, Nicole, 13n

OHIO UNIVERSITY LIBRARY
Please return this book as soon as you have finished with it. In order to avoid a fine it must be returned by the latest date stamped below. All books are subject to recall after two weeks or immediately if needed for reserve.

CF